BORDERLINE CITIZENS

A volume in the series

The United States in the World

Edited by Mark Philip Bradley, David C. Engerman, Amy S. Greenberg, and Paul A. Kramer

A list of titles in this series is available at cornellpress.cornell.edu.

BORDERLINE CITIZENS

The United States, Puerto Rico, and the Politics of Colonial Migration

Robert C. McGreevey

Cornell University Press
Ithaca and London

First published 2018 by Cornell University Press

Printed in the United States of America

Library of Congress Cataloging-in-Publication Data

Names: McGreevey, Robert, author.
Title: Borderline citizens : the United States, Puerto Rico, and the politics of colonial migration / Robert C. McGreevey.
Description: Ithaca : Cornell University Press, 2018. | Series: The United States in the world | Includes bibliographical references and index.
Identifiers: LCCN 2017054548 (print) | LCCN 2017057127 (ebook) | ISBN 9781501716157 (epub/mobi) | ISBN 9781501716164 (pdf) | ISBN 9781501716140 | ISBN 9781501716140 (cloth ; alk. paper)
Subjects: LCSH: Puerto Ricans—United States—History—20th century. | Puerto Ricans—Migrations—History—20th century. | Puerto Rico—Colonial influence. | Puerto Rico—Emigration and immigration—History—20th century. | United States—Emigration and immigration—History—20th century. | Citizenship—United States—History—20th century.
Classification: LCC E184.P85 (ebook) | LCC E184.P85 M38 2018 (print) | DDC 305.868/7295—dc23
LC record available at https://lccn.loc.gov/2017054548

For Miriam

Contents

Acknowledgments

This book began nearly ten years ago. Since then, the United States in the World field has developed rapidly to include exciting new studies that globalize the study of American history. As I have written this book, I have come to know many of those working in this field, and I have incurred many debts. It is a pleasure to thank all of those who have lent me their support and encouragement over the years.

I have been privileged to work with an extraordinary group of historians who have profoundly shaped my view of the world and my career as a historian. At Swarthmore, I thank in particular Timothy Burke, Bruce Dorsey, Pieter Judson, and Marjorie Murphy for opening new worlds to me. At Brandeis, I had the great fortune of working with David Engerman, Jacqueline Jones, Jane Kamensky, and Michael Willrich. Their influence can be seen throughout this book. I also thank Silvia Arrom and Peter Winn for tutoring me in Latin American history and encouraging me in my work. I owe special thanks to Christopher Capozzola for his invaluable feedback as I wrote this book and for becoming a great mentor to me.

For the financial resources needed to travel to archives and write the manuscript, I am grateful for the support of the Crown fellowship from Brandeis University, the Stuart L. Bernath Dissertation Fellowship from the

Society for Historians of American Foreign Relations, and the John Higham Travel Award from the Immigration and Ethnic History Society and the Organization of American Historians. At the College of New Jersey, I thank Provost Jacqueline Taylor and the office of Academic Affairs for supporting my sabbatical leave in 2015–16, as well as a series of summer research assistants and course releases that aided me in completing the revisions. I also thank the editors of the *Journal of the Gilded Age and Progressive Era* for allowing me to reproduce some material that first appeared in my article "Empire and Migration: Coastwise Shipping, National Status, and the Colonial Legal Origins of Puerto Rican Migration to the United States," *Journal of the Gilded Age and Progressive Era* 11, no. 4 (October 2012): 553–73.

I extend my gratitude to the many archivists who have worked with me patiently, even when I asked repeatedly, "Is there another box?" In Puerto Rico, I worked closely with Miguel Vega, librarian of the Collección Puertorriqueña at the University of Puerto Rico, and I am deeply grateful for his expert guidance in navigating the extensive newspaper collection there that is not yet digitized. I also thank María Ordóñez, director of the Collección Puertorriqueña, for welcoming me over several visits. In the Archivo General de Puerto Rico, I owe a special thanks to archivist María Isabelle Rodríguez for helping me track down U.S. colonial records deep within the stacks. During my time in the Archivo, I had many fruitful conversations with other researchers. I thank, in particular, Raquel Rosario Rivera, who lent me her favorite seat in the archive and offered several leads as to where I might find documents related to citizenship, and Fernando Picó for pointing me in the right direction on more than one occasion when I thought I had reached a dead end.

In New York, at the Centro de Estudios Puertorriqueños at Hunter College, I thank Pedro Juan Hernández for his assistance in tracking down numerous manuscript collections and newspapers. I also thank those who helped me in the National Archives Northeast regional branch in Manhattan as well as the staff of the New York Public Library. In Washington, DC, I thank the staff of the Library of Congress. I also owe special thanks to the archivists of the U.S. House and Senate records in the National Archives who took me into the stacks to access committee records rarely used by researchers and worked with me, seemingly around the clock, for many months. In Maryland, I thank the highly efficient staff at the National Archives in College Park and at the George Meany Memorial Archive of the University of Maryland. In Boston, many thanks to the expert staff at Widener Library, Baker Library, Brandeis University Library, Boston Public Library, and the National Archives Northeast Region Headquarters.

For their encouragement, savvy, and good cheer, I thank a wonderful group of colleagues at Brandeis: Clara Altman, Alexis Antracoli, Yoni Applebaum, Noelani Arista, Lindsay Silver Cohen, Denise Damico, Jonathan DeCoster, P. J. Dickson, Robert Heinrich, Benjamin Irvin, Jeremy Kuzmarov, Shane Landrum, Jessica Lepler, Gabriel Loicaono, Molly McCarthy, Hilary Moss, Jason Opal, Matthew Pehl, Greg Renoff, Paul Ringel, Nathan Rives, Eric Schlereth, David Soll, Emily Straus, Frederick Turner, William Walker, Jeff Wiltse, and Lynda Yankaskas.

During my time at Vanderbilt, I had the privilege of getting to know Gary Gerstle, Sarah Igo, and Elizabeth Lunbeck and I am grateful for the welcome they showed me. In the history department at the College of New Jersey, I have had the great fortune of being surrounded by colleagues who are passionately committed to both teaching and research. For their encouragement and stalwart support, I thank Mekala Audain, Dina Boero, Matthew Bender, William Carter, Celia Chazelle, Daniel Crofts, Christopher Fisher, Jo-Ann Gross, Craig Hollander, Alejandra Irigoin, Adam Knobler, Roman Kovalev, Xinru Liu, Michael Marino, Ann Marie Nicolosi, Cynthia Paces, Qin Shao, and Jodi Weinstein. Deans Deborah Compte, Benjamin Rifkin, John Sisko, and Jane Wong offered vital support for my work. For help with the images and bibliography, I thank our humanities librarian, David Murray, as well as Laura Hargreaves, Faith Newins, and Andrew Vitale. I am also grateful to my many students who have taken an interest in this project, in particular Steven Rodriguez and E. Kyle Romero who worked with me as summer research assistants and are now well on their way to becoming historians themselves.

In a variety of conferences, seminars, and more informal conversations, I have benefited from the advice and constructive feedback of many gifted and generous historians, including Eiichiro Azuma, Sven Beckert, Katherine Benton-Cohen, Brooke Blower, Denise Bossy, Alison Bruey, Dale Clifford, Benjamin Coates, Steven Cohen, David Courtwright, Mary Dudziak, Eileen Findlay, Greg Grandin, Julie Greene, Cindy Hahamovitch, Hendrik Hartog, Jesse Hoffnung-Garskof, Kristin Hoganson, Madeline Hsu, Julia Irwin, Noam Maggor, Daniel Margolies, David Montgomery, Mae Ngai, Christopher Nichols, Meredith Oyen, Christina Duffy Ponsa, Gunther Peck, Nicole Phelps, Efrén Rivera Ramos, Lucy Salyer, Aaron Sheehan-Dean, Bryant Simon, Rachel St. John, Alan Taylor, Lorrin Thomas, Andrew Urban, Richard White, and Judy Tzu-Chun Wu.

At Cornell University Press, many thanks to my editor, Michael McGandy, for guiding me through the process of revision with sage advice and good humor. I also thank my production editor, Susan Specter, and her colleagues, Karen Carroll, Lisa DeBoer, William Nelson, and Bethany Wasik for all their help in copyediting the text and preparing the images and maps. I am deeply indebted to the anonymous readers whose insightful comments on earlier drafts made this a significantly better book. I also owe special thanks to Paul Kramer, who showed an interest in this project at a very early stage and has since become a great mentor, guiding me in framing my arguments and clarifying my contributions.

Finally, I thank my friends and family who have made it all possible. To those who have been with me for the duration, housing me during research trips, distracting me when I hit a wall with writing, and generally making my life a lot more fun, I thank Seth Budick, Jill Clark, Catherine Chu, Melissa Dustin, Julie Falk, Matthew and Michelle Halpern, Fatimah Johnson, Dana Lehman, Sam Merabi, Tara Schubert, Heather Schwartz, Jesse Shore, Amy and Peter Sollins, Darian Unger. My parents, Jack and Dianne McGreevey, cultivated my inquisitive nature from a young age. Though my path to eventually becoming a historian took me to far-off places, and my parents might have preferred that I stay closer to home, they have supported me in more ways than I can count and celebrated each of my achievements with love. My brothers John and Michael have been treasured companions, cheering me on from the East and West Coasts. My extended family, Sharon and Michael Clifford, the Godin clan, Carol Hu, Mimi Kavanagh, Gal Kober, and Aaron Shakow have further enriched my life and, thankfully, known when to ask me about my book and when not to. Carol Shakow and Melvin Leiman have become like second parents to me, nourishing me with their Provençale cooking and good conversation, and routinely flying in from Seattle to help take care of the kids. I thank my sons Theo and Jacob, my pride and joy, for bringing a bit of magic to each day. And last but certainly not least, I thank Miriam Shakow who has been with me for the long haul and who has read more drafts of this manuscript than anyone else. This book is dedicated to her.

BORDERLINE CITIZENS

Introduction

Migration and Empire

In March of 1919, leaders of the Porto Rican Club of San Francisco wrote to colonial officials in Washington, DC, with an urgent message: despite the extension of U.S. citizenship to Puerto Ricans under the terms of the 1917 Jones Act, Puerto Ricans in California were not being recognized as U.S. citizens.[1] A mutual aid society working to benefit the 1,200 Puerto Ricans living in San Francisco, the club had formed a "patriotic-social group" during World War I to win support and recognition for the 120 Puerto Ricans from the city who were drafted into the armed services. Yet, despite the service of these men, the best efforts of the club, and the legal force of the Jones Act, the club stated that "we Porto Ricans in California, like those of us in Hawai'i, are classified—in respect to citizenship—with Filipinos, Japanese, or Chinese."[2] Puerto Ricans, they claimed, were treated as Filipino nationals or Japanese and Chinese aliens, instead of as U.S. citizens.

The Club of San Francisco's complaint suggests that Puerto Ricans faced a legal dilemma similar to that faced by a host of other immigrant groups. In the early decades of the twentieth century, various groups, including Filipinos, Japanese and Chinese, were restricted in their rights to become naturalized. U.S.-born members of these groups could be considered "alien citizens": American-born children of immigrant parents, legally U.S. citizens, but assumed to be foreigners by employers and the state.[3] Puerto Ricans faced similar challenges when they struggled to be recognized as citizens after Congress passed the Jones Act in 1917, which granted Puerto Ricans a form of U.S. citizenship that entitled them to more rights than aliens and nationals but still fewer rights than full U.S. citizens. Yet the club's complaint also suggests how Puerto Ricans sought to position themselves favorably against these other groups. At a time when Japanese immigrants in California often claimed superiority over Filipinos by drawing a firm distinction between the independence of Japan and the colonized status of the Philippines, Puerto Ricans, though migrants from a formally recognized U.S. colony, made claims to a higher status than Asian alien citizens.[4]

The misperception of Puerto Ricans as noncitizens was made manifest at the end of World War I. As factory owners and shipyard managers demobilized wartime industries, they justified firing Puerto Rican employees on the basis of their presumed alien status in order to make room for returning white citizens. When Puerto Ricans protested that they were, in fact, U.S. citizens, employers directed them to "bring a paper from the court showing you are a citizen." Those who took their case to the U.S. Circuit Court in San Francisco found that even the court considered them to be aliens. By paying one dollar, they were told, they could obtain official evidence of their "declaration of intention" to become a U.S. citizen. Then, after an additional five years of residence in the United States, they were entitled to pay four dollars more to receive a paper certifying their status as U.S. citizens.[5]

The Club of San Francisco struggled to understand the circuit court's reasoning in order to challenge the decision. For the court to decide that Puerto Ricans in California were legally excluded from the Jones Act, the club members speculated, it must have assumed that Puerto Ricans in California had not been resident on the island of Puerto Rico in 1899. Section 5 of the 1917 Jones Act declared that U.S. citizenship was extended to all Puerto Ricans residing on the island at the time of the ratification of the Treaty of Paris, April 11, 1899, and "all natives of Porto Rico temporarily absent on April 11, 1899, and who have since returned." By this logic, Puerto Ricans who migrated in 1899 to California and did not return to the island would be excluded from the Jones Act. Yet the club argued that the courts in California—and in Hawai'i where the first such judgment was made—failed to recognize that the earliest Puerto Ricans did not migrate to Hawai'i until December 1900, and that the first Puerto Ricans settled in California in 1903. Those who migrated to Hawai'i and California, the club maintained, had all been resident in Puerto Rico in 1899, making them U.S.

citizens under the terms of the 1917 Jones Act. As the club wrote, these Puerto Ricans never returned to the island, nor were they absent from the island in April 1899.

In an effort to more permanently resolve legal questions such as this one that had been brought before the courts on a case-by-case basis, Arcadio Santiago, secretary general of the Porto Rican Club of San Francisco, wrote a petition to the resident commissioner for Puerto Rico in Washington, DC, urging the U.S. government to issue an identification card that Puerto Ricans could carry with them when applying for jobs. In this period before social security cards, Santiago argued that an identity card could prove Puerto Ricans' "just claims to citizenship" to foremen, growers, factory owners, and other employers. In doing so, it would distinguish Puerto Ricans from "other Spanish-speaking races" in California. Such a distinction was critical as U.S. citizenship placed Puerto Ricans on a different legal footing than Mexicans, even as employers routinely conflated the two groups. In making clear Puerto Ricans' status as U.S. citizens, such an identification card would, Santiago wrote, "overcome the mental stupidity which seems to be chronic in the brains of the greater number of our blonde brethren on the continent."[6]

This book is about the intersection of U.S. colonial power and Puerto Rican migration. The conflict in San Francisco was but one in a series of confrontations in the early decades of the twentieth century between colonial migrants seeking work and citizenship in the metropole and various groups—employers, colonial officials, courts, and labor leaders—that policed the borders of the U.S. polity. At a time when U.S. colonial officials sought to reduce citizenship through the definition of Puerto Rico as a U.S. territory, Puerto Ricans tested the limits of colonial law when they migrated to California, Arizona, New York, and other states on the mainland. The incidents and legal cases created when Puerto Ricans migrated to the U.S. mainland serve as essential, if largely overlooked, evidence in understanding the nature of U.S. empire and citizenship.

Colonial migrations to the mainland gave rise to vigorous debates in the United States over whether colonial territories and their subjects should be classified as "foreign" or "domestic." At the turn of the century, several U.S. bodies of law defining the relationship of Puerto Rico and its people to the mainland were at odds with each other. Though the United States had ruled the island as a colony since the War of 1898, immigration laws from 1898 to 1904 governing the entrance of people to the U.S. mainland classified Puerto Ricans with Russians, Greeks, and all other immigrants from foreign nations.

At the same time, shipping laws regulating the movement of goods defined Puerto Rican ports as existing within U.S. domestic shipping channels. Amid these conflicting legal decisions, the Supreme Court in *Gonzales v. Williams* (1904) created a new legal category of belonging, the U.S. national, that defined Puerto Ricans as occupying a status in between citizen and alien. As nationals, residents of U.S. territories could enter the U.S. mainland free from immigration restrictions, but could not formally participate in the polity by voting. The Jones Act of 1917 marked a change in the law as Puerto Ricans were officially granted U.S. citizenship, even as the legal status of Puerto Ricans was continually contested on the ground. I argue that Puerto Ricans who migrated to California and other states were vital protagonists in sparking debate and change in colonial law. Recognition of the central role these migrants played compels a reassessment of the historical relationship between colonialism, law, and migration.

The legal questions colonial migrants raised on the mainland should be understood within the broader context of U.S. rule in Puerto Rico. While war, occupation, and colonial policy brought residents of the island within the bounds of the American economy, shifting legal decisions made Puerto Ricans' status with respect to the polity far from clear. Upon acquiring Puerto Rico from Spain after the War of 1898, the U.S. Congress first defined the island as "coastwise," or part of the eastern U.S. seaboard for the purposes of trade law. Under the terms of the Coastwise Laws, Congress mandated that American steamships transport Puerto Rican goods. Because U.S. steamship companies only operated between Puerto Rico, New York, and New Orleans, these laws effectively cut off trade between the island and Europe. Puerto Rico's primary export of coffee, long prized in Europe, could not compete in the U.S. market against much cheaper coffee imported from Brazil. The legal definition of the island as "coastwise" led to the collapse of the coffee market, Puerto Rico's main industry, and spurred the newly unemployed to seek work in the United States. Yet, at the same time, the Supreme Court ruled that Puerto Ricans, unlike residents of previous territorial acquisitions such as Hawai'i and New Mexico, were not entitled to the protections of the U.S. Constitution. The court's ruling in *Downes v. Bidwell* (1901) broke with long-standing tradition when it defined Puerto Rico as an "unincorporated territory" with no expectation of future statehood or citizenship for Puerto Ricans. Later in the century, the Jones Act of 1917 limited the extension of U.S. citizenship by tying it to the island's territorial status. Colonial officials routinely declined to issue passports or identity cards to

Puerto Ricans as a means of confining U.S. citizenship to the island and limiting migration to the mainland.

How, then, could Puerto Ricans in San Francisco, as migrants from a U.S. colonial territory, claim the right to stand before U.S. courts? What was the role of law in shaping the migration of colonial subjects in the first place? What, more broadly, was the relationship between colonial legal categories and migration?

I address these questions by chronicling the dynamics of colonialism and migration during the early years of U.S. rule in Puerto Rico. In demonstrating the central role of colonial law in shaping migrations, I challenge conventional paradigms of immigration history, such as "uprooted and transplanted," which assume that immigrants crossed a clean line of separation when moving from their home countries to the United States. I argue instead that the boundary between the United States and the rest of the world often blurred as migrants from sites of U.S. empire—that is, countries destabilized by the exercise of U.S. power abroad—moved within one interconnected economy and polity. In the early 1900s, unemployed laborers from Puerto Rico undertook far-flung journeys by rail and steamship to Honolulu, New York, and points in between. Migrants responded to the recruitment efforts of U.S. labor agents who had defined Puerto Ricans as "non-foreign" in order to evade legal prohibitions on the importation of foreign contract labor under the 1885 Foran Act. Migrants also responded to U.S. trade and shipping policies that had devastated Puerto Rico's coffee-based export economy. Instead of framing migrations in terms of discrete national boundaries, I show how a border is constructed, illustrating how some groups perceived as immigrants from distant and separate economies were, in fact, migrants moving within the sphere of U.S. economic and political power.[7]

Yet the exercise of colonial power is only part of this story. Colonized people were central actors as well, both in the very act of migrating and in their vigorous contestations of colonial status, which forced debate and change in colonial law.[8] I explore how colonial migrations have, in fact, been coproduced by the interaction of legal categories, changing political economies, and the demands of migrants themselves. Just as the legal designations of "coastwise" shipping and "non-foreign" labor shaped migration patterns, so too did migrants, in turn, contest and sometimes reshape colonial legal categories. Though initially barred from entering U.S. mainland ports, colonial migrants later made claims on the colonial state to be allowed entry. Through court appeals, migrants won the legal right to enter the mainland under the new legal title of "national." Despite bitter protest from Congress, the 1904 *Gonzales* ruling opened U.S. ports to residents of Puerto Rico and other U.S. territories, including the Philippines. Migration to the mainland would increase again after the Jones Act as Puerto Ricans on the mainland sought to claim full citizenship rights. In this book I invite a rethinking of immigration and imperial histories, two literatures that have long been separated, by demonstrating the mutual shaping of colonial law and migration.

The Narrative

This book is organized chronologically, from the period of the U.S. takeover of Puerto Rico after the War of 1898 through the first two decades of U.S. citizenship in the 1920s and 1930s. This period was one of broad reconfiguration, as U.S. colonial rule, trade policy, and immigration law brought about an increase in migration from the island to the United States. Nonelite actors, such as immigrants traveling to New York in search of work and laborers on the island protesting for the right to unionize, pressured colonial officials to grant them full U.S. citizenship status. Changes in citizenship law, along with severe economic damage caused by colonial rule on the island, gave rise to increasing migration to the mainland. Yet, despite the long history of colonial ties between the island and the mainland, many mainland Americans conceived of Puerto Ricans arriving in the United States as foreign immigrants. Claims of Puerto Rican foreignness peaked in the 1930s when migrants were routinely repatriated to the island despite the protections of U.S. citizenship. But this decade also saw the growing political power of Puerto Ricans on the U.S. mainland, which resulted in the election of their first voting representative to the U.S. House of Representatives in 1934.

I begin by situating U.S. colonial rule on the island within the larger histories of Spanish empire, Puerto Rican resistance movements, U.S. racial politics, and narratives of American exceptionalism. One year prior to the U.S. takeover, Spain signed the 1897 Autonomy Charter, which expanded Puerto Ricans' citizenship rights, including representation in the Spanish Congress, or Cortes, in Madrid.[9] Yet the U.S. Congress withheld citizenship from its new colonial subjects when it passed the Foraker Act in 1900. Framed in a language of tutelage, the decision to withhold citizenship from Puerto

Ricans was shaped, in part, by the regret of some white Americans over having extended the Fifteenth Amendment to southern blacks in 1870. At the same time, congressional leaders placated mainland citizens' fears of colonial migration, economic competition, and the "racial degeneration" of the United States by asserting an overriding confidence in Congress's own plenary power to control the effects of colonialism through legislation. In chapter 1, I examine how, in the early years of U.S. military rule, a variety of colonial policies upended the island economy and spurred Puerto Rican migration to the mainland. Yet, even as Puerto Ricans were drawn into the mainland economy, various groups of whites defined them as foreign immigrants unfit for citizenship. In chapter 2, I explore migrants to the mainland in this period, such as Isabel González, who challenged their status as aliens and helped establish the new legal category of U.S. national.

Labor struggles proved to be an important arena of contestation over colonial law and migration. Included within the United States as residents of an unincorporated territory but denied the full rights of citizenship, Puerto Ricans in the early twentieth century became a quintessential "people without a country." As I detail in chapters 3 and 4, while some elite Puerto Ricans sought independence from U.S. colonial rule, many in the working class struggled instead to become recognized as full citizens of the United States. Labor leaders on the mainland and on the island, such as Samuel Gompers and Santiago Iglesias, adopted long-distance strategies to develop a labor movement on the island despite holding different aims. Iglesias allied with the American Federation of Labor (AFL) in order to protect the nascent labor movement in Puerto Rico from repressive island elites. Gompers, meanwhile, sought to improve labor practices on the island in an attempt to stem the migration of impoverished foreign workers to the mainland who would compete with the native-born. This alliance led to large-scale strikes for better wages and petition campaigns among workers calling for U.S. citizenship. In the context of an extensive U.S. Senate investigation into the uprisings, Congress voted to approve the Jones Act, granting Puerto Ricans U.S. citizenship in 1917. As the United States mobilized to fight World War I "to make the world safe for democracy," President Woodrow Wilson called on Congress to rid the nation of what he called the "embarrassment" of protests by colonial subjects in the American republic. This conjuncture of events during World War I—widespread protest on the island and growing concern in Washington over America's reputation abroad—made the condition of statelessness for Puerto Ricans increasingly untenable. The advent of U.S. citizenship status for island residents, though markedly inferior to mainland citizenship because of the lack of representation in Congress, spurred even greater labor mobility than had national status a decade earlier.

I explore in chapter 5 how Puerto Rican efforts to gain full citizenship began to bear fruit after 1917. Citizenship reinforced the legal loophole allowing Puerto Ricans to freely enter the mainland that had been first opened by national status. More significantly, citizenship made Puerto Rican migrants broadly eligible for employment in the United States, a change in the substantive rights of Puerto Ricans on the mainland. U.S. citizenship, then, laid the legal groundwork for what would become one of the largest-scale migrations of the twentieth century as Puerto Ricans eventually became the second-largest Latino group (after Mexicans) living in the continental United States.

In chapter 6 I examine how, even after Puerto Rican migrants could claim U.S. citizenship, however, various groups in the United States persisted in constructing Puerto Ricans as foreigners for their own purposes. New York charity boards in the 1930s, for example, defined Puerto Ricans as foreign immigrants in order to justify repatriations of impoverished people to the island and thereby shrink their relief rolls. In response, Puerto Rican leaders organized politically in New York, overcoming the restrictions of state literacy laws, to elect political leaders.

Whereas American political culture has long assumed that immigrants come from a world set apart, I reframe our understanding of immigrants—demonstrating how many are actually migrants responding to U.S. influence in their home country and moving within the sphere of America's world economic and political power. By showing how early U.S. colonialism in Puerto Rico gave rise to one of the largest migrations in modern American history, I make clear how U.S. involvement abroad not only affected foreign nations, but also fundamentally changed the United States itself.

In this book I demonstrate that Puerto Rico is an extreme case of a broader phenomenon—that of large-scale migrations from countries profoundly shaped by U.S. power such as Mexico, the Philippines, Cuba, Vietnam, and Iraq, among others.[10] Puerto Rico, as a formal colony administered by the U.S. state, forms a distinct part of the larger U.S. empire that includes corporate enclaves in Latin America and zones of war and occupation in Asia and the Middle East. I use the term "colonial" to describe migrations from U.S. juridical spaces, but throughout this book, I also highlight how colonial migrants had much in common with other groups who migrated from a wide variety of U.S. imperial settings. I show how, for many Puerto

Ricans, as for other peoples affected by U.S. state and corporate expansion overseas, the very act of migration was a form of agency in response to global inequalities.

Context in Scholarship

This book contributes to two emerging bodies of historical scholarship: studies of imperial law and studies of colonial migration. It contributes to debates within both of these literatures while also bridging these traditionally separate fields of scholarship.[11] In so doing, this work aims to show the value of an imperial approach to immigration history.

First, it builds on recent studies of U.S. empire by narrating a history of colonial subjects contesting legal categories. Historians have explored the intersection of law and colonialism extensively, demonstrating how law is an instrument of imperial power.[12] A growing body of scholarship has shown how colonial law wrought a violence of exclusion as the United States created new categorizations such as "foreign in a domestic sense" and "unincorporated territories" as a means of withholding constitutional protections from lands deemed to be sources of wealth for the United States but outside the U.S. "territorial domain."[13] In the context of exclusionary control, there is also an important story of the agency of colonial subjects who challenged such laws, often through migration to the mainland.

The history of migrants such as Arcadio Santiago and Isabel González shows how colonial subjects seeking entrance to the metropole and its polity challenged and helped reshape the legal definitions of unincorporated status and noncitizenship that marked U.S. colonial rule. In the period after 1917, those who moved to the U.S. mainland tested the guarantees of the Jones Act and the delicate balance of colonial policy it had made law. When mainland courts and employers refused to recognize this new citizenship, Puerto Ricans' protest over their status became a federal issue. Precisely because Puerto Ricans moving to the mainland could become residents of a state and, potentially, gain full U.S. citizenship, migration proved to be a central arena of conflict for the colonial regime.

Working-class vulnerabilities pushed many people from the colonies to the forefront of legal battles on the mainland over colonialism, migration, and citizenship. In a telling example of what historian Paul Kramer has described as the "asymmetries of power" that marked imperial migrations, migrants arriving in California, New York, and other states faced the contradiction of being labeled "foreign immigrants" despite having been granted U.S. citizenship.[14] Yet, in asserting claims to citizenship in the mainland, Puerto Ricans challenged the imperial boundaries that limited citizenship through territorial status. The book, then, contributes to the scholarly literature on U.S. empire and legal history by showing how colonial law is a charged political arena in which migrants who were desperate to find work in the domestic United States contested, at times successfully, the colonial legal categories that defined them as foreign.

Second, this book builds on recent cultural studies of imperialism by probing the legal, economic, and political origins of colonial migrations. Historians have only just begun to examine how American empire abroad sparked immigration patterns to the United States.[15] This long-standing gap in the literature can be explained by persistent strains of exceptionalist thinking—that is, the belief, among U.S. historians and the public at large, that the United States is a promised land for immigrants from *distant* and *separate* economies. Recent cultural studies of empire that focused on the United States in the Philippines, for example, have shown how a culture of imperialism shaped Filipino migration to the U.S. mainland as hierarchies of race and nation spurred the movement of colonial subjects to the metropole. U.S. schools in the Philippines not only taught English to Filipinos but also inspired many to pursue higher degrees at mainland universities.[16] Historians of other sites of U.S. empire have shown similar patterns. English-speaking black migrants from the British West Indies, who had worked in the corporate enclaves of the United Fruit company in Central America or in the U.S.-occupied Panama Canal Zone, also migrated to the United States. Many who settled in Harlem became supporters of Marcus Garvey's Universal Negro Improvement Association and the "New Negro" movement.[17]

Understanding these legacies of imperialism and their effects on migration has contributed significantly to our understanding of the sources of migration. But the political and legal origins of colonial migration have not been fully understood. How, for example, did the shift in legal status from alien to "U.S. national" shape the migration of colonial subjects? How did the granting of U.S. citizenship in Puerto Rico and its withholding in the Philippines shape different migration patterns from the colonies? Such questions point to the intertwining of colonial law and migration. As in the history of other empires, such as that of Britain, imperial laws had the effect of shaping migration from the colonies to the metropole.[18] In revealing the central role of colonial legal categories in shaping labor migrations, my work challenges notions of American exceptionalism by demonstrating how U.S. immigration patterns have resembled those of other imperial nations.

In bridging these two literatures, this book suggests the value of an imperial approach to the history of migration. Such an approach draws attention to the legal claims migrants made on the mainland and in so doing highlights an important form of agency often overlooked in histories of U.S. empire.[19] At the same time, this work demonstrates how colonial institutions shaped migration streams through a series of changing legal categories that tracked alongside corporate and government demands for labor mobility.[20] Such histories challenge a binary association of empire with structure and migration with agency that can be seen in the historical literature.[21] By highlighting how colonial structures are critical to understanding migration and how the agency of migrants is necessary to understanding empire, this book explores a history shaped as much by the force of U.S. power overseas as by the claims of colonial migrants within the United States.

Note on Sources

Research in both Puerto Rican and mainland U.S. archives has allowed me to tell a series of new and interconnected stories that span the border between metropole and colony. In researching the experience of Puerto Rican migrants to the mainland during World War I, for example, I found the evidentiary record to be scattered in numerous archives. Research in the U.S. National Archives, including the collections of the Bureau of Insular Affairs and the Quartermaster General, led me to previously unexamined material such as the records of the large-scale recruitment of thousands of Puerto Ricans to work in army camps throughout the U.S. South during the war. These documents make clear how the U.S. Army seized on Puerto Ricans' new U.S. citizenship status in 1917 to satisfy wartime labor demands. Research in the Archivo General de Puerto Rico revealed how Puerto Ricans then struggled to be recognized as U.S. citizens, even after they arrived on the mainland and served in the U.S. Army. At the end of World War I, U.S. employers fired Puerto Rican workers they perceived as aliens in order to make room for returning citizens. Records in the Collección Fortaleza, Oficina del Gobernador of the Archivo, reveal how Puerto Ricans petitioned Washington for identity cards that would make clear their citizenship status. Taken separately, these archival records each tell only part of the story.

Taken together, as an imperial history, these documents show not only how the category of citizenship made wartime migration possible, but also how the experiences of colonial migrants during and after the war compelled them to make claims on the state for full citizenship rights.

I built the narrative in this book from evidence in U.S. and Puerto Rican archives in order to map the relationship between colonialism, law, and migration. I examined colonial policy debates and decisions by examining congressional hearings, committee papers, and correspondence in the legislative records of the National Archives and Records Administration. I also examined court cases, newspapers, and labor and business records in U.S. archives. I examined letters, petitions, and newspaper articles in the Archivo General de Puerto Rico and the Collección Puertorriqueña at the University of Puerto Rico. This range of English- and Spanish-language sources has allowed me to tell the story of both state and nonstate actors as they moved between the island and the mainland.

Chapter 1

America's Caribbean Frontier

U.S. military forces invaded Puerto Rico on July 25, 1898, and established military control of the entire island in October of that year.[1] With the ratification of the Treaty of Paris in Washington on February 6, 1899, and in Madrid one month later, the Spanish flag was lowered on the island and the American flag raised to take its place.[2] From the beginning of the American occupation, many Puerto Ricans assumed American liberties would soon follow. U.S. Major General Nelson A. Miles, in fact, made promises of extending American liberal ideals to Puerto Rico shortly after invading the island in 1898. In a broadside issued throughout the island to win support for the U.S. invasion, Miles proclaimed: "The people of the United States in the cause of liberty, justice and humanity . . . come bearing the banner of freedom, inspired by a noble purpose . . . [to] bring you the fostering arm of a nation of free people, whose greatest power is in justice and humanity to all those living within its fold . . . and to bestow upon you the immunities and blessings of the liberal institutions of our government."[3] U.S. colonial officials boasted, in the first months of the occupation, that Puerto Rico would soon be the "gem of the Antilles," the "best governed, happiest, and most prosperous island in the West Indies."[4] But establishing even the initial political and economic institutions on the island proved to be a challenge as

American officials worked to abolish, alter, or build on preexisting Spanish colonial structures to suit changing American needs.[5]

Spanish Colonialism

Understanding U.S. efforts to incorporate the island begins not in Washington or San Juan but in Madrid.[6] Toward the end of the nineteenth century, Spain faced growing anticolonial resistance in the Caribbean, especially when the Cuban War of Independence gained momentum in 1895 and when the Puerto Rican Autonomist Party called for home rule a year later.[7] Contrary to conventional narratives of Spanish imperial decline, the historian Christopher Schmidt-Nowara has shown that Spain attempted ever more sophisticated efforts to retain colonial control.[8]

One such strategy was the Autonomy Charter of 1897, a measure that did in fact win support from liberal elites in Puerto Rico even as it did little to improve the lot of an increasingly disaffected working class. Luis Muñoz Rivera, a wealthy island-born creole journalist who became head of the Autonomist Party in Puerto Rico, led the push for autonomy within the Spanish empire. Muñoz Rivera represented the interests of large landowners after a split in 1897 with the José Celso Barbosa wing of the autonomist movement, which appealed more to urban artisans and professionals.[9] Muñoz Rivera maintained that despite strong opposition from conservative Spanish-born *peninsulares* in Puerto Rico, Spain was likely to offer Puerto Rico liberal reforms because there had been no anticolonial rebellion on the island as there had been in many other Spanish colonies. Muñoz Rivera reasoned that the Spanish government wanted to show its subjects that it was "not retrograde, that it desires the happiness, wealth, progress of its subjects."[10] Hopes of new freedoms abounded in the liberal island press with some speculating that the Spanish *Cortes* would pass the autonomy measure as soon as the rebellion in Cuba subsided.[11]

The Autonomy Charter was passed at the end of 1897 when the Liberal Party in Spain won control of the Cortes.[12] A cablegram from Madrid on November 24 announced the news: "Decrees were signed establishing the Autonomy in Cuba and Puerto Rico."[13] Editors at *La Democracia*, a newspaper run by Muñoz Rivera and other liberal elites, exclaimed: "We register with profound jubilation the news."[14] The Cortes granted Puerto Rico expanded male suffrage as well as significant control over tariffs and the export trade, allowing for an equal number of deputies from the peninsula and colony to decide on island policies.[15] The charter defined Puerto Ricans as full Spanish citizens with fifteen delegates and five senators representing the island in the Spanish Parliament.[16] Puerto Rican elites placed great hope in the charter, predicting that the "injustices, exclusions and irritating suspicions of which we are victims will end forever."[17]

Though proponents of the charter assumed workers would benefit from autonomists' efforts to "obtain the common well-being," labor papers in December 1897 described a working class increasingly marginalized by Puerto Rican liberal elites.[18] The labor press expressed anger at the elite focus of the Autonomist Party leadership: "Oh! You the tyrants of the worker, masters of capital, nothing stops you from bringing cruel injustices upon us."[19] Though Muñoz Rivera courted workers' support, he was routinely criticized for his paternalistic approach, defining himself as a patriarch protecting the "sons of labor."[20] Such concerns suggest that class inequality among Puerto Ricans, as much as imperial control, shaped working-class concerns.

In February of 1898 when the Spanish government formed a local cabinet known as the Autonomic Council and installed Muñoz Rivera as minister of internal affairs, writers in *Ensayo Obrero*, a working-class paper founded by the labor leader Santiago Iglesias Pantín and published in San Juan, compared the new creole elite to the peninsular elite that had ruled ten years earlier. In 1887 black artisans suffered torture at the hands of Spanish colonial officials but peninsulares in San Juan did little to protect them. In disgust, black leaders such as Sotero Figueroa migrated to New York to found the Club Borinquen and work alongside José Martí for the independence of Cuba and Puerto Rico.[21] "The iron hand that weighed over the worker class in '87 is the same," writers for the *Ensayo Obrero* claimed, "though with a different glove, in 1897."[22] Indeed, Muñoz Rivera moved quickly to exclude from positions of power members of the Orthodox-Reformist Party, a rival party that appealed to urban workers.[23] Complaints that Muñoz Rivera was insulting to workers and power hungry circulated in the labor press, especially after the alliance of autonomists on the island with the monarchical Liberal Party in Spain was made public.[24]

Editorials in the *Ensayo Obrero* lamented the continued "situation of misery" of the working classes in the Spanish autonomist period. In an editorial entitled "Looking toward the Future," Iglesias and the editors of *Ensayo* pointed to two persistent obstacles working people faced under the new autonomist regime: the lack of unions and the high cost of living. "Because we are completely disorganized," they wrote, "we don't have force and enough will to . . . do something grand and lasting, taking advantage of and making use of the freedoms that they give us and the rights that as honorable citizens the new autonomic form gives us." Having been forbidden to organize unions under Spanish colonial control, the advent of autonomy found Puerto Rican workers without an established infrastructure for mobilizing the working class. The editors called on Muñoz Rivera's autonomist government to "see if by means of wise disposition the horrible misery and the lack of necessary food for workers can be diminished, which for being excessively expensive, we can't reach for the meager resources that we have."[25]

Recognizing that the political power of labor had increased with the expansion of suffrage under the Autonomy Charter, the labor leader Iglesias traveled around the island to organize workers. He held large public meetings and expanded the Economic and Social Studies Center he had founded the previous year to hold lectures and other activities in support of the nascent labor movement.[26] Liberal elites, however, grew deeply suspicious of worker radicalism and its potential to unseat autonomists in power.[27] As a result, labor organizers were routinely arrested, blacklisted, and intimidated by officials in the autonomist period.[28] In the early months of 1898, before the U.S. invasion in fact, Muñoz Rivera had Iglesias arrested for organizing a mass meeting of workers, and had the *Ensayo Obrero* fined for criticizing the Catholic Church and the autonomist regime.[29]

U.S. Military Occupation

It was in this context of a newly satisfied liberal elite and a disaffected working class that the U.S. occupation began. Soon after the Spanish-Cuban-American War ended in the summer of 1898, General Guy V. Henry was installed as the U.S. military governor to great acclaim in the island's elite liberal press. Henry spoke of the need to improve public order and sanitation and Muñoz Rivera lent his public support: "We applaud the goals laid out in General Henry's plan."[30] In welcoming the American occupying forces, Muñoz Rivera and his followers expected to attain autonomy quickly, this time within the U.S. empire rather than that of Spain. As the historian Christina Duffy Ponsa has shown, liberal elites in this period understood statehood as perfectly in line with the goals of autonomy.[31] Indeed, in a symbolic gesture Muñoz Rivera renamed his party the Federal Party, signaling his faith that incorporation of Puerto Rico as a state within the American federal system was imminent.[32]

For their part, urban craft workers, who had been dissatisfied with liberal reforms since the early 1890s, seized on the promise of American liberties to form unions and win protections long denied by Spanish rule, the Autonomy Charter, and Puerto Rican elites.[33] As one labor paper exclaimed: "Behold the American people! Our grateful country greets you wanting to live with you and . . . the life of liberty, of justice, and of light." "The American Government, inspired by democratic doctrines," wrote another, "will give the country the laws which the best agree upon for its administration."[34] Workers' expectation that the U.S. takeover meant autonomy from liberal elites led them to push more forcefully for unionization. With persistently high levels of unemployment in this period, reports in the labor press stating that "many workers [were] without work" were often coupled with early calls for organizing unions.[35] Urban artisans, in fact, organized the first labor federation on the island in October 1898.[36] In the early months of the occupation, the Federación Regional de los Trabajadores worked to establish worker circles to allow for the continued education of its members, to raise funds to support their work of fighting against the "tyranny of monopolistic capitalists," and to pressure the new colonial government for the eight-hour day.[37] The goal of the eight-hour day was realized when General Henry adopted the measure on May 1, 1899. Workers responded with great enthusiasm, as can be seen in letters from workers published in labor papers stating that "it fills us with legitimate pride," and "demonstrates the inexorable spirit of justice."[38] When newly formed unions organized strikes against employers who refused to recognize the eight-hour measure, they sought to make real General Henry's promise of American democratic reform.[39]

Indeed, the U.S. occupation opened a political space for workers to organize independently from the elite liberal regime that had so firmly ruled the island in the Spanish autonomy period.[40] The intellectual ferment of worker newspapers, study circles, and newly built lending libraries fueled the labor movement and connected workers on the island to socialists and anarchists overseas.[41] When Santiago Iglesias reached out to the American Socialist Worker's Party in 1899, for instance, Henry Kuhn, the ASWP secretary, responded with enthusiasm: "It is now the time for uniting and properly organizing the socialists of Puerto Rico inside the Socialist Worker's Party of America."[42]

Export Markets and Coastwise Shipping

Yet while the U.S. occupation gave rise to fervent hope within Puerto Rico over the promise of democratic reforms and the fledgling labor movement, it also brought upheaval to the island economy. Under Spanish rule, the Puerto Rican economy had centered on coffee, the primary export of the island, accounting for more than 70 percent of all exports in the late nineteenth century. Grown under ideal conditions in the tropical highlands of the Cordillera Central, Puerto Rican coffee was coveted in Europe for its strong and distinctive flavor, selling in Spain and other parts of Europe for prices equivalent to Mocha and Java beans from Indonesia, the highest-priced coffee in the world. Puerto Rico also sold its coffee to Cuba, a country with little domestic coffee production. As the Cubans preferred the cheaper grades, and Europeans the most expensive, Puerto Rican coffee farmers could routinely export all their yearly harvest, worth seven to eight million dollars.[43] The coffee export trade grew significantly with the rise of coffee prices on the international market after 1885. In 1886 coffee accounted for 49 percent of the island's exports; ten years later, in 1896, coffee accounted for a full 77 percent of all Puerto Rican exports. The year 1896 marked the highest point of coffee production on record with 58,656,826 pounds exported.[44] Such rapid growth of the coffee export trade prompted many to predict a prosperous future. One local observer described the Puerto Rican coffee zone in the late nineteenth century as "silvery mountains that vomit millions, giants of gold that give rise to crazy fortunes, prodigal fountains that nurture an entire people."[45] The decade immediately preceding the U.S. takeover would become known on the island as the "edad de oro," or golden age, for coffee growers, many of whom were small-scale producers.[46]

The U.S. takeover in 1898 devastated Puerto Rico's economy by all but abolishing the coffee trade.[47] With the end of Spanish rule, the island lost access to its protected, and therefore most profitable, export markets in Spain and Cuba. This change could be seen most dramatically in trade statistics. In 1890 only 22 percent of the island's exports were shipped to the United States, but in 1939 exports to the United States had reached 95 percent of the island's exports.[48] Because the U.S. market was already saturated with coffee from Brazil, Puerto Rican coffee, which sold for higher prices for reasons of quality and shipping costs, could not compete. Recognizing the impact on Puerto Rico of losing the Spanish markets without gaining a replacement market in the United States, General George Davis, the American military governor on the island, observed that economic conditions in the first year of the American occupation were "much worse than before the troops landed."[49]

The change of sovereignty also brought the new coastwise shipping laws mandating that American steamers carry all Puerto Rican goods to and from the United States and between the island's ports.[50] "Coastwise" was a nineteenth-century term used to describe commerce that was not "interior" to the continental United States but, instead, between ports on the Atlantic or Pacific coasts and islands "so near thereto and belonging to the several States, as properly to constitute a part of the coast."[51] President McKinley first extended the coastwise designation to Puerto Rico as a military measure during the War of 1898.[52] When the policy was extended after the war, critics who recognized the relative lack of American ships assigned to the Puerto Rico trade (as compared with the far larger number from Spain and Britain) excoriated the measure as a "great blunder," one that fundamentally threatened the island's economy.[53] McKinley temporarily amended the measure in 1899 to allow foreign vessels to also carry goods between the island and the United States, thus buying time for the U.S. steamship trust to develop regular service to Ponce and San Juan.[54]

But by early 1900, with the coastwise laws back in full force, a group of Puerto Rican officials, together with Dr. Azel Ames, a U.S. physician in charge of distributing the smallpox vaccine in Puerto Rico, decried the law as a "grievous hardship" that allowed for American shipmasters to charge exorbitant rates.[55] As American steamship companies no longer had to compete with foreign companies for the transport of Puerto Rican exports to the United States, they held a de facto monopoly on trade, causing shipping rates to rise considerably.[56] U.S. colonial policy thus caused both a rise in shipping prices and the destruction of the coffee export market.

Already made vulnerable by a weakening economy under U.S. rule, Puerto Rico entered a period of acute crisis when hurricane San Ciriaco swept across the island on August 8, 1899.[57] Laying waste to the small subsistence farms of half the population, and the houses of fully one quarter, the hurricane killed thousands of farm animals and some 2,700 people. Surveying the damage, Governor Davis doubted if another people in modern history had ever been "so devastated and overwhelmed as was Puerto Rico in one day of August last."[58] Indeed, the timing of San Ciriaco could not have been more tragic. Coming just before the coffee harvest season was to begin in September, the hurricane decimated nearly all of what had been the island's primary export.[59] Flattening shade trees by the thousands, the hurricane exposed hillside coffee farms to the blistering tropical sun. Without the shade they required, maturing coffee berries quickly shriveled to ruin.

By clearing debris and replacing fallen trees, coffee planters hoped to preserve at least part of their crop for the following year's harvest. But most farmers were unable to find local banks willing to extend them credit. With U.S. trade policies aggravating the impact of the hurricane by leading to both increased costs and decreased selling prices, banks came to view coffee farmers—formerly the chief exporters of the island—as a bad investment. As Governor Davis stated in a hearing before the U.S. Senate, "They are absolutely powerless to secure financial assistance from insular or exterior sources, and are doomed to inaction, decay and disaster unless help be given."[60] Recognizing that the tropical sun and vegetation were quickly consuming what was left of the coffee farms, and that new coffee plants would require five years of growth before bearing fruit, Governor Davis asked Washington to intervene with a loan of ten million dollars. When the loan was denied, Davis pleaded: "The country was paralyzed by this storm; discouragement was almost everywhere. The situation is one of very great gravity. I can not overstate it."[61] The U.S. takeover and the resulting contraction of the coffee export market brought about, in turn, the unwillingness of U.S. banks to extend credit to coffee farmers, leaving most unable to recover from San Ciriaco.[62]

Exclusionary Control

While coastwise shipping, like General Miles's original promises of freedom in 1898, suggested a measure of incorporation into the U.S. polity, other U.S. policies suggested exclusion. In January 1899, for example, President McKinley ordered military officials to begin collecting import duties on goods shipped to the island from the United States, implying that the U.S. Constitution did not necessarily follow the flag.[63] If the Constitution extended to the island, then collecting customs at Puerto Rican ports would violate the Constitution's uniformity clause, which stated that all taxes must be uniform throughout the United States.[64] Still, McKinley required that such duties be collected in San Juan, even after the final ratification of the Treaty of Paris in early 1899. This practice revealed the assumption of the McKinley administration that the Constitution did not extend to Puerto Rico *ex propio vigore*, or automatically.[65]

In fact, U.S. government actions in a wide variety of realms demonstrated the U.S. refusal to extend the Constitution to Puerto Rico but, instead, to build on Spanish colonial practices prior to autonomy to establish American colonial policy. The practice of applying U.S. customs laws to Puerto Rico, for instance, built on long-standing Spanish colonial practice. Rather than relying on taxes on income or real estate, Spain had used tariffs on imports and exports as the main source of revenue for their administration of the island. But McKinley's decision in 1899 to continue this tax regime brought what had been settled Spanish colonial practice into one of the most divisive domains of U.S. legal debate. Legal scholars and the Supreme Court wrestled with the question of empire and the constitutional status of Puerto Rico. Continuing the Spanish practice of charging tariffs would eventually require, after the court ruled on Puerto Rico's status in 1901, defining the island as unincorporated, or outside the jurisdiction of the Constitution.

As with U.S. customs policy, the American form of governance on the island also built on preexisting Spanish colonial institutions. During four centuries of colonial rule, Spain had centralized the island government in the governor appointed by the Spanish Crown. *Alcaldes*, mayors appointed by the governor to govern each of the sixty-nine municipal districts on the island, administered the governor's policies. The Provincial Assembly in San Juan, also known as the Provincial Deputation, was made up of six elected representatives from each region, but it held no legislative power and served solely as an administrative body in charge of running the schools, jails, and public works.[66]

Under the terms of the 1897 Autonomy Charter, Spain had granted each alcalde on the island the "power to frame its own laws regarding public education, highways, public health, municipal finances, as well as to appoint and remove its own employees."[67] Yet even after the Autonomy Charter was passed, Spanish colonial officials proved to be unwilling to cede authority to alcaldes for fear of compromising their own power and patronage networks. In early 1898, for instance, evidence suggests that the Spanish governor overruled alcaldes who tried to make personnel changes within their municipalities.[68] The U.S. military government kept the Spanish system of alcaldes in place, but stripped municipalities of the broad powers granted them in the autonomy period, with the effect of centralizing power in San Juan.[69] Though the U.S. regime allowed for more regular local elections than during the Spanish period and allowed for alcaldes to be sworn into office without the approval of the governor, the alcaldes' power was so constrained that they became mere functionaries of the U.S. colonial bureaucracy.[70]

Like the tariff laws and governance structure, the judicial system in the period of U.S. military occupation was superimposed over Spanish institutions. The Spanish judiciary had taken the form of a supreme court on the island, along with an administrative court, military court, and naval court.

In addition, there were eight "courts of first instance," one in each of the judicial districts.[71] Given that Spanish courts did not provide for the rights of trial by jury, or habeas corpus (protection from unlawful imprisonment), American colonial officials from the beginning of the occupation feared that U.S. investors would not come to the island without the protections of U.S. courts. As the military governor wrote in 1900, U.S. investors worried that they would be "liable at any time to be imprisoned on trumped-up charges and to languish in jail, incommunicado, while the case dragged its slow length along through the local courts."[72] Investors, U.S. citizens already living on the island, and American colonial officials all clamored for U.S. protections. Yet because many U.S. colonial officials assumed that Puerto Ricans would not be extended the full rights of the U.S. Constitution and citizenship, they counseled against converting all the Spanish courts to the American legal system.[73] One solution was the institution of a U.S. district court in San Juan with appellate power. Such an extension of the U.S. legal system abroad built on a nineteenth-century tradition of U.S. consuls deciding cases involving Americans overseas, beginning in China in 1844.[74] The district court in San Juan was established in 1900 to review decisions of local courts that were still structured as under Spanish colonial rule and overturn decisions deemed unjust by American legal precedent.[75] Given the challenge of rewriting the legal system on the island and staffing all its courts with people who were both familiar with American legal traditions and able to speak Spanish, superimposing an American court over the Spanish system seemed, to the U.S. military governor, the most practical solution.[76]

The U.S. military government, which had brought such dramatic changes to the Puerto Rican economy, thus made only minor alterations to the political structure of the island, thereby keeping much of the Spanish colonial system in place. Given that Congress was expected to establish the rules governing the new possession in a few years or months, the U.S. military government assumed that its military rule would be temporary. According to the U.S. War Department, "The tendency of the military government under such circumstances was naturally to abstain from interference with the courts, the laws, and native institutions."[77] Such continuities in colonial law and administration between the late Spanish and early American periods suggest, as Fernando Picó has argued, that 1898 was not the watershed moment it is sometimes thought to be.[78] In this way, the U.S. extended Spanish colonial forms of law and governance while refusing to extend full U.S. constitutional protections to Puerto Ricans.

Movement of people

The Foraker Act

The U.S. Army ceded military control over the island on May 1, 1900, when the "Organic Act for Puerto Rico," commonly known as the Foraker Act, took effect and Charles Allen was installed as the first U.S. civil governor of Puerto Rico. Governor Davis hailed the measure as an act of American benevolence, claiming, "The lack and miseries of the past and of the present will soon be replaced by happiness and abundance."[79] For their part, liberal autonomists like Muñoz Rivera viewed the new colonial government as a tragic setback from the autonomy achieved under Spain. "With the civil regime today, like the military regime yesterday, the Puerto Rican people continue without free will, identity, without right of intervention in the government of the country," lamented writers in the elite newspaper *La Democracia*.[80] "From this point of view," they continued, "we have not progressed at all . . . a frank and expansive autonomy handed over a tight and oppressive centralization, and in this atmosphere we have lived under Governor Davis and we will continue to live under Governor Allen."[81]

Under the terms of section 8 of the Foraker Act, the current laws and ordinances of Puerto Rico—some holdovers of the period of pre-autonomy Spanish rule and some implemented by the U.S. military during the period of occupation—were to remain on the books unless specifically altered or repealed by an act of the U.S. Congress. In the language of the act, "The laws and ordinances of Porto Rico now in force shall continue in full force and effect."[82] Thus, even into the early 1900s, with the advent of civilian rule on the island, U.S. colonial policy continued to be shaped by preexisting colonial Spanish institutions, laws, and practices.

Civil government began on the island just two weeks after the U.S. Congress passed the Foraker Act. The quick order of events and spare detail of the act itself left colonial officials in San Juan with little time and few instructions for bringing about the transition from a military occupation to a civil government. The transition to civilian rule was made all the more difficult by Congress's decision to extend parts of U.S. law to the island and withhold others.

The 1899 Treaty of Paris with Spain had granted U.S. Congress plenary, or near absolute, power in governing the island, stating that "the civil rights and political status of the native inhabitants of the territories hereby ceded to the United States shall be determined by the Congress."[83] While the 1900 Foraker Act transferred some of this power to elected officials on the island, the U.S. Congress retained significant control over the island's affairs, including tariff and immigration policies governing the movement of goods and people between the island and the mainland. Granted such plenary power, Albert Beveridge, Joseph Foraker, and other leaders in Congress expressed great faith in their ability to regulate the effects of colonialism with legislation in Washington. Should Congress elect to regulate the entrance of people or goods from the colonies to the mainland, Foraker claimed in 1900, "it will be simply a question of policy."[84] But Foraker's confidence would prove to be misplaced as congressional decisions made in Washington had often unanticipated effects on both the island and the mainland.

On the question of whether or not the Constitution followed the flag, the Foraker Act extended U.S. statutes to Puerto Rico, except for U.S. laws governing internal revenue, but did not so extend the Constitution of the United States.[85] After rancorous debate in Congress, the act further declared that residents of the island would be "citizens of Porto Rico" but not citizens of the United States. Academics writing in this period understood the island as fundamentally different from the United States, pointing, in particular, to the "enervating effect" of the tropical climate. L. S. Rowe, a professor of political science at the University of Pennsylvania and a member of the U.S. Commission to Revise and Compile the Laws of Porto Rico, wrote that "the energy and assertiveness which are as necessary to the maintenance of civil and political rights as to the attainment of industrial success, have little opportunity for development under the conditions that prevail in the tropics."[86] Rowe and other U.S. observers clearly assumed that the tropical environment—rather than four centuries of Spanish colonial rule—was to blame for Puerto Rico's failure to develop a "progressive civilization."[87]

The Coasting Trade and Currency Reform

While the Constitution and U.S. citizenship were withheld from the island, other parts of U.S. law, such as coastwise shipping laws, were extended to it. Significantly, the extension of coastwise laws to Puerto Rico followed a precedent set in extending such laws to Hawai'i, an incorporated territory.[88] These laws were not extended, however, to the Philippines because of vigorous protests there that the application of coastwise laws, and the requirement that goods be shipped in American steamships, would be disastrous. Because Filipinos depended on foodstuffs shipped between the many islands of the archipelago in non-U.S. ships, Secretary of War William Taft successfully argued that the application of coastwise laws to the Philippines would lead to a "pitiable" condition.[89] No such advocate came forward for Puerto Rico.

With the beginning of civilian rule in 1900, the coastwise shipping mandate in the Foraker Act, which required that American ships carry all goods between the island and the mainland, turned what had originally been a wartime measure into permanent policy. Section 9 of the Foraker Act stated: "The coasting trade between Puerto Rico and the United States shall be regulated in accordance with the provisions of law applicable to such trade between any two great coasting districts of the United States."[90] The Supreme Court ruled on the question of shipping between San Juan and New York shortly after Congress passed the Foraker Act.[91] In the *Huss v. New York and Puerto Rican Steamship Co.* decision, the court ruled in 1901 that Puerto Rico "is properly a part of the domestic trade of the country since the treaty of annexation, and is so recognized by the Puerto Rican or Foraker Act." Thus, McKinley's executive order to apply the coastwise laws to the island as a military measure, the Foraker Act of 1900, and the Huss decision a year later effectively placed Puerto Rico, for the purposes of U.S. shipping law, on the Atlantic coast of the United States. This decision had the dual effect of dramatically increasing costs for Puerto Rican producers as well as increasing costs of living for consumers on the island.

Ironically, Puerto Rico's devastated export economy was made still worse in the early civilian rule period by another reform that was meant to help it: currency reform. Beginning in 1900, the McKinley administration initiated an experiment in currency reform that sought to bring Puerto Rico to the U.S. gold standard in order to promote trade with the mainland. Such an experiment grew out of the late nineteenth-century contest over monetary standards that pitted farmer-led Democrat "Silverites" against business-led Republican "Goldbugs." Both sides argued their case with an eye to expanding trade overseas: Silverites claimed that a silver standard would better promote trade with Asian and Latin American economies that were based on silver; Goldbugs looked to cement ties with England, which was also based on gold, and disparaged silver currency, which they viewed as the mark of "lesser," "uncivilized" countries.[92]

After vigorously campaigning for the gold standard in the 1896 presidential campaign, McKinley signed the Gold Standard Act in 1900, making gold the only legal tender in the United States.[93] That same year, the McKinley administration, along with Republican supporters in Congress, turned their attention to extending the gold standard to the colonies. As the historian Emily Rosenberg points out, these financial missionaries abroad believed

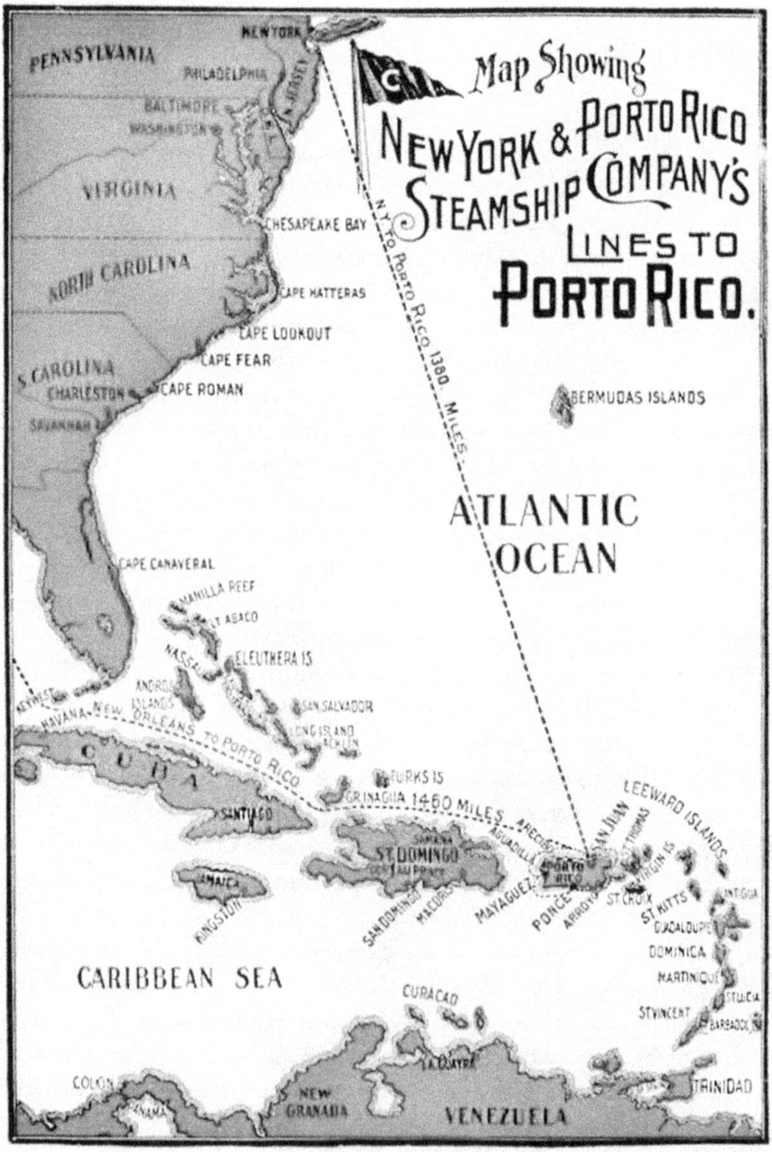

Figure 1.1. "Map Showing New York and Porto Rico Steamship Company's Lines to Porto Rico," c. 1900. Centro de Estudios Puertorriqueños, Hunter College, New York City.

"that rationalizing systems of exchange on the basis of gold would expand markets, attract investment, and bring material progress."[94] Currency reform, then, reflected the twin Progressive-era impulses of rationalization and social uplift.

The Foraker Act brought the gold standard to Puerto Rico. It mandated that Puerto Rican pesos be redeemed for U.S. dollars at a rate of one Puerto Rican peso to $.60 (U.S.).[95] According to the economist Edwin Kemmerer, a contemporary advocate of the gold standard and advisor to the McKinley administration and the U.S. Treasury Department, the exact rate of exchange was highly contested. In Puerto Rico, he found that "creditors as a class, including merchants and bankers, favored a high gold rate; debtors, consisting chiefly of the agricultural population, favored a low gold rate."[96] The rate of one peso to $.60 was derived from surveying creditors and debtors and then pegging the value at a point of compromise in between. Senator John Morgan, a Southern Democrat who was both a leading voice in the Foreign Relations Committee and a staunch white supremacist, objected to the exchange rate, presumably out of an interest in promoting consumption of U.S. goods overseas. Morgan worried about the effect of the exchange rate on Puerto Rican workers: "Can we take from these people, poor as they are represented to be, this 40 cents in every dollar and put it in the treasury of the U.S., and go home and go to bed and sleep with our consciences?"[97]

Though the full impact of the currency reform could not be known in March 1900, Morgan had good reason to worry. Indeed, the gold standard provision of the Foraker Act spawned a number of unintended consequences, the most significant of which was a dramatic rise in the cost of living. As one observer wrote, "Merchants are trying to make the consumers pay the difference in the exchange of money by increasing the price of food." Workers throughout the island echoed this concern, asking the governor to prevent merchants from raising prices of "the necessaries of life."[98] As General Davis observed in 1900, while a "poor peon" who had saved ten pesos was given only six dollars, merchants "would seek to put him off with as little codfish, rice, or rum as he would have gotten the day before for his pesos."[99] Another observed: "Bakers gave no larger loaf of bread for an American cent than for a Porto Rican centavo."[100] This phenomenon of selling the same goods for higher prices extended to rents and transportation costs as well as food: omnibus fares in San Juan, for example, were changed from ten centavos to ten cents in August 1900.[101] Similarly, rents rose as "a dollar was extracted after August 1 for every peso that had been collected the month before."[102] Thus the currency was devalued a stunning 40 percent—by practice if not by law.

Currency reformers had touted the gold standard as a progressive reform that would benefit workers by expanding purchasing power.[103] In practice, however, rising prices far outstripped rising wages. General Davis lamented in terms both condescending and sympathetic that the "dense ignorance of 80 per cent of the inhabitants and their general helplessness was taken advantage of by the merchants, local bankers, and employers of labor."[104] Most coffee laborers, McKinley's adviser Edwin Kemmerer admitted, faced only deepening poverty: "A peon on a coffee plantation whose wages of P 15 a month were reduced to $9 as the result of the [exchange of money], and who found the prices of the goods he bought unchanged, irrevocably lost 40% of his monthly wage; and his loss was repeated each month until there was a readjustment through an increase in his wage, a reduction in prices or both."[105] Sugar workers generally fared better, with some even winning wage conversion at par.[106] Yet while wages rose for some, prices rose for all, leading one observer to estimate a general rise in the cost of living of 10–15 percent in 1900.[107]

The *canje*, or exchange of money, shaped the lives not only of coffee day laborers and sugar workers but owners of small farms as well. The average farm size on the island in this period was 12.5 acres.[108] Owners of these farms, who mostly grew coffee, routinely bought the supplies they needed at the start of the growing season from local storekeepers on credit. With a term of credit usually lasting the length of the growing season, farmers would settle their accounts at harvest time by paying the storekeeper in crops. The storekeeper, in turn, settled his debt with suppliers and merchants by paying them with produce he received from the farmer. The change in the value of money affected all these transactions—even when no money changed hands—as it reset the prices of goods bought and sold. Thus coffee farmers dealing in credit saw the same upward pressure on prices that others saw when dealing in cash. Coming on the heels of the devastating 1898 loss of the Spanish markets, and the 1899 hurricane, such pressure all but wiped out the coffee sector.

Debating Free Trade

Puerto Ricans did not passively accept the massive economic disruption brought by U.S. colonialism. The loss of the coffee market, the lack of government emergency aid after San Ciriaco, and the rising cost of living all drove workers to petition the colonial state for aid. One petitioner complained that attempts to mitigate the effect of the hurricane have been "fruitless" and that the "exchange in the Puerto Rico currency for American money will be a new cyclone."[109] Isidor González, president of the Labor Union of Carolina, Puerto Rico, representing some four hundred workers, wrote to the governor in May asking that "something be done to relieve the distress caused by the change of money, their wages being cut 50 centavos per day, and the price of provisions rising." Workers, he continued, were not able to support their families, and "unless they are protected by the government, their suffering will be unbearable." Governor Allen was unsympathetic. He wrote that while he could not interfere with contracts established between employers and employees, he hoped that "the rate of wages will accommodate itself to the changed conditions." With rampant unemployment, he urged workers to be content with work "at any price," adding "all these deprivations must be borne patiently."[110] Allen, who would resign the governorship in 1902 and later become president of the American Sugar Refining Company, in fact regularly favored the interests of business over labor. "Puerto Rico has plenty of laborers and poor people generally," he stated. "What the island needs is men with capital, energy, and enterprise."[111]

In the context of the ongoing economic crisis, many Puerto Ricans called for free trade with the United States. As early as February 1900, when the Foraker bill was still being debated, Tulio Larrinaga, a civil engineer who had been appointed assistant secretary of the interior under the insular government, wrote a petition along with twelve other Puerto Ricans to Congress. Describing themselves as "children [of the U.S.] by late adoption," they asked Congress, "Who are we, what are we? Are we citizens or are we subjects?" Decrying the fact that they had "no voice in the government" and "no markets where to dispose of their goods," they maintained that only the intervention of the U.S. Congress could keep Puerto Ricans from the "starvation and ruin before them." Recognizing the impact of the decimated coffee industry, Larrinaga wrote that the island found its "props and mainstays cut from beneath her whole commercial structure." Larrinaga saw only one way out of this crisis: free trade between Puerto Rico and the United States. Such a policy, he reasoned, would both expand Puerto Rico's export market, particularly for coffee, and allow food staples to be imported at lower prices, creating, he hoped, "abundant food for the islanders, who are now starving."[112] The editors of *La Democracia*, though highly critical of most of the

Foraker Act, did support the free trade measure, noting "it may be able to bring benefits to our despondent situation."[113]

But the question of free trade proved to be divisive among American farmers and corporations, Puerto Rican producers, and the steamship companies who relied on trade between them. As one of the largest trusts in the United States, the American Sugar Refining Company was perhaps the most powerful backer of free trade with the island, exerting great influence in Washington. If the company could import tens of thousands of tons of raw sugar without tariffs for refining in New York, it stood to save millions of dollars. The sugar trust was joined in its pro–free trade stance by another powerful American trust: the New York and Porto Rico Steamship Company. As the main carrier of people and cargo between San Juan and New York, the Steamship Company operated daily voyages from each port. In the midst of the coffee crisis on the island, however, steamship freight had dropped precipitously, with ships routinely returning from San Juan empty, or in ballast. In a letter to Congress, the Steamship Company asserted that free trade, which was sure to increase sugar exports, and thereby increase its profits, was also essential to Puerto Rico's economic security. Strategically emphasizing the projected benefits to the island over its own self-interest, the Steamship Company asserted that without free trade Puerto Rico would "remain practically bankrupt."[114] With the increase in shipping costs brought about by the coastwise laws, importers in New York also stood to gain from a decrease in import duties that would come with free trade.[115]

For their part, Puerto Rican business leaders looked on free trade as an economic necessity. George Finlay, a representative of the Puerto Rican Chamber of Commerce, called for free trade as a means of rescuing an economy devastated by the coffee crisis: "Merchants have been compelled to limit their operations, banks have suspended making advances, agricultural properties are heavily mortgaged, and in many ways the work has been suspended; laborers are out of employment, whole families are in misery, and hunger threatens everywhere, the poor farm laborers being in such a state of destitution as they never have been before in the history of the island."[116] Thus Puerto Rican business leaders and U.S. merchants both supported free trade.

But while American importers, steamship and sugar refining companies, and Puerto Ricans generally all supported free trade, those opposing it also had powerful backers, namely, American farmers. Herbert Myrick, chair of the League of Domestic Producers representing three million U.S. farmers, denounced the precedent free trade with Puerto Rico would set. U.S.

farmers, he contended, could not compete with tropical farmers in sugar, tobacco, and semitropical fruits and vegetables.[117] In a petition to Congress he wrote: "Free trade with the tropics would thus introduce entirely new economic conditions."

The most powerful opponent of free trade was the domestic beet sugar industry, which routinely opposed policies that encouraged foreign competition in sugar cane.[118] Henry Oxnard, president of the Oxnard Beet Sugar Company in Oxnard, California, which extracted sugar from white beets grown in the U.S. Southwest, was the industry's most vocal spokesman. Citing a dramatic wage differential—mainland sugar workers were paid thirty cents an hour and Puerto Rican sugar workers were paid thirty cents a day—he argued that, "with the low price of labor down there we can not expect to develop a beet-sugar industry in the U.S. in competition; it is impossible."[119]

Oxnard supported his position against free trade with an appeal to racial ideologies, a clear example of how race could be deployed for specific political purposes. Calling for caution when extending freedoms to the colonies, he claimed that "the latin race, after years of the rule of despotism, suddenly given too much power, is a troublesome if not a dangerous factor with which to deal."[120] Though nativists like Oxnard made few distinctions between Puerto Rico and the Philippines, American colonial officials, much like Spanish officials before them, in fact incorporated Puerto Rico to a greater degree than the Philippines. In contrast to U.S. colonial practice in Puerto Rico, the United States defined the Philippines as a foreign port and did not establish a district court there or introduce U.S. currency.[121]

Democrats from southern and western states also favored tariffs for reasons of economics and racial nativism. Senator Francis G. Newlands of Nevada opposed the rise of East Coast monopolies such as the American Sugar Refining Company and the attendant rise of colonial sugar cane plantations that relied on cheap nonwhite labor. He favored, instead, protective tariffs to support small-scale beet sugar farms in the Southwest that could be worked by whites in the model of Jefferson's agrarian ideal. The historian April Merleaux argues that "populist anti-imperialists" such as Newlands and others, including Senator Ben Tillman of South Carolina, opposed free trade on economic and racial nativist grounds.[122]

Against the protest of Oxnard, domestic farmers, and Democrats from the South and West, the Foraker Act of 1900 allowed for the possibility of free trade with Puerto Rico in the future.[123] When the act was passed, its supporters understood the collection of tariffs on trade between Puerto

Rico and the United States as a temporary measure, one that would eventually be repealed once the island legislature devised a way of supporting the government through local taxation. The Foraker Act stipulated that by March 1, 1902, the Legislative Assembly should decide on the question of the tariff. Once the assembly passed a resolution certifying the successful operation of local taxation and requested the end of the tariff, then the president of the United States could sign into law free trade between the island and the mainland.[124] On July 4, 1901, the Legislative Assembly met for a joint session, lasting three hours, to decide on the question. After voting unanimously in support of free trade, Governor Allen signed the resolution before a large crowd of spectators in Assembly Hall in San Juan. Governor Allen then delivered the resolution to President McKinley and asked for his final approval.

Supporters on the island requested that the president sign the measure on the anniversary of the U.S. takeover of Puerto Rico in order to make a political point: by abolishing tariffs, the U.S. Constitution would begin to follow the flag to the island. Critics in Washington, however, noted the unusual process by which this free trade measure came into being: "It is almost certain that Congress could not have been induced to do by legislation what the President has done by Executive action."[125] Though Congress had allowed for the possibility of free trade through the passage of the Foraker Act of 1900, opinions on the matter had long been divided in Washington. Indeed, the Supreme Court's May 1901 decision in *Downes v. Bidwell* to uphold the legality of the tariff and declare, in effect, that the Constitution did not follow the flag, suggested the possibility that Congress would have voted against free trade and in favor of continuing the tariff.[126]

Ships carrying raw sugar from Puerto Rico to refineries in Brooklyn idled outside New York Harbor waiting for McKinley to sign the measure. Sugar merchants in New York directed the *Mannie Swan*, for instance, to cruise slowly along the eastern coast with its cargo of sugar until the measure was signed. By delaying its arrival in New York Harbor until July 25, merchants unloading the *Mannie Swan*'s cargo stood to save an estimated six thousand dollars, the beginning of sizable savings for U.S. sugar refiners and other merchants involved in the Puerto Rico trade.[127] President McKinley approved the resolution and proclaimed the official beginning of free trade on July 25, 1901, the day marked locally as the anniversary of the arrival of the American flag.[128]

The uneven benefits of this free trade policy, however, shaped the success as well as the failure of various agro-export industries on the island.

Ironically, coffee farmers—those most desperate for a new market in the United States—won no advantage at all. Because coffee was placed on the "free list" for all countries, free trade status gave Puerto Rico coffee farmers no price advantage over Brazil when selling in the U.S. market. Free trade did, however, confer significant advantages to the Puerto Rican sugar industry. Indeed, free trade made Puerto Rico exempt from the sugar tariff, a tax imposed on all other sugar imports to the mainland.[129] The same was true of fruits (at issue in *Downes v. Bidwell*) and early spring vegetables. As one observer explained, free trade positioned Puerto Rican farmers inside America's "ring fence," giving them an advantage over competitors who had to pay import duties.[130] Thus, while free trade led to growth in sugar, fruit, and vegetable exports, it failed to save the coffee industry.

Creating a Legal Borderland

Yet even as free trade and coastwise shipping brought Puerto Rico's economy within the "domestic trade" of the United States, other parts of the Foraker Act suspended the island's political structure in a legal borderland. Puerto Rico's legislative branch, for example, was designed as a kind of hybrid of republican and colonial forms of government. The act established the Puerto Rican House of Delegates as a legislative chamber that was elected by the people. It consisted of thirty-five delegates, elected locally in each of the districts of the island. At the same time, the act set up a second legislative chamber, known as the Executive Council, which was nonelective. The Council comprised eleven members, the majority of whom were appointed by the U.S. president. Members of both island parties, Federals and Republicans, were appointed to Council seats. Federals, the elite party with roots in the autonomy period, held broad support among rural landowners, including both sugar owners who had benefited under U.S. rule and coffee owners who were impoverished by U.S. trade policies but sought relief from the U.S. government.[131] Federals expected to be favored much like they had been under the autonomy regime of Spain. When officials in the McKinley administration drew voting districts on the island that favored island Republicans, however, Federals sought new alliances with mainland U.S. Democrats.[132] The Foraker Act granted the Legislative Assembly, consisting of both the Executive Council and the House of Delegates, full legislative authority for the island but made its laws subject to veto by the U.S.-appointed governor and to revision by the U.S. Congress.[133] In a clear departure from Spanish practice under the Autonomy Charter, the Foraker Act established the position of resident commissioner, a representative of Puerto Rico who would serve in the U.S. House of Representatives as a nonvoting member.

The hybrid nature of the Foraker Act could also be seen in the design for the executive and judicial branches of government. The act established a civil governor, as opposed to a military one, but the governor would still be appointed by the U.S. president, instead of being elected by the residents of the island. Drawing on the idea of the Black Legend, whereby Americans accentuated the antidemocratic features of Spanish colonialism, U.S. colonials justified a centralized regime under the Foraker Act in order to support Puerto Rican tutelage in citizenship.[134] In the judicial branch, the act established the U.S. District Court in San Juan. The district court was analogous to district and circuit courts in the United States, with appeals to decisions made by the court heard by the Supreme Court of the United States. All trials and proceedings were conducted in English, effectively limiting this court to cases involving American citizens and business interests. The U.S. District Court was established alongside a preexisting Spanish judiciary. One hundred courts, known collectively as the "Insular Courts," remained in operation, even after the Foraker Act was passed, as a holdover from the period of Spanish rule.[135]

The Foraker Act's incorporation of Spanish colonial and U.S. political forms raised fundamental questions for U.S. interests and Puerto Ricans of all social classes about the place of a colonial territory in a republic. One of the most pressing questions concerned the applicability of the U.S. Bill of Rights to the island. While the Foraker Act clearly withheld the Constitution and U.S. citizenship from the island, whether or not it withheld the Bill of Rights remained unclear.[136]

J. W. Burgess, a law professor at Columbia University who was regarded as one of the most influential political scientists at the turn of the century, argued in September 1900, after the passage of the Foraker Act but before the Supreme Court heard various legal challenges to the act in 1901, that the Bill of Rights applied to U.S. territories under the terms of the Fourteenth Amendment. In an article in *Political Science Quarterly* entitled "The Relations of the Constitution of the United States to Newly Acquired Territory," he wrote: "All of the provisions of the Constitution defensive of civil liberty against the government of the United States apply with the same force and uniformity throughout all territory under the sovereignty of the United States in which civil government exists."[137] Burgess reasoned that it made no difference whether Puerto Rico was called a territory, district, or colony; the Bill of Rights extended to it all the same.[138]

These and other assumptions about the reach of U.S. law would be tested in the Supreme Court. Beginning in 1901, much of the Foraker Act was brought before the court in the landmark Insular Cases. The Supreme Court decided *Downes v. Bidwell*, one of the most consequential of these cases, on May 27, 1901, just two months before the free trade provision of the Foraker Act went into effect. S. B. Downes & Co. was a merchant firm based in New York that imported oranges from Puerto Rico. After the passage of the Foraker Act in early May 1900, Downes brought suit against the customs collector in the Port of New York, asking that the duties of $659.35 he had paid earlier in the year be returned. Given that the island was a territory of the United States, Downes claimed, duties could not be rightfully charged on goods brought from the island. When the Circuit Court of the United States for the Southern District of New York upheld the right of the customs collector to charge duties on goods brought from the island, Downes brought his case to the U.S. Supreme Court.[139]

The court split 5 to 4 in favor of Congress's right to impose duties on products imported from Puerto Rico. The court's decision, as expressed in the five concurring opinions, upheld the lower court's decision by arguing that charging customs did not violate the Constitution because the Constitution did not extend to the island. Section 8 of the U.S. Constitution states: "All Duties, imposts, excises shall be uniform throughout the United States." Thus, in order to argue that the tax on oranges did not violate the uniformity clause, the court had to argue that the Constitution did not extend to Puerto Rico—that the Constitution did not follow the flag. Justice White described the court's reasoning most famously: "In an international sense Porto Rico was not a foreign country, since it was owned by the United States, it was foreign to the United States in a domestic sense, because the island had not been incorporated into the United States, but was merely appurtenant thereto as a possession."[140]

White's doctrine of incorporation was key. By designating Puerto Rico as an unincorporated territory of the United States, the court defined Puerto Rico, and by extension the Philippines, as different from previous U.S. territories, which had all been incorporated. Incorporated territories were acquired with the promise of eventual statehood; unincorporated territories were acquired as colonies with no expectation of statehood or citizenship.[141] The only precedent for Congress to rule indefinitely with plenary power was in the District of Columbia and in Indian tribal lands.[142] In these cases, Congress ruled over territories that were not expected to become states. But as the historian Christina Duffy Ponsa has shown, Congress wielded even more complete power over Puerto Rico and the Philippines, reserving the right to determine each island's final status as an independent nation, a U.S. state, or something in between.[143]

Those who argued for the need to create a new category of territories explained their reasoning partly in terms of prior Spanish colonial structures. Supreme Court Justice Brown maintained in *Downes* that the Constitution should not be extended to the island because the application of income and property taxes to its residents would be "too burdensome for a population not accustomed to such taxes under Spain."[144] Indeed, Spain had only taxed imports and exports in Puerto Rico. The United States continued this practice through McKinley's executive order to collect customs and through the 1900 Foraker Act's stipulation that customs collected in Puerto Rico on goods imported from the United States and all other countries would be used to fund the island government.[145] Similarly, customs collected in U.S. mainland ports on goods imported from Puerto Rico were returned to the island treasury.[146] Thus the island government's operating budget depended, under the terms of the Foraker Act, on extensive trade with the United States, and on Puerto Rico being classified as a foreign country. The funding of the colonial administration and officials' salaries all relied on a definition of Puerto Rico as foreign. In 1900, officials in Washington expected such an arrangement to make the island a self-paying and therefore self-sufficient colony: a source of wealth and prestige at no financial cost.

Yet the logic of unincorporated status was as much racial as it was legal and economic.[147] As Justice Brown wrote in his opinion, "If those possessions are inhabited by alien races, differing from us in religion, customs, laws, methods of taxation and modes of thought, the administration of government and justice, according to Anglo-Saxon principles, may for a time be impossible."[148] Brown built on the logic of Simeon Baldwin, a Yale law professor, who had contended in 1899 that "[It would be unwise] to give . . . the ignorant and lawless brigands that infest Puerto Rico . . . the benefit[s] of [the Constitution]."[149] Such views were shared by a number of prominent legal scholars, including Abbott Lowell and James Thayer, who justified unincorporated status with racial arguments in the *Harvard Law Review* in 1899.[150] Thus, in the case of Puerto Rico and the Philippines, as in the Panama Canal Zone and a variety of sites of U.S. empire, U.S. legal experts justified imperial control with a language of civilizing nonwhite peoples perceived to be lazy and backward. Such racial arguments also informed international law that, together with U.S. constitutional law, helped make the U.S. empire possible.[151]

For their part, the four dissenting justices in the *Downes* decision reasoned in a joint dissent that the designation of Puerto Rico as an unincorporated territory allowed for Congress to exercise the "exertion of arbitrary power," without the limits required by the Constitution.[152] Justice Harlan further objected in a separate dissent to the new distinction between incorporated and unincorporated territories. "Porto Rico," Harlan argued, "became, at least after the ratification of the treaty with Spain, a part of and subject to the jurisdiction of the United States."[153]

After the Insular Cases of the Supreme Court in 1901, the political scientist J. W. Burgess's earlier claim that the Bill of Rights automatically extended to Puerto Rico was thrown into question. In 1904, another political scientist, L. S. Rowe, argued that because the Foraker Act declared Puerto Ricans not citizens of the United States but rather citizens of Puerto Rico, and because the Insular Cases ruled that the Constitution did not follow the flag, the Bill of Rights did not apply as long as the territory was unincorporated.

The Insular Cases upset several decades of legal decisions and this shift was justified by reference to racial ideologies. By 1898 American jurisprudence had established the precedent that the Bill of Rights extended automatically, or *ex proprio vigore*, to the territories.[154] In a series of cases in the late nineteenth century, the Supreme Court had decided that various parts of the Bill of Rights applied to the residents of the territories. In *Reynolds v. United States* (1878) and *Callan v. Wilson* (1887), it was decided that the Sixth Amendment right of trial by jury should be extended to residents of the Territory of Utah and the District of Columbia.[155] Burgess, in 1900, argued that such a precedent would then be extended to Puerto Rico. But the Insular Decisions in 1901 put a stop to this practice. Indeed, because the Sixth Amendment was not considered applicable to the island, it was legislated by the Puerto Rican House of Delegates in its first legislative session in 1900–1901.[156] L. S. Rowe approved of this break from previous practice and understood it in terms of race. "American rule in Porto Rico and the Philippines has taught us," he wrote, "that the Bill of Rights as formulated in the amendments to the constitution, occupies an important place in our constitutional system because it rests upon traditions which are part of the racial history of the people. The mental and moral qualities necessary to prevent the possession of these rights from becoming a menace to the peace and safety of society cannot be developed in a day."[157] It was primarily because of such racial arguments that Burgess's earlier prediction of the automatic application of the Bill of Rights to Puerto Rico was not borne out.

As the traffic in goods between the island and the mainland increased with the advent of free trade in July 1901, some in Washington worried that the increased movement of people was not far behind. Guidebooks published in this period emphasized the proximity of the island: "The center of the island is exactly south of the eastern part of Maine," said one; "The distance from New York to Puerto Rico is about 1,350 miles, or nearly the same as from New York to Topeka, Kansas," said another.[158] Those who were opposed to taking Puerto Rico in the first place routinely evoked the specter of colonial migrants streaming into U.S. ports. Anti-imperialists were a varied lot, of course, and migration was but one of several concerns. Mugwumps, a group of political independents with ties to the founding of the Free Soil Party in the mid-nineteenth century, for example, feared for the loss of America's democratic tradition. Anti-imperialism was one of the last great issues that animated Mugwumps, many of whom feared that the beginning American empire would soon bring the United States to resemble England.[159] One of the most outspoken anti-imperialist Mugwumps was Charles Eliot Norton. Born in Cambridge, Massachusetts, in 1827, Norton became both a successful merchant in the East India trade and a prominent writer, contributing regularly to the *Atlantic Monthly, North American Review*, and the *Nation*. In a lament typical of his anti-imperialist contemporaries, Norton wrote that the War of 1898 "sounded the close of the America exceptionally blessed among the nations."[160] Such writings were often reprinted in anti-American Puerto Rican papers such as *La Democracia*, which ran a piece warning of the Republican Party's imperial ambitions in 1900: "The Puerto Rican people are beginning to recognize the horrible reality that if the Republican party continues to hold power the country will be turned into a colony, governed by enterprising and exploitative Americans that suppose that the American flag does not signify dignity and liberty for those for whom it covers."[161]

But for two of the most powerful anti-imperialist lobbies—organized labor and Southern Democrats—the fear of colonial immigration of nonwhite peoples trumped all other rationales. Samuel Gompers, president of the American Federation of Labor, opposed imperialism publicly in 1898 and 1899. This position was largely based on racialized fears of "semi-savage races" and "slave laborers" migrating from the Philippines and Puerto Rico to the metropole.[162] It was these racial fears about labor competition that led the AFL to pass, after contentious debate in its 1899 convention in Detroit, a resolution calling for Philippine independence, the high-water mark of anti-imperialism for organized labor.[163]

Like organized labor, Southern Democrats, during the congressional debates in early 1900 over the Foraker Act, routinely evoked the specter of colonial migrants entering the mainland. Speaking with reference to Puerto Rico and the Philippines, Representative Stanyarne Wilson of South Carolina declared on February 22, 1900, that "the moment those islands are by Congress declared to be territory of the United States the rights and privileges of American Citizenship will vest in their inhabitants, and the Supreme Court must so hold. Our ports will be open to them. American labor will be brought in direct competition with the cheapest on earth. The corporations and trusts, which are the foster fathers of the party in power and of the Administration, will not hesitate to import and employ it whenever they have grown sufficiently powerful to defy public sentiment. They will be the beneficiaries at the expense of our labor and institutions."[164] Wilson, like other Southern Democrats, feared an invasion of large numbers of non-white people from the colonies. Such views were reinforced by a spate of American guidebooks published in 1898 and 1899 with the aim of surveying America's new possessions. One such guide likened Puerto Rican farmers to those in the U.S. South: "The farming class is about on a par with the poor darkies down South, and varies much even in race and color, ranging from Spanish white trash to full-blooded Ethiopians."[165]

Supporters of U.S. imperialism, however, dismissed such fears with an overwhelming faith in the power of Congress to protect the mainland from any such invasion of colonial migrants, drawing on examples from European colonial powers. As Republican Senator Albert Beveridge said on the floor of the Senate: "Those who see disaster in every forward step of the Republic prophesy that Philippine labor will overrun our country or starve our workingmen. But the Javanese have not so overrun Holland . . . and India's millions of surplus labor have not so overrun England. Whips of scorpions could not lash the Filipinos to this land of fervid enterprise, sleepless industry, and rigid order."[166] Convinced of such racial nativist logic, and of the plenary power of Congress, imperialists maintained that colonial subjects would never be allowed to enter the United States.

Ultimately, the arguments of Beveridge and other imperialists won out. In the period 1900–1902, in fact, the AFL's calls to end imperialism, as seen in convention resolutions and official publications such as the *American Federationist*, sharply declined.[167] This decline reflected an accommodation to imperial policies that began after the reelection of McKinley to the White

House in 1900. As the historian Richard Welch has shown, Samuel Gompers and other U.S. labor leaders became convinced by the McKinley administration and members of Congress that the possession of colonial territories would in no way compromise established barriers to immigration and contract labor, the principal reason many objected to imperialism in the first place. But the AFL's faith in the ability of officials in Washington to keep colonial migrants at bay would soon unravel, when, in 1904, the Supreme Court defined Puerto Ricans as nationals exempt from immigration restrictions when entering the mainland, even as it defended the decision that the Constitution did not extend to the island.

The U.S. Supreme Court's 1901 decision in *Downes v. Bidwell* was perhaps most emblematic of America's colonial policy insofar as it encapsulated elements of both continuity and change in the colonial administration of the island. In defining the island as unincorporated, the court exempted Puerto Ricans from paying property and income taxes under the U.S. tax code, taxes that had not been imposed under Spanish rule. Unincorporated status also reflected racialized thinking as the Supreme Court and other legal scholars drew on ideas of Anglo-Saxon superiority to justify keeping Puerto Ricans outside the U.S. polity. Yet despite the conceit of U.S. officials that Congress, in wielding plenary power, could fully control the effects of colonialism, U.S. rule on the island sparked a number of unintended consequences, including the collapse of the island's primary export sector. In the face of economic ruin and political exclusion, Puerto Ricans would begin migrating in growing numbers to the U.S. mainland.

Chapter 2

The Rise of National Status

It was late March 1900 when Jorge Cruz, a twenty-five-year-old day laborer in San Juan, boarded the steamship *Caracas* for New York. Having signed a contract to work as an assistant truckman for the *New York Herald*, Cruz traveled north for six days, arriving in the Port of New York on April 3.[1] As a resident of a newly acquired territory, Cruz might have expected to pass quickly through the immigration station on Ellis Island. His entry was met with immediate protest, however, as W. F. Dorflinger, a representative of the American Federation of Labor, appeared before the U.S. immigration inspector to argue that Cruz was an *alien* contract laborer forbidden entry under the 1885 Foran Act.[2]

Arrested aboard the *Caracas*, Cruz was taken in handcuffs to a barge office in New York Harbor. There, floating between the Statue of Liberty and the *Herald*'s corporate headquarters, the Bureau of Immigration's Board of Special Inquiry met to decide Cruz's fate.[3] Immigration Inspector Robert Wacliorn opened the proceedings by referring to the bureau's decision the previous year that immigrants from Puerto Rico "are in all respects on a footing with aliens from any other country."[4] "There is nothing for us to do," Inspector Moler responded, "if the [Bureau of Immigration] says that the immigrant is to be treated the same as immigrants from Russia, we have to sit here and do that." Chairman Weihe concurred: "If we don't settle it they may bring more." Voting unanimously to deport Cruz, the board ordered him held in detention on Ellis Island.[5]

But given that Congress was at that very moment debating the Foraker Act, which set out to define the citizenship status of Puerto Ricans, the decision in New York Harbor was far from final. The following day, in fact, authorities in Washington moved quickly to intervene. Treasury Secretary Lyman Gage, charged with overseeing the Bureau of Immigration, reevaluated Cruz's status. According to the 1885 Foran Act, which prohibited foreign workers from entering the United States under labor contracts, Cruz was subject to immediate deportation. Yet the U.S. takeover of Puerto Rico had raised questions regarding the very foreignness of Puerto Ricans arriving in New York. Faced with a dilemma, Gage ruled that Puerto Ricans were neither foreigners nor citizens. He ordered that Cruz be allowed entrance under the condition that the federal government could deport him at any time.[6]

At the barge office in New York Harbor, between America's beacon of freedom and emerging center of capitalism, Jorge Cruz confronted both restrictive ideals of citizenship and corporate imperatives to secure cheap labor. Indeed, the case of Jorge Cruz neatly encapsulates the central tension of America's early twentieth-century expansion overseas: its new colonial subjects were recognized as workers but not as citizens.

Legal wrangling over the status of Jorge Cruz was part of a larger debate about the rights of colonial migrants in the early years of U.S. rule. Would colonial subjects be understood as citizens or aliens, or something in between? Debates over the U.S. government's constitutional and administrative treatment of the people of Puerto Rico began with the question of voting rights on the island but quickly turned to the question of migration to and labor on the mainland. As America's new colonial subjects were excluded from the body politic but included as laborers in the U.S. economy, tensions mounted between colonial migrants, U.S. labor unions, and colonial officials. Even as Puerto Ricans were increasingly drawn into the U.S. economic sphere—first as residents on the island and later as migrants to Hawai'i and the mainland—various groups of U.S. whites defined them as foreigners unfit for U.S. citizenship. Migrants in this period, however, challenged their status as "aliens" and eventually helped establish the new legal category of U.S. national. In the debates over Puerto Ricans' political status, imperial law proved to be a contentious political domain as migrants challenged the colonial categories that defined them as foreign in order to secure work in the domestic United States.

A number of historians have shown how colonial law generated exclusionary legal categorizations such as "foreign in a domestic sense" and "unincorporated territories" as a means of withholding constitutional protections from colonial subjects.[7] In the context of this colonial power so ably demonstrated by other scholars, there is also evidence of the agency of colonial subjects, most notably as migrants to the U.S. mainland challenged colonial laws designed to exclude them from the polity.[8] In seeking entrance to the metropole, Jorge Cruz and others raised new legal dilemmas about the status of colonial subjects under U.S. rule. Pressures on working people pushed many from the colonies to the forefront of legal battles on the mainland. Ultimately, I argue, key decisions that determined the status of Puerto Ricans living in Puerto Rico emerged as a result of the dilemmas created by the migration of working-class Puerto Ricans to the mainland, a migration shaped by the economic integration of the island, but threatening to organized labor and racial nationalists alike.

The Limits of Colonial Voting Laws

In the early period of U.S. rule, debates over the political standing of Puerto Ricans began with the question of whether or not voting rights on the island should extend beyond a literate and propertied elite. During the U.S. military occupation in Puerto Rico from 1898 to 1900, colonial officials expressed concern over the fitness of Puerto Ricans for American citizenship, defined in terms of class as well as race. Of the 201,071 Puerto Rican males of voting age in 1899, only an educated white minority of 54,937 was deemed literate by the U.S. military census.[9] Colonial officials justified limiting voting to this minority by pointing to the persistent challenge for the U.S. government of improving literacy rates in the Spanish-speaking U.S. Southwest. The U.S. governor of Puerto Rico maintained that even after significant school spending in the territory of New Mexico, for example, there remained a large number of school-age children who could not speak English, four decades after the Mexican American War. With school spending in Puerto Rico at one-third the level in New Mexico, and with the island's distance from the mainland making the settlement of large numbers of English-speaking Americans unlikely, the military governor predicted that Puerto Ricans would be "no more fitted for citizenship than were and are the natives of the region conquered from Mexico in 1846." With most of the voting age population illiterate, he reasoned, politicians on the island, like political bosses in the United States, would manipulate working-class voters and "prostitute the ballot."[10]

Along with a literacy requirement, colonial officials asserted the need for a property qualification to further limit voting rights by class. They contended that restricting voting to the "intelligent and well-to-do" would prevent politicians from buying the votes of the working class. In this way, the propertied class would ensure the proper functioning of the government and the lucrative investment of foreign capital on the island that would follow. As the U.S. military governor George W. Davis wrote in his 1900 report, a property qualification was necessary because "manhood suffrage presupposes a basis of real, true manhood," which he implied Puerto Rican men lacked.[11] In linking together property ownership, masculinity, and suffrage, colonial officials defined the majority of Puerto Rican men, by virtue of being poor and illiterate, as politically unfit.[12]

These anxieties about the political standing of working-class colonial subjects were reinforced by white racial nationalists' claims of Puerto Rican racial incapacity. The historian Gary Gerstle has argued that racial nationalism in this period was a "potent ideological inheritance," one that "conceives of America in ethnoracial terms, as a people held together by common blood and skin color and by an inherited fitness for self-government."[13] U.S. officials repeatedly drew on this inheritance—and the link between race and fitness for self-government—when describing America's new colonial subjects. Asked by Congress to describe the intelligence of Puerto Ricans, for example, Governor Davis asserted: "The trouble with the Latin race so far as I have had an opportunity to observe it in Mexico, New Mexico, Central America, Cuba, and Porto Rico, is that . . . they seem to have very little conception of political responsibility and the obligation of all to bow to the will of the majority."[14] Henry Curtis, a member of the Insular Commission, concurred, claiming that Puerto Ricans are "a people who are swayed by all sorts of passions—by rum, some of them, and by bribery."[15]

Racial nationalists justified withholding universal male suffrage by drawing explicitly racial comparisons between Puerto Ricans, Native Americans, and Chinese immigrants. In 1900 Governor Davis maintained that Puerto Ricans were comparable to Native Americans, a group defined as wards of the state since the early nineteenth century.[16] Puerto Ricans, he stated, were "no more fit to take part in self-government than are our reservation Indians, from whom the suffrage is withheld unless they pay taxes." The governor also argued that Puerto Ricans were "far inferior in the social, intellectual, and industrial scale" to the Chinese, a group barred from entering the United States since passage of the 1880s exclusion laws. Given the vehement anti-Chinese sentiment at the turn of the century, such a comparison likened Puerto Ricans to uncivilized barbarians. Expanding suffrage on the island, the governor asserted, would only slow U.S. business investment: "Foreign capital will never jeopardize itself in Porto Rico if the island is to be governed by a horde of human beings called civilized, but who are only a few steps removed from a primitive state of nature."[17]

Colonial officials further described Puerto Ricans' fitness for citizenship as inferior to that of other recently annexed peoples, notably Hawai'ians. Governor Allen maintained in 1901 that Puerto Rico was an island inhabited by "a race of people of different language, religion, customs and habits." Unlike Hawai'i, which had a much smaller population and a longer history of contact with Americans, Puerto Rico, he predicted, would prove to be resistant to Americanization efforts because of its large and dense population. But Allen took this argument further, stating that these differences were based in race. Puerto Ricans, he argued, were "a people, unfitted to at once assume, without careful training and preparation, the management of their own affairs."[18] He reasoned that the lack of fitness for self-government was determined partly by the climate: "where the temperature ranges between 70 and 85 degrees . . . where a man can lie in a hammock, pick a banana with one hand, and dig a sweet potato with one foot, the incentive to idleness is easy to yield to and brings its inevitable consequences." The only hope for change on the island, he asserted, was the introduction of "fresh blood" and "that indomitable thrift and industry which have always marked the pathway of the Anglo-Saxon."[19] Following common tropes of the time, he conflated environment and human biology.

U.S. colonial officials charged with surveying the island in 1899 were in fact confounded by its racial composition, most especially by people whose self-identification lay outside the dominant racial categories of the U.S. mainland. Whitelaw Reid, a U.S. official who negotiated the Treaty of Paris with Spain at the end of the Spanish-Cuban-American War, wrote disparagingly of Puerto Rico's "mixed population," and declared in 1900 that the "enemy is at the gates."[20] As Gary Okihiro has shown, U.S. officials saw Puerto Ricans as threatening because the mixed population of the island defied "the logic of white supremacy by embodying the falsity and perversity of racial categories and boundaries, especially the binary of black and white."[21] Indeed, Puerto Ricans hired to work as enumerators in the 1899 War Department

Census of Puerto Rico included the category of "mulatto." Surveying the island population, the census classified 304,352 people as "mulattoes," 59,465 as "negroes," and 589,426 as "white." Of a total population of close to one million, then, 38.2 percent were classified as "colored," a category that grouped blacks and mulattoes together.[22]

Yet the rhetoric of Puerto Rican incapacity relied on conceptions of the entire island's people as racially inferior to Anglo-Saxons. Such rhetoric racialized Puerto Ricans as uniformly nonwhite and non–Anglo-Saxon. The U.S. military governor claimed in 1900 that the concentration of power under Spanish rule had left Puerto Ricans—even white subjects—without the experience of self-government.[23] Given the extent of the Spanish governor's power in appointing mayors (alcaldes) throughout the island, he maintained that Puerto Ricans had "no conception of any government that did not require of them compliance and submission." Skeptical of their capacity for self-rule, he wrote: "It is a melancholy reflection that there is no instance when the Spanish race, through an honest exercise of the elective franchise, has been able to establish and maintain [good] government."[24] Conflating the experience of Spanish colonialism with perceived racial characteristics, he stated that Puerto Ricans "can not be metamorphosed into Anglo-Saxons."

Such rhetoric failed to take into account the expansion of Puerto Rican political participation that had begun just before the U.S. takeover. In the late nineteenth century, voting was limited to males of Spanish descent who were at least twenty-five years old and who were either civil employees or members of the professions or could pay five pesos in a voting tax. This limited the voting population in the 1870s and 1880s to approximately 20,000 people and gave elites born on the Iberian Peninsula greater political power than Spaniards born in Puerto Rico.[25] With the Autonomy Charter of 1897, however, the Spanish government expanded suffrage to include any male of Spanish descent who was twenty-five (the age of majority in Spanish law) or older and who had resided for a minimum of two years on the island, excluding criminals and bankrupts. This brought the voting population to over 150,000—a majority of Puerto Rican men of voting age.[26] The charter instituted a local legislature on the island for the first time in early 1898, shortly before the beginning of the Spanish-Cuban-American War.[27] This legislature was given the power to pass laws on issues of domestic concern, including taxation. The charter built on a long-standing Spanish imperial practice of allowing colonial subjects to elect representatives to the Cortes in Madrid.

In 1873, in fact, Puerto Ricans won the right to elect four senators and twelve deputies to represent them in the Spanish Cortes.[28]

The history of political representation and expanded suffrage under Spanish rule directly contradicted U.S. racial nationalists' perceptions of Puerto Ricans as colonial subjects unfit for citizenship. Drawing on their recent experience of citizenship under Spain, Puerto Ricans who supported autonomist politics regularly contested U.S. claims of Puerto Rican incapacity. As an editorial published in the autonomist island newspaper *La Democracia* urged: "Do not argue to us that we are inferior to Hawai'i [in capabilities]. Puerto Rico has the capacity to govern itself in the breast of the fullest democracy. This was demonstrated during the Spanish [colonial] system on various occasions."[29] Similarly, Lucas Amadeo, a Puerto Rican coffee planter, testified before the U.S. Senate hearings on the Foraker Bill: "I have not the least doubt that the Puerto Ricans are capable of governing themselves."[30] Pointing to the experience of Puerto Ricans who were granted universal Spaniard suffrage under Spanish rule, Amadeo stated that even those who are illiterate, "have a very good common sense, and understand government better than a great many who can read and write."[31] Such arguments reflected the political commitment of the Autonomist Party to universal manhood suffrage and home rule as a means of winning the support of workers and countering the power of the conservative Spanish-born merchant class.[32]

But by 1899, American concerns over Puerto Rican incapacity won out, as U.S. officials limited suffrage during the period of military occupation. After repealing the liberal suffrage law that Spain had enacted as part of the 1897 Autonomy Charter, the U.S. military governor instituted property and education qualifications for voting. In 1899, during the first elections under U.S. military rule, colonial officials required that voters be male and twenty-one years of age (the age of majority in the United States) or older. In addition, voters were required to own property or demonstrate the ability to read and write in either Spanish or English.[33]

The restriction of voting rights in Puerto Rico was shaped in part by white regret over extending voting rights to African Americans after the Civil War. Abbott Lawrence Lowell, a professor of political science at Harvard University, observed that the impulse to withhold universal suffrage from Puerto Ricans was consistent with late nineteenth-century thinking on race and citizenship. In an influential 1899 essay in the *Atlantic Monthly*, entitled "The Colonial Expansion of the United States," Lowell asserted that by the 1890s white Americans no longer supported the ideas of racial political equality that were central to the Fourteenth and Fifteenth Amendments.[34] In his words, "we have reached the point that the theory of universal political equality does not apply to tribal Indians, to Chinese, or to negroes under all conditions." Citing the Chinese Exclusion Acts of the 1880s and Jim Crow laws in the 1890s, he argued, the Fifteenth Amendment's extension of political equality was premature.

Making this argument in 1899, Lowell recognized that Mississippi, South Carolina, and Louisiana had all recently amended their state constitutions in order to require that voters be able to read and interpret the Constitution. Though the effect of these laws was to disenfranchise the black population in the three states where blacks outnumbered whites, the Supreme Court upheld the legality of the state constitutions. In the case of *Williams vs. State of Mississippi*, the court ruled that such laws did not, on their face, deny the suffrage to blacks. Lowell interpreted these Jim Crow laws, the Supreme Court's decision, and the subsequent lack of northern protest, all as proof of a new acceptance of racial inequality.[35]

Applying this racial logic to the question of American expansion, Lowell contended that it would be a mistake to extend the rights of political participation (as the Fourteenth and Fifteenth Amendments had done to blacks in the South) to the people of Puerto Rico and the Philippines. He stated that all men are not "fitted to govern themselves," and that the theory of universal political equality "seems to apply rigorously only to our own race, and to those people whom we can assimilate rapidly."[36] Regarding the art of self-government, he wrote, "The Anglo-Saxon race was prepared for it by centuries of discipline under the supremacy of law."

It was in these racial nationalist terms that Lowell distinguished between America's previous territorial acquisitions, which were regarded as "infant states," and the new acquisitions of Puerto Rico and the Philippines, which were acquired without the promise of statehood or citizenship. In the case of America's westward expansion, he argued, Anglo-Saxon settlers moving west quickly assimilated the new populations. But, he warned, the same could not be accomplished in America's new island possessions, whose dense nonwhite populations stood at geographic remove from the mainland. In the Philippines, the granting of self-government would be "sheer cruelty both to them and to the white men at Manila." Similarly, in the case of Puerto Rico, he asserted, "self-government must be gradual and tentative, if it is to be a success."[37] Lowell's racial justification for setting the Philippines and Puerto Rico apart from previous territorial acquisitions found a large audience through the *Atlantic* article. Lowell also won the attention of prominent judges, lawyers, and legal scholars in an 1899 essay in the *Harvard Law Review* wherein he used much of the same logic to make a distinction between previous incorporated territories in which the Constitution applied, and new unincorporated territories, such as Puerto Rico and the Philippines, in which it did not.[38]

Migrants at the Margins of the United States

But even as U.S. officials sought to quell the debate over Puerto Rican citizenship by imposing stringent voting qualifications and withholding U.S. citizenship on the island on racist grounds, migrants moving off the island posed a challenge to racial nationalists who sought to exclude them. Migrations from colonies to metropoles had long been routine. In the late Spanish colonial period, Puerto Ricans of different classes and races regularly acquired passports from the Spanish colonial government to gain entry to Europe, Latin America, and the United States. Though passports could often be used to regulate and restrict movement across borders, the Spanish passport in this period appears to have facilitated the migration of diverse colonial subjects.[39] Records of the Spanish colonial government reveal numerous examples of Puerto Ricans from across the class spectrum successfully acquiring passports for travel overseas. Vicente Lopez, for instance, a twenty-four-year-old day laborer, acquired a passport to Spain in 1888; Jose Frigo Verde, a twenty-nine-year-old merchant, acquired a passport to Spain in 1887.[40] While a significant number traveled to Spain, as well as Cuba and other parts of the Spanish-speaking world, some traveled to the United States. Before 1898, small numbers of Puerto Ricans had migrated to the United States as merchants, students, workers, and political exiles, with laborers making up the largest percentage.[41]

A young student of mixed European and African ancestry named José Celso Barbosa was among those who made their way to New York in the last three decades of the nineteenth century. Barbosa's journey highlights the intersection of colonialism and migration in the period before 1898. Barbosa was born in 1857 in Bayamón, Puerto Rico, and was the first racially mixed student to attend the prestigious Jesuit Seminary on the island. He then migrated to New York in 1875 to study English and applied two years later to the College of Physicians and Surgeons, the forerunner of Columbia University Medical School, but was denied admission on the basis of race. In 1877 he enrolled at the University of Michigan as the first Puerto Rican student there, earning a medical degree in 1880. Soon after enrolling at Michigan, the student magazine, the *Chronicle*, commented on Barbosa's arrival: "All young gentlemen of sufficient ability are admitted on equal footing irrespective of complexion. It not being the pigment matter deposited in the skin that is sought after; but the quantity and quality of the brains in the cranium."[42] Barbosa's experience with race in the post–Civil War United States shaped his political outlook as he returned to Puerto Rico to practice medicine. Finding himself surrounded by a white peninsular elite in the medical profession, he became active in the autonomist movement in support of increased creole political power under Spain. Though the majority of *autonomistas* supported Luis Muñoz Rivera, Barbosa led a smaller but more progressive wing of the movement that called for fuller representation within the Spanish colonial government in 1897.[43] Both wings of the autonomist movement adopted a paternalistic vision of an empowered Puerto Rican elite that could bring uplift and tutelage to the working classes and secure local control over the island's economy and government.[44]

As an elite migrant to the United States and a member of the island's creole professional class, Barbosa and people like him faced a measure of discrimination that was tempered by acceptance and opportunity before 1898. In the period of U.S. rule, however, when working-class migrants to the U.S. mainland and Hawai'i posed the question of Puerto Ricans' legal status, they were seen as vexing to racial nationalists in the United States. In the context of political disenfranchisement and economic crisis on the island, U.S. companies in search of cheap labor began recruiting workers from San Juan and Ponce.[45] Created and supported by the colonial integration of the island within the United States, these early migrations eventually proved threatening to organized labor and racial nationalists alike. Out of the dilemmas raised by migrants' efforts to reach Hawai'i and the mainland in search of work emerged key decisions about the legal status of Puerto Ricans under U.S. rule.

While Puerto Ricans were excluded from the U.S. body politic under the terms of the 1900 Foraker Act, labor recruitment illustrated that they were increasingly included as workers within the U.S. economy. Labor agents were hired by American companies concerned about rising wages on the mainland. From San Juan and Ponce, they recruited—and sometimes coerced and tricked—workers to migrate to the United States.[46] In December of 1900, eight months after the passage of the Foraker Act, some two hundred workers boarded a steamship in Ponce for what they thought was nothing more than a trip to the other side of the island in search of work. Far from circling the Caribbean island, however, they soon found themselves heading west toward America's Hawai'ian Territory.[47] After a turbulent voyage lasting six days, these men, women, and children arrived in New Orleans. There, labor agents, who had been hired by Spreckels Sugar Company of Honolulu to bring 2,500 Puerto Ricans to Hawai'i to work on contract, boarded the Puerto Ricans onto two Southern Pacific train cars heading west.[48] Stopping along the way in remote locations, hundreds of miles from the nearest cities, they traveled through the Southwest en route to San Francisco with the aim of avoiding detection by Bureau of Immigration agents. Halfway through the journey, the labor agents stopped the train in the middle of a desert three hundred miles from El Paso, Texas, in an effort to avoid a long layover waiting for the steamship in San Francisco.[49] Waiting in the city of San Francisco, they feared, would give workers a good chance to escape. After the five-day rail journey, they arrived on schedule, and, with careful timing, hurried their charges onto a steamship to cross the Pacific, arriving in Hawai'i seven days later.[50]

The very route of this migration—Ponce, New Orleans, El Paso, San Francisco, Honolulu—reflected the changing contours of labor recruitment

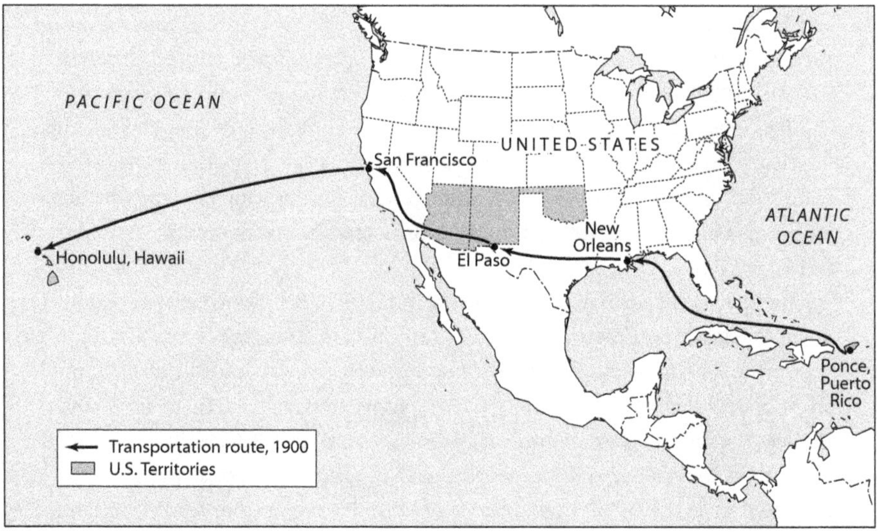

Figure 2.1. Migration Route from Ponce to Honolulu. In 1900, whereas Arizona, Hawai'i, Oklahoma, and New Mexico were incorporated territories, Puerto Rico was designated an unincorporated territory.

in America's new age of empire. Puerto Rican port cities like Ponce were flooded with workers from the interior coffee region who were desperate for work. And as part of a U.S. colonial territory, Ponce was an attractive site of labor recruitment for U.S. companies wary of the Foran Act's prohibition on foreign contract labor. Yet the definition of Puerto Ricans' foreignness was still being debated in 1900. Indeed, the case of Jorge Cruz earlier that year suggested that Puerto Ricans were neither foreigners nor citizens. Given their destination far west of Puerto Rico, and Cruz's much-publicized detention in New York, labor agents opted for entering the mainland through New Orleans, the only other city besides New York serviced by steamships sailing from the island.

Uncertain of their charges' nonforeign status, labor agents moved strategically between New Orleans and Hawai'i. Their choice to stay outside the city of El Paso reflected their wariness of the U.S. Bureau of Immigration. While the Foran Act was difficult to enforce, almost a third of the federal cases against the importation of foreign contract labor originated in El Paso, the center of U.S. corporate recruitment efforts for Mexican labor.[51] Labor agents traveling with contracted laborers from Ponce, and unclear about Puerto Ricans' official status, surely sought to avoid one of the mainland's most heavily trafficked and policed border cities. And as the commercial hub of Hawai'i, Honolulu served as a gateway to sugar plantations throughout the Hawai'ian Islands. Annexed as a U.S. territory with congressional approval of the Newlands Resolution in 1898, Hawai'i was still a U.S. territory in 1900.[52] During this period, the Hawai'ian Sugar Planters Association (HSPA) exerted tremendous influence over the governor of the Hawai'ian Territory and strongly favored the continuation of territorial status over statehood, since it allowed for the importation of low-paid foreign contract laborers, a practice prohibited in the U.S. states but not in territories under the Foran Act.[53]

As Puerto Ricans navigated the structures of U.S. colonialism, including deceptive labor contractors, they also demonstrated resistance and strategic accommodation. Some Puerto Ricans reported being coerced onto steamships bound for Hawai'i. In 1901, labor agents signed some three thousand Puerto Ricans to work as contract laborers on plantations of the HSPA.[54] But letters these Puerto Rican workers sent to the governor of Puerto Rico alleged that many of them were recruited under false pretenses. Victoriana Sánchez of San Juan, for example, claimed that her two sons, Justo and Leon, twenty and nineteen years old respectively, had been "lured to Hawaii by the Emigration Company."[55] Likewise, Bernardino Milan alleged that his son,

Ramon Milan, who was not yet twenty years old, left Ponce for Hawai'i after being "lured by an unkind person."[56] Parents' claims that their sons were lured by labor agents reflected emerging colonial discourses about what constituted legitimate worker complaints. Colonial officials continually rejected worker complaints by insisting that all movement out of the island was voluntary.[57] In this context, workers and their families strategically used the term "lured" to counter official colonial claims and cast their own complaints as legitimate.

Claims of kidnapping were coupled with requests that the colonial government take steps to monitor labor migration. Rodulfo Medina and Manuel Serrano of Yauco urged the Puerto Rican governor to "prohibit the emigration to Hawai'i and other places, of persons under 20 years of age."[58] Taking such reforms a step further, Councilman Jimenez of the Aguadilla city council proposed that a committee of prominent citizens inspect all steamships leaving for the United States in order to see that "all emigrants taking part in the expeditions do so of their free will and that no person be compelled to take the trip if before the boat sails he has changed his mind."[59] Puerto Rican officials eventually responded to working-class and elite calls for reform by taking a more active role in regulating passenger traffic out of its ports. On March 2, 1901, for instance, the mayor of Ponce solicited the help of Governor Allen to delay customs clearance of the S.S. *California* bound for New Orleans. When the governor ordered the collector of customs to halt the ship's departure, customs officials questioned the passengers on board and found seven minors. Only after these migrants were withdrawn, was the steamship released.[60]

Petitions for Labor Rights

Foreign labor contracts proved to be a vital necessity for many. Indeed, for those unable to find work in San Juan and Ponce, such contracts often served as a last resort. As one observer noted in 1901, "The situation of the mass of workers was distressing. Emigration or suicide seemed the only remedies for their misfortunes."[61] On March 2 of that year, some four hundred workers protested outside Ponce's city hall when, after three days of trying to secure contracts with foreign labor agents, they were denied space on a steamship carrying laborers abroad. Left without jobs in Ponce or contracts to work abroad, they complained bitterly of being "roofless and without money with which to buy food."[62] Some went to great lengths to migrate as contract laborers, even when their families protested. One young man, for example, escaped his family's notice by traveling to Hawai'i under an assumed name so as not to "awaken his mother's suspicions."[63] Likewise, several men on board a steamship set to depart for Hawai'i in 1901 were found to be "abandoning their wives."[64] And in at least one case, a woman left for Hawai'i without her husband's approval. In January 1902, Pascual Jordan of Cabo Rojo complained that his wife and children left for a plantation in Maui "without his consent" and asked the governor to arrange for their return.[65]

Those who did make it onto steamships, whether voluntarily or involuntarily, traveled for an average of eighteen days, by ship and train, to reach Hawai'i. Soon after arriving, many in both groups found their working conditions intolerable and sent petitions for redress back to the governor of Puerto Rico who, in turn, forwarded their complaints to the secretary of the interior in Washington.[66] Julio Agostiny, for example, a Puerto Rican from the Borinquen province who was working on the Paulilo Plantation in Hamakua, Island of Hawai'i, claimed in a petition to the governor of Puerto Rico, "[We] have met our perdition in the territories of Oceania, which although under the dominion of the stars and stripes, we do not consider as under your orders."[67] By highlighting the contradictions of a republic with colonial subjects, Agostiny framed the exploitation of Puerto Rican migrants as a threat to American democratic principles. He also flagged a level of mistreatment potentially threatening to American standards of living: "We cannot longer resist the savagery that is coming to every one of us Puerto Ricans; they are every day inflicting more barbarities on us."[68] At a time when U.S. labor leaders asserted that the "standard of living is the measure of civilization," and decried the low wages accepted by "uncivilized" immigrants, Agostiny argued that American colonialism allowed for labor's unwanted barbarities to persist.[69] Such language revealed the highly situated and strategic nature of Puerto Rican migrants' complaints in the early years of U.S. rule.

Agostiny's petition prompted a heated exchange between government officials in San Juan, Washington, and Honolulu. Charles Hortzell, secretary of Porto Rico, in a letter to Thomas Ryan, acting secretary of the interior in Washington, DC, asked that the U.S. government investigate the Puerto Ricans' condition and possibly pay for the cost of these workers to return to Puerto Rico. He asserted that, "owing to their hopeless condition, being entirely without means to leave the Hawai'ian Islands, [the Puerto Ricans] are compelled to submit to the indignities which are placed upon them."[70] Thomas Ryan then forwarded the request to Sanford Dole, governor of

Hawai'i, who directed his assistant, A. G. Hawes Jr. to investigate the conditions of Puerto Rican workers in Hawai'i.[71]

Leaving Honolulu on October 14, 1902, Hawes arrived at the Paulilo Plantation two days later and began interviewing Puerto Rican workers one by one in the plantation office.[72] Wary of recriminations, a few who were interviewed made no complaint at all.[73] Most, however, offered veiled protest as in the case of Nicolas Camacho who, when asked if he had any complaints to make regarding the company store, responded, "No, only that the prices are too high."[74] Similarly, Zolio Esponda commented, when asked if he was getting paid the wage he contracted for, "Yes more, but I did not know the provisions were so high."[75] Julio Agostiny, lead author of the petition, amplified these complaints, arguing that half of their daily wage was paid in credit at the company store. "They give us supplies," he said, "and then deduct them from our month's pay and the prices are too high."[76] Agostiny asserted that the prices of the staples of their diet—codfish and rice—"are too high" and more than at a neighboring "Chinaman's store." Because they were paid in plantation store credit, however, they could not buy their supplies outside the plantation.

Revealing a network of sugar workers across plantations, Agostiny claimed that workers on other plantations earned higher wages. "My friends on other plantations ask me how much I get," he maintained, "and when I tell them they say they get more than I."[77] When asked why he did not then go work on a higher-paying plantation, he responded, "I cannot get work at other plantations unless I get a dismissal card and they will not give me one." Having contracted to work for three years, Agostiny and the thousands of other Puerto Ricans working in Hawai'i were constrained in their movement by the organized power of the HSPA. "Agreement was made in the Planters' Association," Mr. Lidgate, the manager of the Paulilo plantation, confirmed, "to the effect that no Porto Rican should be employed by any other plantation in the association unless he had received discharge papers."[78]

After interviewing close to a dozen sugar workers and the plantation manager, Hawes returned to Honolulu to prepare his report. Citing the expense the plantation had undertaken to pay for their workers' initial travel to the Pacific as well as their housing on the plantation, Hawes stressed the benevolent paternalism of the plantation manager, claiming the Puerto Ricans "are favored on account of their inability to take care of themselves."[79] In his final comments, addressed to Governor Dole, he minimized the plight of Puerto Rican contract laborers in Hawai'i: "Their dissatisfaction seems to be mainly that they are homesick and miss the life of their own country."

"Probably if they were returned to Puerto Rico," he speculated, "they would regret leaving the islands."[80]

Yet, despite Hawes's prediction, many of the Puerto Rican workers in Hawai'i continued to protest their working conditions by petitioning the governor in large numbers, quitting their jobs in droves, and, increasingly, demanding free passage back home. In one indication of workers' widespread discontent, the HSPA wrote to the governor of Puerto Rico: "Great difficulty has been experienced in locating the Porto Ricans for the reason that but few of them remained upon the plantations to which they were originally assigned."[81] Among the many presumed missing were several who had been contracted to work on plantations on the islands of Hawai'i and Oahu, including Martín Medina, Manuel and José Feliciano, Julio Silva, José Ramon Milan, José Bernardino Milan, Manuel Morales Milan, and Gregorio Santiago.[82] While officials of the HSPA could confirm the arrival of these workers, they knew nothing of their current location. The plantation manager of Oahu Sugar Company, for example, admitted that though he knew Medina had arrived on an expedition from Puerto Rico, he did not "know of his whereabouts."[83]

At least one among the missing was later found. In a letter Martín Medina sent to his mother, he described how he, together with Ramon Rivera, another Puerto Rican who had migrated to Hawai'i, found his way back to San Francisco where he was staying at 27A Indey Alley. Having left Hawai'i "on account of sickness," but without money to travel all the way back to Puerto Rico, he was stranded in San Francisco.[84] As the case of Medina suggests, many of those who contracted to work in Hawai'i found the conditions so unbearable that they were willing to risk making it on their own elsewhere in Hawai'i or on the mainland, even with only a few dollars in hand and without the support of family and kin networks.

Increasingly, letters of complaint arrived at the governor's office from organized groups, not just individuals and their family members. The Free Federation of Workingmen, in one example, protested against the "unmerciful treatment of Porto Ricans in the Hawaiian Islands."[85] Even members of the Supreme Lodge of Puerto Rico petitioned the governor "in the name of the universal Masonry, of which George Washington was a member," to offer redress to the "unfortunate Porto Ricans who have become the slaves and victims of outrages in Hawaii."[86]

With protest mounting, the governor of Puerto Rico requested that the governor of Hawai'i and the HSPA further investigate the situation. In response, William O. Smith, secretary of the HSPA, issued a report that investigated working conditions among Puerto Ricans in Hawai'i more fully than the Hawes Report. According to the terms of their contracts, Smith reported, the Puerto Ricans would work six days a week, ten hours a day, for a wage of $16 per month in the first year, $17 in the second, and $18 in the third. Lodging and medical care were to be included free of charge.[87] Still, many workers found these conditions unsatisfactory and left their rural plantations in large numbers in order to travel to Honolulu in search of better jobs.

Seeking to minimize evidence of discontent, Smith asserted that workers abandoned the plantations not because of deplorable working conditions but rather because of a handful of "mischief makers" who incited workers to mobilize work stoppages as well as migrations to Honolulu.[88] Similarly, Smith blamed the Puerto Ricans themselves for their own misfortune. Drawing on class prejudice toward seemingly shiftless and improvident Puerto Rican workers, he maintained that "the restlessness and dissatisfaction created among these people by the malcontents resulted in so large a number of them coming to Honolulu, that they were unable to find employment and were in great distress."[89] Interestingly, Smith's own evidence can be read against his suggestion that only a few workers were dissatisfied. As Smith himself points out, of the 2,930 workers who arrived in Hawai'i in 1901, only 1,851 remained working on the plantations at the end of February 1902.[90]

Hawai'ian police records suggest that workers' discontent was, in fact, widespread. Santiago Granda, a Mexican who had traveled with the Puerto Ricans to Hawai'i, solicited one-dollar payments from workers who were interested in booking return passage to Puerto Rico. While planters cited such examples as evidence of how outside agitators created unrest, the Granda example also speaks to the difficult working conditions of Puerto Ricans in Hawai'i. Just a few months after their arrival, many workers on plantations around Hilo, Hawai'i, desired to leave and paid the one-dollar fee. Once these workers quit their plantation jobs and traveled to the town center of Hilo, however, they found there was no steamship waiting for them. Without a job or a way back to Puerto Rico, the mass of workers was quickly "reduced to a starving condition," with many resorting to "burglaries, larcenies, and highway robberies." Frustrations rose in early 1902 when plantation owners refused to hire back employees who were said to have left "without good cause." Riots broke out throughout Hilo over the next few months, with police making several arrests for disorderly conduct. Some appealed to the police for aid by begging for food, medical treatment, and help finding jobs;

the most desperate actually asked to be arrested and sentenced to prison where they could be sure to be fed and, if need be, sent to the Hilo hospital for treatment.[91]

Migrants' letters revealed the vulnerability of people removed by thousands of miles from the support of family and extended kin networks. Lucia Cruz of Ponce wrote the governor of Puerto Rico asking that her younger sister be returned from Hawai'i Island on account of her being severely beaten by her brother, Antonio. As Lucia wrote, her sister had been "persuaded by her brother Antonio and unprotected against his ill treatment which has reached to the extremity of her being sent to the hospital from his severe brutality."[92] Separated from her extended family by more than 5,000 miles, Cruz's sister struggled to find the support she needed. Similarly, Miguel Serrano of Ponce wrote the governor's office decrying the fact that his daughter Rosalia was alone in her grief after her husband, Isidor, who had emigrated to Hawai'i with her, had died. As Serrano wrote: "She is suffering great misery owing to the death of her husband, and begs her father to send for her as she longs to be back with her folks."[93]

But petitioners did more than protest their isolation and working conditions: they also sought to show a pattern of race and class prejudice. Several protested the fact that three hundred Puerto Ricans had been jailed throughout the Hawai'ian Islands for no other crime, they claimed, than "not being willing to work for small wages." Similarly, they asserted that while "thieveries are committed on these islands mostly by Canacas, Chinese, Japanese, Portuguese, and other foreigners, Porto Ricans alone are held responsible." Calling for justice, they asserted that "some of our poor countrywomen who would rather starve than steal are accused of robbery." Though such claims were, of course, partisan in nature, and blind to how other groups were also racially targeted, they demonstrated Puerto Ricans' heightened sense of injustice. Unlike Japanese, Chinese, and Portuguese workers in Hawai'i, Puerto Ricans could claim—however tenuously—to be part of the United States. "It is a shame to all . . . that today when we are under the domain of the United States, we are compelled to emigrate to a place void of enlightenment and ideals, to live oppressed and without hope."[94] Thus, Puerto Ricans pointed to the contradictions of American empire and their own ambiguous position within it as a means of winning support.

Seeking to downplay reports of mistreatment, the HSPA contacted Federico Degetau, resident commissioner for Puerto Rico serving in the U.S. House in Washington, to assure him of their intent to treat Puerto Ricans fairly, adding, significantly: "Puerto Ricans should enjoy full citizenship privileges."

But the fact that so many Puerto Ricans were arrested on vagrancy charges in 1901 and 1902, well after the vagrancy law in Hawai'i had been officially repealed in 1900, showed just how elusive that goal remained.[95]

In the end, because coercion and mistreatment were in fact so easily documented, the U.S. government paid the cost of most of the Puerto Rican workers in Hawai'i who were brought back to Puerto Rico.[96] J. C. Bills, chief of the Bureau of Labor in Puerto Rico, reflected years later that "the emigration to Hawaii was thoroughly a failure." But Bills understood the misfit between Puerto Rican workers and Hawai'ian plantations in terms of class and race, rather than the extremity of the plantation system's exploitation of contract workers. This failure, he asserted, was "partly because the Porto Ricans who were taken to those islands were largely gathered among the worst classes," and, he continued, "partly because they were, upon arrival in the Hawaiian Islands, thrown into competition with Asiatics, a hardier type with lower standards of living."[97]

The Invention of National Status

In the years immediately following the U.S. takeover, then, Puerto Ricans moved at the margins of the United States, migrating from the Caribbean to the Pacific. Such migrations remained largely out of view of U.S. mainland observers, partly because Hawai'i, though of a higher territorial status than Puerto Rico, was still ambiguously incorporated into the United States. Puerto Ricans in these years did not trouble the various political factions seeking to limit entry of migrants, either those with racial nationalist goals or those hoping to eliminate contract labor in the United States.

This would soon change, however, as more and more migrants began seeking entry to the U.S. mainland. Driven by the increasingly ravaged economy on the island, and pulled by the need for cheap labor, Puerto Ricans migrated to New York, St. Louis, and Washington. At the same time that Puerto Ricans were increasingly incorporated into the U.S. economy as workers, they were kept outside of the polity. Indeed, the 1900 Jorge Cruz ruling, the 1900 Foraker Act, which declared Puerto Ricans were not U.S. citizens, and the 1902 Treasury Department Circular, which declared that immigration laws limiting entry to the mainland United States applied to residents of Puerto Rico, all defined Puerto Ricans as noncitizens.

Like those in the Hawai'ian Territory, migrants to the mainland both encountered exploitation and drew on the contradictions of American empire to protest their noncitizen status. When Mary Coy arrived on Ellis Island from Puerto Rico in 1902, for example, she provoked many of the same questions about her right of entry as Jorge Cruz had two years earlier. A native of Puerto Rico, Coy traveled from the island to New York, where she was detained on Ellis Island and ordered to be deported. Commissioner Degetau objected to Coy's deportation with arguments that directly questioned the contradictory status of Puerto Ricans, stating: "I protest against the application of the restrictions of the immigration laws to the natives and residents of the Territory of Porto Rico."[98] Degetau asserted that the Department of Treasury Circular of August 2, 1902, violated the Treaty of Paris and the Constitution of the United States. And given that the Supreme Court had declared in *Downes v. Bidwell* (1901) that Puerto Rico was a territory of the United States, Degetau asserted, "it is beyond my comprehension how a native born of a territory of the U.S. . . . can be declared to be an alien."[99]

But it was the case of Isabel González that ultimately brought the contradictions of Puerto Rican citizenship status before the Supreme Court. On August 4, 1902, Isabel González, a twenty-year-old pregnant widow, arrived in New York on the S.S. *Philadelphia* from Puerto Rico. With eleven dollars in hand after having paid her own passage, she looked out at the New York skyline eager to meet up with her brother, Louis, who had arrived six months earlier to work in a linoleum factory on Staten Island.[100] Immigration inspectors at Ellis Island quickly detained González, however, alleging that she was "likely to become a public charge," a ruling that routinely barred foreigners from entry under immigration law.[101]

To determine whether González should be allowed entry, the Bureau of Immigration's Board of Special Inquiry held a series of hearings on Ellis Island. Domingo Collazo, a relative of González and naturalized citizen of the United States who had lived in New York City for fifteen years, appeared before the board to state that he and his wife would provide for González, allowing her to stay in their home.[102] Upon further questioning, Immigration Inspector Semsey determined that González was traveling to be reunited not just with her brother, but with a new husband as well. "Why didn't her husband come here for her?" Semsey asked incredulously. While Collazo attempted to explain, Semsey remained unmoved, "But his wife is here and he should come here for her."[103] González's brother, Louis, clarified the point by revealing that his sister was not yet married. When asked why her husband-to-be had still not come to meet her, Louis responded, "He does not want to marry her." Yet, Louis continued, their aunt "is sure of making a reconciliation."[104] Despite such assurances, Inspector Holman moved to exclude González on the basis of her being likely to become a public charge.

Determined to protect his niece, Domingo Collazo filed a petition for habeas corpus on behalf of González at the U.S. Circuit Court for the Southern District of New York. In it he claimed that "Isabel González is imprisoned or restrained in her liberty in Ellis Island, illegally." Asserting that González had a right to enter the United States, Collazo argued that "she should not be treated as an 'alien immigrant,' and that she is not likely to become a public charge."[105]

For his part, William Anderson, counsel for the U.S. commissioner of immigration, countered that, unlike previous treaties by which the United States acquired territory—including the 1803 Louisiana Purchase, the 1819 Florida Purchase, the 1848 Treaty with Mexico, and the 1867 Alaska Purchase—the Treaty of Paris did not declare Puerto Ricans to be citizens of the United States. Anderson further based his logic on the prospect that extending citizenship to Puerto Ricans would open the floodgates to immigrants from other U.S. colonies, particularly the Philippines. He stated that, whereas Puerto Ricans may be civilized, educated, and capable of self-government, "Philippinos are not."[106] Far from supporting Puerto Rican citizenship, Anderson appealed to this racial hierarchy in order to flag the "dangerous" prospect of Filipino immigration if Puerto Ricans were granted free entry to the United States. Responding to such arguments, Judge E. Henry Lacombe of the U.S. Circuit Court for the Southern District of New York denied González's request on the grounds that she was foreign-born and not naturalized.[107] González was remanded to the custody of William Williams, U.S. commissioner of immigration for the Port of New York.[108] The Lacombe decision met with approval in the Bureau of Immigration as E. P. Sargent, commissioner-general, declared that the decision was "exceedingly gratifying to the Bureau."[109]

But González and her family pushed back. In February of 1903, Collazo hired the Courdert brothers, attorneys who would appeal the case and eventually argue it before the U.S. Supreme Court. In their petition for González they wrote: "Your petitioner denies that she is an alien and asserts her right to entry into the U.S."[110] In a motion to advance the Supreme Court hearing, they predicted that the González case would be "the test case upon which will probably be determined the question as to whether citizens of Porto Rico and certain others of our insular possessions are aliens within the purview of the Constitution and laws of the U.S."[111]

The González appeal in 1904 did prove a test case, one that drew focused attention from opposing groups. Wary that admitting González would mean an open-door U.S. policy toward Filipinos, the U.S. attorney general wrote to Geo. B. Cortelyou, secretary of the Bureau of Immigration: "The question of Immigration from the Philippines is involved, and it would seem that no hasty action in opposition to the views of the lower court in the González case should be taken."[112] In contrast, Commissioner Degetau filed an amicus brief in support of Isabel González before the U.S. Supreme Court. Having taken an oath upon entering office to support the Constitution of the United States, Degetau declared he found that the decision to deny González admission to the United States was "inconsistent with the Constitution of the United States and the laws I have sworn to support."[113]

Finding for González, and agreeing with the logic of Degetau, the Supreme Court reversed the decision of the lower court on January 4, 1904. In his opinion for the majority, Chief Justice Melville Fuller put to the side the broader question of citizenship in order to decide only the question of González's alien status. "The question," Fuller claimed, "is the narrow one whether González was an alien within the meaning of that term as used in the act of 1891."[114] Because of the earlier Supreme Court decision, *Downes v. Bidwell* (1901), which resolved the question of import duties by declaring that Puerto Rico was a dependency of the United States, the court decided that residents of a dependency were neither U.S. citizens nor foreigners. The court granted González the right of admission to the United States on the grounds that as a resident of an insular territory she was not an alien. The court also ordered that González be entitled to recover $71.90 for wrongful detention from William Williams, U.S. commissioner of immigration at the Port of New York.

This remarkable decision created a new legal category of belonging: U.S. nationals. Neither aliens nor citizens, nationals owed allegiance to the United States and were granted freedom of movement within U.S. borders.[115] But they were also denied the most basic citizenship rights, including the right of voting representation in Congress.[116] Indeed, national status was the perfect legal expression of the fundamental tension in U.S. colonial policy, as Puerto Ricans were made part of the U.S. economy but kept outside the polity. This case shows how Puerto Rican migrants asserted their agency within the domain of U.S. imperial law.

Reacting to the ruling, the editors of the *Nation* magazine expressed deep anxiety on behalf of organized labor. While supporting Puerto Rican's "promotion from an anomalous position," the editors, like Bureau of

Immigration officials, worried that the case would allow for Filipino immigration. Predicting that after the González ruling, Filipinos could not be legally excluded, they warned: "Here is only a hint of the embarrassments of a republic which injects into its body politic a great class of people who are neither citizens nor aliens."[117]

Indeed, because of the González ruling, and in spite of opponents' protests, contract laborers entered the United States from Puerto Rico and the Philippines in growing numbers beginning in 1904. In March of that year, in fact, 239 Filipinos arrived in the port of Tacoma, Washington, en route to work in St. Louis under contract. The surgeon of the U.S. Marine Hospital stationed at Tacoma Port examined the immigrants and found thirty-five to be infected with trachoma. "This represents about fifteen per cent of the Filipinos arriving," George B. Cortelyou, secretary of the Bureau of Immigration, reported, "affected with a dangerous contagious disease."[118] Cortelyou asserted that such a condition would have justified exclusion for Mexicans, Chinese, and most other immigrants seeking entrance into the United States. But because the 1904 González case had ruled that "citizens of our insular possessions must be admitted to the U.S., without reference to the provisions of the immigration laws," even these sick Filipinos were admitted. Frustrated that the "sanitary purpose" of the immigration laws could be so willfully bypassed, Cortelyou urged Senator William Dillingham, chair of the Committee on Immigration and a powerful ally of eugenicists, to "declare in express terms that the provisions of the immigration laws extend to all persons not actually citizens of this country."[119] In calling for the immigration laws to apply to insular citizens, Cortelyou sought an effective reversal of the González decision, to allow for the prohibition of "infectious subjects" and contract laborers.

Business owners and labor agents eagerly recruited nationals who were exempt from immigration restrictions, however. After *Gonzales v. Williams*, Puerto Ricans were increasingly recruited to American states—not just territories—to work on contract.[120] Francis Lynch, a hired labor agent of the St. Louis Cordage Company, traveled to Puerto Rico to recruit workers for his client in June 1904. After signing contracts and buying second-class tickets from the New York and Puerto Rico Steamship Company, Lynch and twenty-four Puerto Ricans—twenty-two unmarried women and one widow with her young son—set sail on the S.S. *San Juan* for New Orleans on June 13th. Upon delivering his charges to the rope factory in Missouri, Lynch sailed back to Puerto Rico to recruit additional workers, returning with thirty-five more women and one nine-year-old girl in October.

Migrants continued to find ways to fight against economic exploitation even as they were excluded from the full rights of U.S. citizenship. In January 1905, arguing that their working conditions were intolerable, several of the women hired by St. Louis Cordage Company wrote a letter of protest to the governor of Puerto Rico. "The conditions which we were placed in when we reached this city," they explained, "were very different from those which Mr. Lynch had promised we should be surrounded by."[121] Claiming that working conditions had deteriorated over their four months in St. Louis, the petitioners cited the company's dismissal of their matron, Mrs. J. Reyes de Rosales, who had accompanied them from Puerto Rico.[122] More alarming, the women reported that "in midwinter, we have been thrown into the street, where the snow lies one-half yard deep."[123] In using a language of abandonment, these petitioners spoke to broader concerns within American organized labor. Labor advocates who sought to defend the American standard of living had long held that women workers were the most easily exploited because they had "no" standards at all and because they were "likely to become a public charge."[124] In the context of their own seemingly desperate situation and ambiguous citizenship status, as well as the broader patriarchal values of American labor, these women strategically petitioned the governor of Puerto Rico for help in redressing their grievances with their U.S. mainland employer.[125]

The petitions of these women attracted attention in St. Louis and San Juan. N. C. Dauron, a Puerto Rican living in St. Louis, wrote to the governor of the island in mid-January to alert him to the conditions of the women in the rope factory. "Without any notice," he claimed, "[St. Louis Cordage Company] has turned fifteen out into the city streets, penniless, hungry and without a shelter."[126] While the St. Louis police decided to shelter the workers, Dauron called on "kindhearted citizens of this country, Porto Rico, or the Government" to lend aid.[127] Maria Casalduo, writing from Utuado, Puerto Rico, also wrote the governor: "Among the girls abandoned in St. Louis is my sister."[128] Demanding that her sister and the other women who had been mistreated be brought back to Puerto Rico at the government's expense, she urged the governor to "see that the tears may be dried which are now being shed by families full of grief."[129] Arturo Córdova, a prominent citizen of San Juan, declared that local newspaper articles and the many letters of protest he had received from the women themselves impelled him to write to the governor on their behalf. Decrying the plight of young women who were treated so poorly in America, he questioned how this could happen in "a land that is no doubt noble and grand."[130]

Like other Puerto Ricans on the island, in Hawai'i, and on the mainland, Córdova brought into focus the contradiction of unfree labor in the post–Civil War United States. Indeed, since the 1885 Foran Act, American political culture had regarded contract labor, marked by the inability to negotiate wages and working conditions, as dangerously close to slavery and as the very opposite of free labor.

In response to such pleas for help, the House of Delegates of Puerto Rico appointed a commission in late January to investigate the conditions of the contract laborers in St. Louis.[131] Responding to inquiries from San Juan, Benj. G. Crosby, president of the St. Louis Cordage Company, admitted, "It is true that some of the girls who came from Porto Rico with Mr. Lynch left our employ."[132] "But," he quickly added, "reports that they were in destitute circumstances were not true."[133] Despite these improbable claims, the majority of women who contracted with the St. Louis Cordage Company returned to Puerto Rico before their contracts came due. By the end of January, Lynch himself returned to the island with twenty of the women. Six more returned by way of New York in early February. Only eight of the original fifty-four remained working for the company by the end of 1905.[134] Migrations between Puerto Rico and the U.S. mainland, in this example, were shaped by both labor recruitment and migrants' strategic efforts to navigate economic exploitation and political exclusion in the U.S. empire.

The case of Juan Rodríguez also illuminates the tensions and contradictions inherent in national status. A day laborer who migrated from Puerto Rico to New York, Rodríguez later found his way to Washington, DC, where he applied for employment at the U.S. Navy Yard on Capitol Hill. When the Board of Labor Employment responded that he could not file for employment because he was not a citizen of the United States, he asked for help from Commissioner Degetau. Degetau took up the case in 1904, filed for a writ of Mandamus, and eventually represented Rodríguez before the Supreme Court. But despite his arguments that the Treaty of Paris, the Foraker Act, and the Supreme Court's ruling in the *Gonzales* case earlier that year all protected Rodríguez's right to be considered for employment in the United States, the Supreme Court ruled against him, citing the fact that the rules governing the employment of workers at the navy yard made no allowances for nationals.[135]

National status usually, however, allowed for Puerto Ricans to be even further incorporated into the U.S. economy. Driven by crippling U.S. trade policies on the island and extensive recruitment by American companies, workers migrated first to U.S. territories and, increasingly after 1904, to states. Yet national status also allowed for Puerto Ricans to be defined as foreigners. Indeed, while the new legal category of national offered Puerto Ricans broadened rights on paper, these rights continued to be circumscribed in practice.

National status enshrined in law America's deep ambivalence toward its new colonial subjects. Included in the economy, but legally defined as outside the polity, Puerto Rican nationals were permitted to work as contract laborers with private employers but not allowed to seek employment with the U.S. government. Such restrictions on the freedom of labor were seemingly at odds with the protections of the Thirteenth and Fourteenth Amendments, passed on the heels of the Civil War with the aim of making slavery, and other forms of coercive labor, except in prisons, illegal. Indeed, when these civil rights amendments were passed, many legal experts understood the chance to freely seek employment as a basic right of American citizenship. In the words of Supreme Court Justice Joseph P. Bradley, one of four dissenters in the 1873 *Slaughterhouse Cases*: "The right of any citizen to follow whatever lawful employment he chooses to adopt (submitting himself to all lawful regulations) is one of his most valuable rights."[136] But the Supreme Court's decision in the Rodríguez case constrained the freedom of nationals to seek employment at will. In 1905, seven years after the U.S. occupation began, Puerto Rican migrants to the mainland found themselves to be stateless workers in America's new empire, caught between concern over making foreigners citizens, and the needs of a still volatile post–Civil War labor market.[137] In the years after *Gonzales*, when workers entered the U.S. mainland free of immigration restrictions, labor proved to be a central arena of colonial conflict as mainland labor unions sought to discipline migration to the United States.

Chapter 3

Labor Networks

With the rise of national status in 1904, racial nationalists sought various ways to stem the flow of migrants from the colonies. With many of these migrants, including Isabel González, Jorge Cruz, and Mary Coy, among others, coming from the working classes, labor proved to be a central domain of conflict for those concerned about the deleterious effects of colonial migration on the republic. Part of this conflict involved the role of mainland employers and labor agents in recruiting cheap labor and the struggles of the U.S. government to enforce the 1885 Foran Act's prohibition on importing contract labor. Yet organized labor, both in the United States and in Puerto Rico, played just as important a role as capital and the state in shaping migration patterns to the mainland. In the period from 1904 to 1912, organized labor, including the American Federation of Labor's first foreign affiliate in San Juan, mobilized workers in island-wide strikes in an effort to improve conditions on the island and slow migration to the United States. At the same time, Puerto Rican laborers organized massive petition drives for full U.S. citizenship. Such mobilizations would set the stage for the Jones Act of 1917, which opened the door to broad employment opportunities in the United States, thereby promoting increased migration to the mainland. Thus organized labor, despite the

AFL's original nativist intentions, played an important role in channeling colonial migration from Puerto Rico to the United States.

On September 26, 1900, Santiago Iglesias Pantín, a labor leader based in San Juan, boarded the steamship S.S. *Philadelphia* for New York City, with the aim, as he stated at the time, of building "solidarity with organized labor in America."[1] In New York he made contact with Samuel Gompers, president of the American Federation of Labor. Gompers pledged support for the Puerto Rican labor movement, opening the AFL's affiliate in San Juan in 1901, and later traveling to the island to investigate economic conditions in 1904. Over the next decade, Iglesias and Gompers responded to U.S. colonial expansion on the island by building a labor movement involving workers on the island and the mainland. This movement, known as the Federación Libre de Trabajadores (FLT), became the most powerful labor organization on the island in the early 1900s.[2]

As a colonial labor movement, the federación in Puerto Rico developed within the dense field of interaction between the United States and Puerto Rico. Iglesias and Gompers each had their own distinct motivations for organizing beyond the U.S. mainland. Iglesias, though a socialist, adopted the "pure and simple" antisocialist trade unionism of the AFL as a pragmatic strategy for building the labor movement on the island and overcoming repressive Spanish labor laws. Gompers's support of Iglesias, by contrast, sprang from multiple, and sometimes conflicting, sentiments.[3] He originally supported Iglesias out of professed humanitarian concern for the rights of Puerto Rican workers. Yet, after U.S. national status allowed Puerto Ricans unrestricted entrance into the mainland in 1904, Gompers was forced to square his support for colonial subjects with the conservative AFL's nativist stance against immigrant workers.[4] Gompers seemingly reconciled these divergent concerns by supporting organizing on the island as a way of reducing Puerto Rican migration to the United States.[5] With their different and conflicting motivations, the movement Gompers and Iglesias built relied on shared and sometimes contradictory strategies of resistance, ranging from label campaigns on the mainland encouraging U.S. workers to buy Puerto Rican coffee to petition drives on the island calling on Congress to grant Puerto Ricans U.S. citizenship.

Recent scholarship on the intersection of labor and empire has shed new light on the complexities of workers' agency. In rejecting simple binaries of "solidarity and complicity," the historians Daniel Bender and Jana Lipman have argued that "workers often engaged in actions that simultaneously buttressed and destabilized imperial networks."[6] Such was the case in Puerto

Rico, where workers living under American rule allied with a conservative AFL in ways that U.S. union leaders and government officials surely hoped would check both migration to the United States and further radicalization on the island. Yet imperial designs were rarely, if ever, fully realized. In forging a labor network with ties to the U.S. mainland, Puerto Ricans at times helped to stabilize the colonial arrangement, but they also expressed various forms of protest deemed unwelcome by American colonial officials.

Understanding the labor movement that Gompers and Iglesias launched is critical to making sense of the dynamic relationship between colonialism and migration.[7] These leaders and the thousands of workers they organized in island-wide strikes and petition drives helped bring the question of Puerto Rican citizenship before the U.S. Congress through a massive campaign for citizenship in 1912. When Congress later granted U.S. citizenship to Puerto Ricans through the Jones Act of 1917, migration to the mainland sharply increased.[8] Ironically, then, the labor movement Gompers supported as a means of improving working conditions on the island and slowing out-migration eventually helped spur migration to the mainland. This dynamic history of labor networks suggests that migrations from Puerto Rico, and a variety of imperial settings, could be shaped and disciplined not just by the mobility of capital and the state, but also by that of organized labor.[9]

Forging Labor Networks

Born in La Coruña, Spain, in 1872, Santiago Iglesias was first exposed to currents of socialist and anarchist thought as an apprentice carpenter and active member of workers' centers. As a young activist, Iglesias moved to Havana, Cuba, in 1887 and joined the Cuban revolutionary movement headed by José Martí and Máximo Gómez. The founder and editor of the radical newspapers *La Alarma* and *Archivo Social*, Iglesias worked under the threat of censorship and suppression by Spanish colonial officials. When the Spanish general of Cuba issued an order for his arrest in 1896, Iglesias fled Cuba for Puerto Rico. There, he built on the radical worker culture centered in the cigar-making shops of San Juan.[10] Tobacco-rollers had a long tradition of hiring readers to read newspapers and essays by radical thinkers on the shop floor. It was in this context that Iglesias and others, including the radical feminist Luisa Capetillo, helped form early labor unions on the island and found the labor newspaper *Ensayo Obrero*.[11]

The origins of Iglesias's collaboration with Samuel Gompers lie in the 1900 currency crisis, one of the earliest conflicts during U.S. rule on the island.[12] In early August of that year, thousands of Puerto Ricans in San Juan rallied outside the governor's mansion to protest the rising cost of living. Just months after the U.S. Treasury Department in Washington initiated its first currency reform overseas with the exchange of Puerto Rican pesos for U.S. dollars, workers on the island expressed discontent with the fact that their wages now bought significantly less of the "necessaries of life."[13] Santiago Iglesias helped organize a general strike on August 1, 1900, with the hope of winning support from employers and the governor on the island. Lasting several days, and spreading out across the island, the strike shut down much of the island's businesses and government offices before the Insular Police of Puerto Rico suppressed the protests.[14] Seeing how the new U.S. colonial regime could undercut the labor movement as much as the autonomist regime before it, Santiago Iglesias recognized the need to seek support outside Puerto Rico.

In 1900 Iglesias traveled to New York to work as a carpenter in Brooklyn, study English, and seek out the advice of labor leaders and socialists in the city. Theodore Cuno, an intellectual in New York working on the radical publication *New Yorker Volkszeitung*, was the first to suggest that Iglesias meet with Samuel Gompers.[15] Though Gompers and the AFL deliberately rejected socialism in favor of trade unionism, Iglesias understood the necessity of first securing the basic rights of workers before building a socialist movement. In 1897, in fact, when the leader of the Spanish Socialist Party suggested that Iglesias found a chapter of the party in San Juan, Iglesias declined, preferring to organize for labor protections still lacking under Spanish rule.[16] At the 1900 AFL annual meeting in Louisville, Kentucky, and in a private meeting with Iglesias at the AFL headquarters in Washington DC, Gompers pledged to support the labor movement on the island. Iglesias later returned to San Juan to work as a paid AFL organizer.

Shortly after arriving home in December of 1901, however, Iglesias was arrested, charged, and sentenced for allegedly organizing a "conspiracy to raise the price of labor" in the 1900 strike. Under Spanish law, union activity in support of higher wages was deemed a conspiracy in violation of the law.[17] Autonomist leaders such as Luis Muñoz Rivera remained politically powerful in the early years of U.S. rule and opposed the work of Iglesias and others, claiming such activity was disorderly and even unpatriotic.[18] Given that the U.S. colonial government maintained some Spanish laws and courts, autonomists could legally charge labor leaders with conspiracy as late as 1901, long after unionization was legalized in the United States.[19]

American labor leaders were outraged by Iglesias's arrest, particularly because the charge that union activity was unlawful was one the AFL had been fighting on the mainland since the passage of the 1890 Sherman Antitrust Act.[20] Gompers declared that the Iglesias arrest had "shocked the sense of fairness and the justness of the entire American people."[21] Indeed, even the conservative *New York Evening Post* published an editorial stating, "If we have annexed a lot of barbarous, medieval statutes which deprive men of their liberty . . . those statutes must be stamped out like yellow fever or any other tropical plague."[22] Likely because he was in the midst of the AFL's own campaign against similar charges on the mainland, Gompers moved quickly to intervene, cabling five hundred dollars in gold to pay Iglesias's bail.[23] After Iglesias's sentence had been appealed to the island's highest court and reversed, President Theodore Roosevelt personally called on the Puerto Rican legislature to change the legal code in order to make worker organizations lawful.[24] Such a bill declaring that unions would no longer be regarded as "conspiracies in restraint of trade" passed the Puerto Rican House of Delegates and became law in 1902.[25] The legalization of unions reflected both U.S. imperial interests in stabilizing the colony and Puerto Rican workers' agency in struggling for basic rights.

The story of Iglesias's struggle to win the right to organize illustrates how Puerto Ricans acted within a web of colonial ties in America's post-1898 overseas empire where developments on the island and mainland were mutually constitutive. Currency reform legislated in Washington prompted protest among island workers, and when that protest was suppressed, Puerto Ricans turned to the mainland labor movement for support. Similarly, when elite autonomist leaders on the island like Muñoz Rivera defined union activity as illegal, the AFL stepped up its support as part of its own struggle for protective labor legislation on the mainland.

But concern over the conspiracy charge as a threat to workers on the mainland was likely just one of Gompers's many reasons for expanding the AFL beyond U.S. continental borders. Born to a Jewish family in 1850 in Spitalfields, the manufacturing center of London, Gompers immigrated to New York with his family when he was thirteen years old. In London and New York his parents sent him to Jewish schools to learn Hebrew but he turned against religious orthodoxy as an adolescent when he joined the Ethical Cultural Society. Gompers claimed to be drawn to the society's teachings, particularly the idea that good was to be achieved "not by divine intervention, but by the exertions of men."[26]

As a young man, Gompers worked as a cigar maker in several of the cigar factories of New York. He became increasingly aware of union politics as locals protested the introduction of cigar molds, which led to a dramatic decline in wages.[27] He dabbled in socialist and Marxist circles but ultimately developed a philosophy of "pure and simple" trade unionism that was more focused on raising wages and limiting hours than building a large-scale political movement.[28]

Gompers's own turn away from socialism may have made him especially receptive to Santiago Iglesias, who also emphasized the pragmatic benefits of a trade union approach. In his autobiography, Gompers described his first meeting with Iglesias at the AFL headquarters in Washington, DC, in 1900. As Gompers remembered it, Theodore Cuno, though a prominent socialist, "thoroughly understood that the only agency that could help develop the labor movement in Porto Rico was the American trade union movement."[29]

Yet Gompers's support for labor organizing in Puerto Rico was surprising given his stated opposition to imperialism on the grounds that it would

Figure 3.1. Earliest known photograph of both Samuel Gompers, seated center, and Santiago Iglesias, seated far right. Pan-American Federation of Labor. Representatives of the Pan-American Federation of Labor, Mexican Federation of Labor and American Federation of Labor in El Paso, Texas, October 25–29, 1924. Folder 14, box 2, series 4, AFL-CIO Still Images, Photographic Prints (2014-001-RG96-001), Special Collections and University Archives, University of Maryland Libraries.

increase immigration to the U.S. mainland. In 1898 Gompers staunchly opposed U.S. expansion into Puerto Rico and the Philippines, a position largely based on the fear of what he called "semi-savage races" and "slave laborers" migrating from the colonies to the mainland.[30] Gompers and the AFL viewed two possibilities in particular as potential setbacks for organized labor: first, opening the United States to Asiatic immigration from the Philippines after the passage of the 1880s Chinese Exclusion Laws; and, second, allowing the entrance of cheap contract laborers from Puerto Rico after the passage of the 1885 Alien Contract Labor Law prohibiting foreign contract laborers from legally entering U.S. ports. Indeed, for Gompers and other American labor leaders, concerns over migration from Puerto Rico and the Philippines were often linked. The Bureau of Immigration's decision in 1900 to allow the Puerto Rican Jorge Cruz entry at the Port of New York aroused suspicion among American workers concerned that alien contract laborers would drive down the price of labor.[31] "Once we admit that Porto Rico is a part of the U.S.," American labor sympathizers lamented in the *Nation*, "it will be impossible to hold that the Philippine Islands are not also."[32]

Such sentiments reflected a larger racial nationalist impulse at the turn of the twentieth century, when American workers and farmers generally opposed immigration from outside Western Europe. Gompers and the American Federation of Labor opposed foreign immigration and routinely called for immigration restriction. At the 1909 meeting of the International Secretariat, a European federation of trade unions, Gompers proposed that an important objective of labor movements throughout the world should be to prevent their workers from migrating to other countries in search of work (the secretariat declined to pass this resolution).[33] Similarly, T. J. Brooks, president of the Farmers' Educational and Cooperative Union, which represented some three million farmers in the South and West, called on the U.S. Congress for more stringent controls at Ellis Island. Responding to a proposal to distribute immigrants throughout the agricultural states of the South and West, Brooks stated in 1910 that his association would only accept Europeans, a group he described as "more desirable."[34]

Support for immigration restriction was expressed in terms of both racial ideologies and economic competition, demonstrating how economic fears could be rationalized via racial prejudices. Reflecting Social Darwinist ideas, Brooks claimed that non-Europeans were uncivilized: "The Indian was unable to sustain the civilization the white man presented to him in this country. The Negro was transplanted from Africa here into the bosom of civilization and he will be unable to sustain that civilization."[35] After Brooks detailed a hierarchy of races in which Irish, Germans, and British were deemed superior to Italians, Greeks, Asians, blacks, and Indians, Congressman Adolph Sabath, a Democrat from Illinois, asked Brooks on what grounds he made these distinctions. Brooks explained that these groups were marred by a history of "conquering inferior people and bringing them home as slaves and later allowing them to enter into their citizenship [which] caused the better element to be submerged." Congressman Sabath responded with more than a hint of irony: "We have been doing a little conquering ourselves of late, have we not?" Congressman Gustav Kusterman, a Republican from Wisconsin, seemingly unconvinced by Brooks's argument, pressed the logic of his distinctions: "Could you not just as well ask us to keep out all the people who are red haired and have freckles on their faces as being undesirable, because if you read novels you will always find the villain with red hair?" Brooks maintained his position, stating plainly, on behalf of his constituents: "[The farmers] do not desire foreign immigration."[36]

As immigrants from southern and eastern Europe entered the country in greater numbers during the first decade of the twentieth century, the nation's peak decade of immigration, the AFL described the United States as "an asylum whose dormitories are full up."[37] In an article in the *American Federationist*, the AFL's magazine, entitled "Problems of Immigration," Edward McSweeney, assistant U.S. commissioner of immigration at the Port of New York, lamented the various ways alien contract labor agents managed to subvert the 1885 Contract Labor Law, which prohibited importing contract laborers. "Those persons in whose interest it was to bring in contract laborers," he wrote, "immediately bestirred themselves to find a way to evade the law. Aliens were instructed to deny coming under contract, and many violators of the law were able to gain admission."[38] Unionized workers and farmers in the early years of the twentieth century thus agreed that immigration restrictions—which in the early 1900s extended to alien contract laborers and anarchists, as well as Chinese immigrants—were neither sufficiently restrictive nor properly enforced.

When Gompers and AFL leaders contended that non–Western European immigrants were enemies of organized labor who threatened to cheapen American work, they relied on languages of racial difference and economic competition.[39] John Commons, a professor of labor economics at the University of Wisconsin described this sentiment most succinctly in his 1907 book *Races and Immigrants in America*: "The race with the lowest necessities displaces the others."[40] According to this logic, racial groups with a lower standard of living lacked the ambition to improve their lot. This, Gompers and other AFL leaders maintained, created downward pressure on wages for native white workers.

But if foreign immigrants were the object of such fears, so too were colonial subjects. Though the U.S. War Department Census of 1899 defined Puerto Rico as a majority white country, Gompers declared Puerto Ricans as in need of Anglo-Saxon tutelage. After visiting the island, Gompers claimed that Puerto Ricans were "impulsive, enthusiastic . . . and indolent," insisting that "they must be taught a little of the American Anglo-Saxon characteristics of persistency and application and punctuality."[41] In the case of the Philippines, the AFL leaders stated that Filipinos—who held the same national status as Puerto Ricans after 1904—were unassimilable on the basis of their race, and later lobbied Congress to exclude Filipino immigrants.[42]

Such distinctions were reinforced by popular cultural representations of America's new colonial subjects, which typically positioned Puerto Ricans as superior to Filipinos but inferior to Anglo-Saxons. A clear racial hierarchy was made manifest in political cartoons of the turn of the century depicting America's new colonial subjects as children. In one cartoon published in *Harper's Weekly*, entitled "Uncle Sam's New Class in the Art of Self-Government," a young girl representing Puerto Rico is portrayed as a good student sitting at the front of the classroom. In contrast, a young boy representing the Philippines is portrayed as disobedient, standing with a dunce's cap at the back of the room. Degraded on account of their Asiatic origin and violent opposition to U.S. colonialism, "bad" Filipinos were often racialized in cartoons of this period with a darker complexion than Puerto Ricans.[43] But however differences between Puerto Ricans and Filipinos were portrayed, they were both always depicted as children under the tutelage and discipline of Uncle Sam. As the historian Lanny Thompson has shown, the colonial project was justified with "notions of difference not only *between* the United States and the subject peoples but also *among* the subject peoples themselves."[44] In this context, AFL leaders may have been inclined to accept Puerto Rican workers on the island as members of the American labor movement, in part because they could be defined as racially superior to Filipinos.

After Iglesias initiated contact with Gompers in 1900, the AFL passed three consecutive resolutions to send a representative to the island in order to undertake a broad investigation of the economic conditions there.[45] Gompers planned to travel south himself in 1903, only to cancel his plans after the sudden death of his son. Finally setting sail in February 1904, Gompers's journey to Puerto Rico came one month after the U.S. Supreme Court decided the *Gonzales* case.

Figure 3.2. Political cartoon depicting Puerto Rico in the back right next to a female figure representing Hawai'i. William Allan Rogers, "Uncle Sam's New Class in the Art of Self Government," *Harper's Weekly*, August 27, 1898.

Gompers Arrives in Puerto Rico

Traveling aboard the steamship S.S. *Coamo* from New York to San Juan, Gompers surely carried with him American workers' fears of large-scale foreign, particularly non-European, migration to the mainland. Traveling south at a rate of roughly three hundred miles per day, Gompers spent the five-day journey writing in his journal and talking with fellow passengers.[46] In conversations with others on board, many of whom were U.S. businessmen and investors, Gompers heard repeatedly of the unreliability and indolence of Puerto Rican workers. Preferring to make his own judgments, Gompers recorded in his diary, he desired to see for himself the conditions of workers on the island before allowing his mind "to become pregnant with prejudice."[47] He vowed to make a thorough investigation of working conditions, arguing that Puerto Rican workers could "not live isolated from the American movements."[48]

By his own account, Gompers was met with an enormous outpouring of enthusiasm from Puerto Rican workers. Though he arrived ahead of schedule, Gompers was met at the steamship dock in San Juan by a large crowd of workers and government officials. Checking in to the Hotel Inglaterra, he quickly organized a series of meetings with labor leaders and local officials throughout the island. Traveling by horse-drawn buggy, Gompers left San Juan early the next morning to head south toward Ponce along the U.S. military road, the best-maintained road on the island. Leaving the city at five in the morning, he reached the town of Cayey shortly thereafter. Though it was not on his itinerary, Gompers stopped to greet a large group of workers who had gathered in the town center to give him a petition describing the "impoverished condition of the people."[49] Traveling on to Ponce over a winding mountain pass above the Aibonito Valley lined by tobacco plantations, Gompers and his entourage reached Ponce the next morning. There, Gompers was met with parades, petitions, flags and banners hanging from wrought-iron balconies, and a theater filled "to the rafters" with workers awaiting Gompers's speech. After cabling for a new team of horses, Gompers left Ponce later that day and traveled to Arecibo where, "in the drenching rain, thousands were waiting . . . keeping as near to the coach as they could, shouting, hurrahing until the hotel was reached."[50] Gompers remembered being overwhelmed by his welcome: "In the experience of many years in the labor movement and demonstrations of all sorts in all parts of the country," he wrote, "I never saw such earnest, yearning, hopeful expression and such genuine, hearty souls of welcome and expectant gazes in the eyes of men and women as I saw in all the towns and roads along Puerto Rico, and particularly Arecibo."[51] In these examples, Gompers's own narrative of his visit to the island suggests genuine sympathy for Puerto Rican workers.

As president of the AFL during a period of widespread social unrest in the United States, Gompers was acutely aware of workers' struggles against unemployment and poverty on the mainland. By 1904 he was familiar with the failed 1892 Homestead Strike in Pennsylvania, the arrest in 1894 of Coxey's army of the unemployed in Washington, DC, the violent suppression of the Pullman strikers in Chicago that same year, and the desperation of Mexican and Japanese farm laborers striking in 1903 against the Oxnard Sugar Beet Plantation in California.[52]

Yet nothing in his experience prepared him for the destitution he saw in Puerto Rico, he wrote. "I saw more misery and hunger stamped upon the faces of the men and women and children in Porto Rico than I have ever seen in all my life, and I hope I may be spared from seeing the like again."[53] "You can not walk in the streets," he continued, "or you can not ride along the country, you can not stop at a station, you can not buy a newspaper, you can not buy anything, anywhere, unless you are met by some poor man or woman or child, often the three of them together, holding out their hands and asking for a cent."[54] Estimating that some 15,000 men were out of work throughout the island, Gompers reported that it was impossible for the unemployed to travel to work sites in other parts of the island because train fares were prohibitively expensive.[55] In this regard, he stated, workers "are as much bound to the soil as were the serfs in old time guilds when the lords and barons held their sway."[56] Such a situation, he maintained, left people desperate for work with little alternative other than to sign contracts with U.S. labor agents who offered to pay the cost of their steamship fare to the mainland.

Seemingly startled by the widespread hunger and destitution—and the potential for large-scale migration to the mainland—Gompers grasped for different ways to understand the causes of Puerto Rican poverty. Comparing malnourished workers to soldiers in the Puerto Rican infantry of the U.S. Army in San Juan, he made his own observations on the physical fitness of different groups. While both groups were underfed at the outset, the soldiers, who ate significantly more than the workers, "developed greater muscular and physical strength." As if to prove that race was not a factor in developing physical strength, Gompers declared: "It is plainly a question of proper food."[57] Still, Gompers clearly conceived of a strict hierarchy in which Anglo-Saxons were superior to uncivilized island peoples. In a speech

Figure 3.3. Photograph of Samuel Gompers in San Juan. Puerto Ricans gathered as Samuel Gompers entered the Teatro Municipal Tapia in San Juan in 1904. Box 3, folder 14 (2014-001-RG96-001), George Meany Memorial AFL-CIO Archive, Special Collections and University Archives, University of Maryland Libraries.

in Ponce, he declared his hope that Puerto Rican workers would make up "their minds that four, five, six, seven or eight people living in one room shall come to an end" in order to "live as becomes a higher civilized nation of people."[58] Implying that poverty was caused by faults of culture and character rather than the colonial economy, Gompers asserted that workers on the island were "easily persuaded, easily influenced, and—hungry."[59]

Gompers encountered suspicion among Puerto Ricans who were concerned about their position in America's racial hierarchy. During his 1904 visit, Gompers responded to a number of questions from Puerto Rican workers about the position of blacks in the American labor movement. "There is prejudice," Gompers admitted, "among the white men against the black men in the United States." Nevertheless, he insisted, "the working people of the world must unite, regardless of color, politics, religion, or nationality."[60] Making these statements in 1904, years before the Great Migration of blacks from the South to northern cities had increased pressure on the AFL to end its racial exclusion, Gompers spoke more from the perceived need to improve the standard of living on the island—and thereby slow the Puerto Rican migration north—than from any actual experience of racial unity on the mainland.[61]

In fact, the AFL's publications from this period portrayed southern blacks in the United States much like they had Filipinos, as an inferior racial group who had "allowed themselves to be regarded as 'cheap men.'"[62] Such attitudes toward blacks were shaped by the history of slavery and Reconstruction. As Samuel Gompers explained in an editorial in the *American Federationist*, "the unpreparedness of the colored people as a whole for fully exercising and enjoying possibilities existing in trade unionism" was clearly related to the fact that they were just "a little more than half a century from a condition of slavery."[63] Ironically, though Puerto Rican slaves were emancipated in 1873, a decade *after* southern blacks, Gompers lent more enthusiastic support in the early 1900s to organizing Puerto Ricans than to southern blacks. Indeed, while the AFL would largely fail to live up to Gompers's rhetoric of racial inclusion on the mainland, it continued to support laborers in Puerto Rico by working to extend labor protections to the island.

Such consistently racist stances toward Filipinos and southern blacks throw into stark relief the paradoxes of Gompers's rhetoric of racial inclusion in Puerto Rico. These different rhetorical positions can be understood in relation to the AFL's predominantly northern membership and their perception of threats to their livelihood. In the early 1900s, AFL members had little reason to believe that the Filipinos and southern blacks would migrate north and thus did not make organizing these groups a priority. But the case of Puerto Rico was different. After Jorge Cruz entered New York City in 1900, and after the Supreme Court ruled in *Gonzales v. Williams* (1904) that Puerto Ricans could enter the U.S. without restriction, the AFL leadership and rank and file denounced increased migration from Puerto Rico. It was only when they were faced with the rampant poverty of the island and the growing possibility of large-scale migration to the mainland that the AFL stepped up its support for workers in Puerto Rico. In this context, their attempts to back Puerto Ricans' unionization efforts appear to have been aimed at strengthening the economy and reducing the number of migrants. AFL inclusion of island workers can thus be seen as an act of racialized exclusion from the mainland. Though much of Gompers's racial thought vis-à-vis the mainland was dedicated to protecting white workers from competition with black workers, he seemed content to adapt to the Puerto Rican context in which organized labor did not rely on such racial distinctions precisely because he sought to exclude all Puerto Ricans, independent of race, from competing with white Americans. Such efforts to reduce migration from Puerto Rico were part of a larger process of racial sorting and labor segmentation throughout the U.S. empire, which the historians Daniel Bender and Jana Lipman have described as "a shared racialized system of labor recruitment, immigration restriction, deportation, and racial segregation."[64]

It was because of Gompers's intent to insulate white American workers from competition with all workers in Puerto Rico, regardless of race, that his support of the Puerto Rican working class was so substantial. Yet Gompers's efforts to extend labor protections to residents of the island faced stiff resistance. Though he had lobbied for an eight-hour workday law on the island as early as 1900, for example, the Puerto Rican Executive Council in San Juan, a nonelective body largely appointed by the U.S. president, took no action until the day after Gompers announced he would visit the island in 1904. During his tour of the island, Gompers met with the Executive Council to review the terms of the bill. Speaking with William Willoughby, treasurer of Puerto Rico, Gompers asked him to amend the bill to guard against employers extending the workday beyond eight hours. "I called his attention," Gompers recalled, "to the experience we had in the U.S. with unsympathetic administrative officers who very easily found an 'emergency' to have the men work longer than 8 hours . . . and I suggested that he insert the word 'extraordinary' before 'emergency.'" Willoughby answered, "I regret, Mr. Gompers, that you should ask anything like that of me, because I could not offer the amendment, for I am opposed to the bill."[65] AFL-backed labor reforms, in this case, ran up against the intransigence of U.S.-appointed colonial officials who opposed labor protections.

In spite of such opposition, however, Gompers's visit to the island succeeded in expanding interest in organized labor among Puerto Rican workers. Under Spanish rule, Iglesias explained to the AFL Convention in San Francisco in 1904, "the people of Puerto Rico had no freedom of the press, had no freedom to express their thoughts in meetings on the streets or in halls, and such a thing as labor unions would have been disbanded by the police."[66] Though the U.S. Congress denied Puerto Ricans the right to be represented in national politics, with the AFL's support certain civil rights did expand at the local level. "We [now] have a right," Iglesias noted, "to speak and to associate ourselves together."[67] "But," he added, in light of how the island economy had been upended under U.S. rule, "we have no work."[68] The growth of economic and political rights did not track together; instead, new rights to organize gave vent to growing frustrations with an economy radically transformed by U.S. corporate expansion on the island, especially in the sugar sector.

U.S. corporations had invested heavily in the island sugar trade soon after the U.S. occupation began. The U.S-based companies South Porto Rico, Central Aguirre, Fajardo, and United Porto Rico eventually acquired about a quarter of the island's sugar plantations. Production soared from 81,000 tons in 1900 to 349,000 tons in 1910, an increase of over 300 percent. The early effects of this economic transformation could already be seen by the time of Gompers's visit as laborers worked grueling twelve-hour days cutting cane in the intense heat of the six-month harvest season and then struggled to survive without work during the *tiempo muerto*, or off season. As sugar companies expanded across vast swaths of the island, workers had less access to land for subsistence and became increasingly wage dependent. Though company owners, both U.S. and Puerto Rican, reaped growing profits in this period, real wages for sugar workers remained flat. In contrast to coffee, which was less capital intensive and grown on small- and medium-sized farms, sugar required heavy investment and large plantations, thereby inviting foreign corporate ownership.[69]

Upon his return from the island in 1904, Gompers sought to build support among U.S. officials for the Puerto Rican union drive. Even with considerable evidence of poverty and suffering on the island, some colonial officials in San Juan and Washington tried to discredit his observations. William Willoughby, for example, stated publicly that Puerto Ricans were living in shacks and huts that were "more healthful than many of the crowded tenements of the United States."[70] Willoughby, who strongly opposed attempts by the American Federation of Labor to organize Puerto Rican workers, aimed to portray island working conditions in the best possible light. To this, Gompers retorted, "I want to know, if we were to ask for more improved conditions of the tenement houses in our great cities, would Mr. Willoughby say that they are more healthful than the shacks of Porto Rico?"[71]

By 1905, however, Gompers's reports of extreme poverty were accepted by officials in Washington, including President Taft. As part of an AFL declaration that American workers—instead of foreign workers—should be employed in building the Panama Canal, Gompers recommended that the thousands of unemployed in Puerto Rico be hired. Gompers's proposal served the twin goals of addressing the problem of unemployment on the island and keeping Puerto Ricans out of the U.S. mainland. President Taft and Governor Beekman Winthrop at first lent their support to the proposal. But by October 1905, President Taft had changed his mind, stating: "I looked into the matter of the employment of Porto Ricans and found that so many of them were afflicted with anemia of a contagious character that we would not very well run the risk of employing them on the canal."[72] Though frustrated by Taft's response, Gompers noted that the decision served to publicly confirm his own report of widespread hunger and poverty on the island.[73] "A sad commentary," he said, "upon the benevolence of our assimilation."[74]

Strategies of Resistance

Puerto Ricans were not alone in their effort to build links with the American labor movement. Workers in a variety of locations throughout the U.S. empire responded to workplace intimidation by allying with U.S. mainland unions. In the Panama Canal Zone, U.S. government officials used police spies, vagrancy laws, and race- and skill-based segregation laws to impede labor organizing. Under the terms of the U.S. military occupation of the Canal Zone, U.S. officials could even deport workers, including white Americans citizens. General George Davis, the last military governor of Puerto Rico and the first military governor of the Panama Canal Zone, encouraged the use of deportation against U.S. citizens who threatened to strike in the Canal Zone. Laboring under these constraints, skilled white Americans working the steam shovels and cranes to build the canal turned to unions on the mainland United States to assert their workplace demands in Washington.[75]

Though the proposal to hire Puerto Ricans to work on the Panama Canal failed in 1905, Puerto Rican workers on the island capitalized on the AFL's support and organized forty-three unions that same year and three times that number by 1915, a remarkable feat given the political obstacles to organizing in the rural zones.[76] As Santiago Iglesias explained, workers who participated in unions lived in fear of "dismissal from work or [from] their humble huts, usually built on the property of the plantation."[77] Because most employers on the sugar plantations actively opposed union organizing, it was only "with great difficulty and risk that our organizers succeed[ed]."[78] Another challenge to organizing the growing rural proletariat was the fact that Iglesias and other labor leaders, like Luisa Capetillo and Julio Aybar, had been limited in their organizing experience to urban craft unions.[79]

Drawing on mainland union support became a central strategy of Puerto Rican workers beginning in 1905. In April of that year the FLT, the official AFL affiliate on the island, declared a strike in the southern coastal sugar region. Within a few days, nearly 14,000 workers left their jobs, petitioning that their workday be reduced from 14 hours to 9 and that their daily wage be increased from 40 cents to 75. Before striking against the Porto Rico Sugar Company, Santiago Iglesias delivered a letter to the head of the company asking for wage increases and hours reductions. "Strike is the natural course of defense and does not mean to attack properties or injure their owners," he wrote.[80] Iglesias further justified the strike by arguing that the causes were well known: "a deep disgust exists among those unfortunate peasants. The life of the country laborer in Porto Rico is anything but human."[81] But when the company denied these requests, Iglesias urged the strikers to stand their ground as the AFL was sending two shiploads of supplies from New York to aid those on strike.[82]

When the Insular Police suppressed the strike with brutal force, workers again looked to the mainland for support. On April 16, 1905, the Insular Police—who had been ordered by Governor Winthrop to intervene after multiple sugar company owners, both U.S. and Puerto Rican, appealed to him for protection—opened fire on a nonviolent meeting of workers in Ponce's central plaza.[83] In the midst of a speech by labor leader Ignacio Sanchez, police charged the crowd, wielding revolvers, sabers, and clubs. As one observer remembered: "The terrorized and panic-stricken people fled wildly from the scene, and in the confusion that followed, several citizens were badly hurt."[84] The Insular Police arrested some three hundred strikers and prohibited them from taking part in public meetings or interfering with the sugar harvest.[85] After strike leaders cabled reports of such repression to AFL leaders in Washington, Gompers exclaimed in an editorial in the *Washington Star*, "A tragedy is being enacted in Porto Rico under the very folds of the American flag and in utter defiance of the American Constitution."[86] By highlighting the growing tension between American ideals and colonial practices, Gompers sought to win public support in the United States for Puerto Rican unionized workers on the island. As the historian Julie Greene has observed, such patriotic rhetoric could prove as powerful as workplace protests in U.S. colonial contexts.[87]

At the same time that Puerto Rican workers sought support from the metropole, island employers borrowed coercive—even violent—tactics of repression from the mainland. Amid rumors that sugar workers had set cane fires in protest, Charles Hartzell, general counsel for the Porto Rico Sugar Company, and former secretary of Puerto Rico, petitioned Puerto Rican courts, arguing that the strike should be stopped on the grounds that it was costing the company three thousand dollars a day.[88] Following a practice established by U.S. courts on the mainland, Justice Charles F. MacKenna of the U.S. District Court in San Juan granted the Porto Rico Sugar Company an injunction on April 24, 1905.[89] Injunctions against striking workers had been used with legal sanction on the mainland since the passage of the 1890 Sherman Antitrust Act. In 1894, for example, U.S. Army troops clashed violently with Pullman railroad workers when U.S. Attorney General Richard Olney obtained a court order effectively outlawing the Pullman Strike outside Chicago. Similarly, though Iglesias appealed directly to President Roosevelt for redress, the court order effectively broke the strike against the Porto Rico Sugar Company. Workers were prohibited from striking through June 1 in order to allow for the end of the grinding season.[90] Still, by early May, in an example of the incremental gains Puerto Rican workers made through strike efforts, sugar companies agreed to increase wages by 10 to 30 percent and reduce the workday to ten hours.[91]

While sometimes stymied by the power of business, colonial strategies of resistance proved increasingly effective for Puerto Rican sugar workers seeking to check the power of American sugar trusts. By late 1905, *El Águila*, a bilingual daily newspaper based in Ponce, reported that workers throughout the sugar zone were increasingly well organized.[92] Organizers for the AFL and FLT circulated pamphlets in Arecibo and other plantation towns calling on workers to prepare for a general strike by contributing ten cents a day to the strike fund. With an estimated 70,000 men working in the sugar fields and mills, and another 150,000 women and children dependent on their wages, fully one-quarter of the island's people braced themselves for the hardship such a strike would entail. Seeking to mitigate suffering and encourage workers to go ahead and strike, AFL leaders in Washington, DC, pledged to pay each union member on strike $4 per week for up to six weeks. Union membership required payment of monthly dues totaling 50 cents, with 40 cents going to the local union and 10 cents to the AFL. But because most workers could not afford to pay this amount out of their already-meager wages—in fact, only 10,000 of the 70,000 sugar workers were dues-paying union members in good standing—the mainland AFL leadership instructed its members on the island to expect to divide their $4 a week with three others as a means of supporting nonunion men and their families.[93]

Sugar workers were not the only Puerto Ricans using such strategies to improve their lot in the colonial agro-export economy; coffee workers and longshoremen were also mobilizing in this period across vast distances.[94] Coffee workers, still floundering after the loss of European markets and without an adequate share of the U.S. market to take its place, pressured Washington and the local media for change. The editors at *El Águila* undertook a campaign in its pages in 1905 to justify tariff protection of Puerto Rican coffee in the U.S. market, similar to what Brazil had enjoyed since 1870.[95] Other newspaper editors agreed on the need for protection, especially given Puerto Rico's position, albeit tenuous, within U.S. borders. "We let in Brazil's chief product, coffee, free," one editor explained, "while thousands of acres of our coffee growing lands are lying idle in the Philippines and Puerto Rico," because tariffs made those exports more expensive.[96]

Responding to the growing concern of coffee workers on the island, Puerto Rico's resident commissioner Tulio Larrinaga made coffee his number one priority in Washington. When America's new colonial possessions stood ready to produce much of the coffee Americans consumed, Larrinaga asserted, keeping Brazilian coffee duty-free was both unnecessary and unfair. The tremendous American coffee market had opened up to Brazil in the 1870s when Congress placed coffee on the free list as part of a series of tariff bills aimed at lowering the cost of the "poor man's breakfast." Because of the extended suffering of Puerto Rican coffee producers, and because the beef and sugar trusts routinely raised their prices, Larrinaga urged, the U.S. Congress should reinstate the tax on coffee imported from outside the United States, thereby giving producers in America's colonies a price advantage.[97]

In addition to lobbying in Washington by way of the Puerto Rican press and the resident commissioner, coffee farm owners and laborers worked to increase consumption among workers on the mainland through other strategies such as AFL label campaigns and boycotts. Beginning in 1904, the FLT arranged to attach the AFL label to Puerto Rican coffee sold in the United States, thereby encouraging American workers to buy Puerto Rican coffee over that imported from Brazil.[98] And by 1906 a movement had begun on the island to boycott imported American rice until Congress agreed to protect Puerto Rican coffee.[99]

Longshoremen working the docks in San Juan harbor also adopted long-distance strategies of resistance. As employees of the American-owned New York and Porto Rico Steamship Company, longshoreman in San Juan were critically important to the expansion of American businesses on the island. Workers loaded sacks of sugar, coffee, tobacco, and fruit onto steamships headed for New York and unloaded rice, wheat, beef, and manufactured goods arriving in San Juan. Even a short strike could disrupt hundreds of thousands of dollars' worth of trade.

Such protests, however, ran up against corporate demands for cheap labor and the conservatism of the mainland AFL leadership. When the dockworkers decided to walk out on June 24, 1905—after their request for a ten-cent raise for day and night shift workers was turned down—the New Jersey–based New York and Porto Rico Steamship Company shipped in replacement workers from Ponce.[100] After a violent clash between strikers and the Insular Police, a riot broke out throughout San Juan during the night of August 1, 1905. Reading of the violence in the *Washington Star* the following day, Samuel Gompers immediately sent a letter to Iglesias in San Juan inquiring as to the nature of the violence during what he called "the negro riot in San Juan." While expressing hope that the *Washington Star*'s account had exaggerated the role of workers in prompting the riots, Gompers was quick to admonish Iglesias that violence threatened the very reputation of the AFL and was in no way condoned by its leadership.[101] The strike ended with a thirty-day truce negotiated by strikers, steamship company executives, and city officials on August 6. But one month later, with calls for wage increases unheeded, workers again mobilized and launched a strike on September 22.[102] Insular Police Chief Colonel Hamill dispatched plainclothes policemen among the strikers. Though peaceful, this second strike of the longshoremen again proved unsuccessful.[103]

Frustrated by injunctions and other tactics against longshoremen and sugar workers, Puerto Rican laborers campaigned for the establishment of a new government office in support of island workers: a Puerto Rican Bureau of Labor. One AFL affiliate, the Women's Protective Local of San Juan, petitioned Congress to establish a bureau with the same power as other departments in the Executive Council in order to "protect the agricultural and labor interests in the island of Porto Rico."[104] Similar petitions were signed by thousands of workers on the island.[105]

Puerto Rican workers' efforts to organize within the U.S. empire included petitions to the U.S. president. While aboard a steamship traveling from San Juan to New York, Iglesias explained the pressing need for a Puerto Rican labor bureau in a letter to President Taft: "The Union Party in power is committed against the enactment of labor laws to improve the condition of the working people."[106] Without government support of labor, he explained, business and banking elites turned a blind eye to the needs of working people, contributing to the increasing impoverishment that was, by then, acknowledged in Washington.[107] "The banks on the island," for example, "will advance money only on large plantations and practically all of these are in the hands of the very wealthy and of corporations."[108] Such limited access to loans had devastating effects for small coffee farmers. To make his case understood by a mainland audience, Iglesias likened Puerto

Rican coffee farmers on the island to small-scale farmers in the American South. "Thousands upon thousands of small land holders in the Southern states," he explained, "get their provisions and supplies from their merchants on credit or borrow money from the bank to run them through the year and pay it back with their first bales of cotton. Imagine what those farmers would do if such credit should cease and at the same time it should become possible for some foreign country to produce cotton much cheaper."[109] With intense competition from Brazilian coffee in the American market, and without bank loans readily available, small coffee farmers on the island continued to languish. Iglesias maintained that American and other foreign-owned corporations relied on "many thousands of serfs." A bureau of labor, Iglesias urged President Taft, could help make loans available to small farmers.[110]

Racial nativists from both the U.S. government and AFL anticipated that a bureau of labor could also serve to diminish migration to the mainland. Secretary of War Henry Stimson, one of the bureau's supporters, stated that a labor bureau could reduce government expenses, as when the government had paid for the return of emigrant laborers stranded in Hawai'i in 1901, and St. Louis in 1905.[111] Citing Puerto Rico's pervasive poverty, Frank McIntyre, assistant to the chief of the Bureau of Insular Affairs (BIA) recommended that a labor bureau be charged with overseeing labor migrations out of Puerto Rico.[112] "People who have not been to Puerto Rico," he added, "do not understand how miserable some hundreds of thousands of these people are. I have seen the Mexicans on the Rio Grande River 25 years ago, and I have seen the negroes in the South, and I must say that even in the plantations which have been abandoned by their owners and turned over to the negro tenants for 10 to 20 years without looking after them, the most miserable negro is much better off than these people I have referred to."[113]

Samuel Gompers agreed, stating that a Puerto Rican labor bureau would enjoy the full support of the American workers.[114] At the same time, the AFL argued against the U.S. government–led recruitment of immigrant workers. When the U.S. Division of Information, an agency within the U.S. Department of Commerce and Labor's Bureau of Immigration, began recruiting laborers from Europe to work in parts of the rural United States in need of seasonal labor in 1907, the AFL denounced the move as promoting immigration.[115] Yet, as the Panama proposal of 1905 suggests, the AFL did support state-led distribution of colonial labor in the period after the *Gonzales* ruling as an alternative means of limiting migration to the United States.

The Question of Citizenship

Alongside mobilizations in support of unions and a labor bureau on the island, Gompers and Iglesias jointly called on the U.S. Congress to grant Puerto Ricans U.S. citizenship. Beginning in 1902, the AFL pledged its support annually for granting Puerto Ricans U.S. citizenship.[116] AFL secretary Frank Morrison, in a letter to U.S. senators asking for support of U.S. citizenship in Puerto Rico, decried the fact that "the people of the island are practically without a country that they may call their own."[117]

The AFL promoted U.S. citizenship for Puerto Ricans by appealing to American democratic ideals and prevailing racial ideologies. On the occasion of George Washington's birthday in February 1904, for example, Gompers pledged during his visit to the island that the "guarantees of the American Constitution . . . and . . . all the rights of American citizenship, of American manhood and womanhood, must come to you and belong to Porto Rico."[118] Calling for full representation in Congress, Gompers declared in an address to union members in Washington, DC: "It is an outrage, to my way of thinking, when we continue to treat Porto Rico as a stepchild in the family of Uncle Sam."[119] In a speech in San Juan, he promised to work toward a "day of human salvation for the people of Porto Rico . . . stamping out injustice. That is the highest conception of the spirit of the Declaration of Independence. That is the spirit of the guarantee of the Constitution of the United States. That is the spirit of the American Federation of Labor."[120] At the same time, AFL leaders also argued for citizenship in terms of racial fitness for self-government, stating that the "people of Porto Rico have given evidence of self-control under awful poverty, misery, great injustice and provocation."[121] Comparing Puerto Ricans to Cubans, the AFL stated that the Puerto Ricans were "fully as capable, if not more so, of self-restraint and self-government."[122]

The quest for U.S. citizenship became an important part of workers' efforts to organize unions on the island during the period between 1905 and 1917. When early efforts to secure citizenship failed, the gap between expectations of expanded rights and the reality of colonial subjugation only deepened, giving rise to growing anti-American sentiment among Puerto Ricans.[123] In fact, this frustration at being denied citizenship prompted some Puerto Ricans to reject the AFL and instead support the elite pro-independence movement on the island.[124] As Gompers reported at the AFL national convention in Atlanta in 1911, Puerto Ricans expressed their frustration by refusing to take part in American institutions, including the American Federation of Labor: "The dissatisfied Puerto Ricans make their protests felt by refusing to give voluntary assistance to any national organization or institution of the U.S."[125] Such discontent, Iglesias agreed, "is certainly accountable for the obstacles met with in the general development of the labor movement throughout Puerto Rico."[126]

For the AFL and its FLT affiliates on the island, then, U.S. political citizenship proved to be the key to winning Puerto Rican laborers' confidence in American institutions, thereby enabling the AFL to increase its membership and, in turn, build a labor movement capable of improving the standard of living. In recognition of the growing anti-American sentiment, Gompers and Iglesias decided to focus their attention on the citizenship question in 1912. That year, in fact, the AFL published a special report, *A People without a Country*, prepared by Santiago Iglesias. He made a case for citizenship through collected excerpts from various groups on the island and the mainland in support of U.S. citizenship for Puerto Ricans. Mainland U.S. workers registered their support for extending U.S. citizenship to Puerto Rico. The Central Federated Union of Greater New York and Vicinity, for example, wrote Congress in support of citizenship as well as the creation of a department of labor for the island.[127] The 1912 citizenship campaign shows the complexity of labor networks that drew together Puerto Rican workers fighting for full citizenship rights and AFL mainland unions interested in stabilizing a volatile colonial economy.

The campaign for citizenship in 1912 must also be understood as a response to the changing political dynamics in the metropole. In that year, Woodrow Wilson became the first Democrat in the White House since Grover Cleveland left office in 1896. During his campaign, Wilson publicly entertained the possibility of granting the Philippines independence.[128] Wilson and other Democratic leaders in Washington began to set the Philippines on a path distinct from that of Puerto Rico, with the Democratic Party calling for Philippine independence in 1912, and Congress later codifying that promise in the 1916 Second Organic Act.[129] Given the AFL's long-standing concern that policies in Puerto Rico would set a precedent for policies in the Philippines—a territory with eight times the population of Puerto Rico and one marred, in the view of racial nationalists, by Asiatic origin and violent opposition to U.S. rule—the uncoupling of America's two colonies was a significant development for mainland organizers. Having reason to expect eventual independence for the Philippines, the AFL mounted its most extensive lobbying effort in support of U.S. citizenship in Puerto Rico, no longer concerned that such a policy would ever be enacted in the Philippines.

Yet again, however, Gompers's and the AFL's efforts combined support with exclusion. While promoting citizenship for Puerto Rico, the AFL also lobbied Congress to pass restrictive immigration laws. Testifying before the U.S. Immigration Commission, or "Dillingham Commission," in 1911, Gompers stated that American workers no longer believed that the United States could "go on indefinitely absorbing the entire possible stream of immigration." Now, he stated, the AFL supported immigration restriction as "simply a case of the self-preservation of the American working classes."[130] AFL fears of foreignization permeated its lobbying efforts in Washington throughout the first decades of the twentieth century. The AFL passed a resolution calling for a literacy test to limit the influx of immigrants in 1909; Congress passed the Literacy Act in 1917.[131]

But because Puerto Ricans were nationals exempt from immigration restrictions, the AFL could do little to stop Puerto Ricans from entering the United States. Denied a legal basis for excluding Puerto Rican laborers from the mainland, the AFL lent significant and increasing support to organizing efforts on the island in order to stem the flow of migrants north. By 1912 this strategy of treating the immigration problem at its source extended to lobbying Congress for the granting of U.S. citizenship to Puerto Ricans.

Notwithstanding AFL support for the citizenship cause in 1912, it was Puerto Ricans' own efforts that drove the campaign. Petitions of laborers in support of citizenship poured into Washington. The Men's Protective Local of Cabo-Rojo, Porto Rico, in one of the several hundred petitions submitted, contested the ideology that defined Puerto Ricans as inferior to Anglo-Saxons and unfit for U.S. citizenship: "Our people [have] nothing in their character incompatible with the national American life."[132] Such mobilizations suggest, in the words of the historian Christopher Capozzola, the "centrality of labor politics to the ongoing contest over the terms of colonial rule."[133]

Ultimately, this history of Puerto Rican labor networks suggests the ways in which the mobility of organized labor, as much as capital and the state, could shape migrations within the U.S. empire. Iglesias and Gompers each had their own distinct reasons for building a colonial labor movement. In allying with the AFL, Iglesias sought protection against autonomist island elites who continued to impose Spanish anti-labor laws in the early years of U.S. rule. In supporting the FLT, Gompers combined humanitarian concern for Puerto Rican workers with an interest in mitigating migration to the mainland. The movement these leaders built involved organizing across vast distances: shipping supplies from New York in support of striking workers in San Juan and organizing consumer buying campaigns and boycotts on the mainland with the aim of reviving the flagging coffee sector on the island. The labor movement of the FLT and AFL laid the foundation for large-scale mobilizations of island workers in support of basic rights, mobilizations that would later prove to be a powerful force behind the granting of U.S. citizenship in 1917 and increased migration to the metropole.

Chapter 4

Citizenship and Statelessness

Puerto Rican workers' demands for U.S. citizenship intensified in the period of World War I, even as U.S. racial nationalists defined Puerto Ricans as unfit for citizenship. In this chapter, I explore the struggle between colonial laborers who supported citizenship and racial nationalists who opposed it. I argue that the compromise position that emerged in the Jones Act of 1917, which granted a form of second-class citizenship to Puerto Ricans, opened the door for increased migration to the U.S. mainland. Thus, despite nativist efforts to confine colonial subjects to the island, labor mobilizations and changing citizenship laws helped shape a growing colonial migration to the metropole.

American colonial officials' concern about the fitness of Puerto Ricans for citizenship can be traced to the earliest days of the U.S. occupation. Shortly after taking over the island, in fact, the U.S. Army began training Puerto Ricans to serve in two battalions in San Juan and Cayey. The official goal of raising these battalions, according to General Guy V. Henry, the first American military governor of the island, was less to build military strength than to develop citizens. Equating citizenship with manhood proven through military service, Henry stated that the aim of the U.S. military was to transform Puerto Ricans, who he claimed were "not real men," into "good American citizens." As early as 1902, Henry asserted that nothing would do more to turn Puerto Ricans into U.S. citizens than "wearing the U.S. army uniform."[1]

The arrival of a *Harper's Weekly* reporter in 1902 prompted Henry and other U.S. Army officials in Puerto Rico to reflect on the impact of the first few years of training. Officials described the opening days of the training camps during which Puerto Ricans first entered as "unclean natives" who were reluctant to bathe. Major Swift remembered "driving men like sheep" to a nearby stream, stripping the recruits of their clothes, and forcing them into the water. After three years of training, army captains spoke with pride about how the soldiers had acquired American habits of hygiene, claiming that the open-air shower-bath at a camp in Cayey was now "always filled." Officials related the pride they took in providing uniforms to their new recruits. U.S. Army Captain Maginess recalled how Puerto Ricans at first seemed bewildered by army-issue "under-drawers." Unable to explain the garment in Spanish, Maginess resorted to lowering his own pants in order to instruct the soldiers on how to wear them. Years later, army captains boasted that their "natty-looking native troops" inspired a "greater love of clothing" among the Puerto Rican population at large.[2]

Such a narrative of paternalism, tutelage, and uplift reflected widespread American attitudes toward their new colonial subjects. The claim that military service was a necessary means of training Puerto Ricans for U.S. citizenship was based on the assumption that Puerto Ricans were unfit for citizenship and therefore in need of tutoring in the art of self-government. This claim also drew on the common trope equating citizenship with manhood, leaving women out of such narratives altogether.[3]

The withholding of citizenship in the pre-1917 period resulted in a condition of insecure legal status for residents of the island, a condition resembling the statelessness of political refugees who lacked citizenship. Indeed, the Supreme Court's 1901 *Downes v. Bidwell* decision served to legally codify Puerto Ricans' noncitizen status by defining the island as an unincorporated territory. Setting Puerto Rico apart from incorporated territories acquired before 1898, the court created a new category of territorial acquisition, one not subject to constitutional protections. Commonly expressed as the dictum the "Constitution did not follow the flag," the *Downes v. Bidwell* decision, the most significant of the Insular Cases, established a legal basis for colonialism: the United States could rule over a territory (by planting the flag) without granting its residents basic citizenship rights (by extending the Constitution). Included within the United States as residents of an unincorporated territory but denied the full rights of citizenship, Puerto Ricans in the early twentieth century became the quintessential "people without a country."[4]

Large numbers of Puerto Ricans contested their legal status, especially after the U.S. Supreme Court defined Puerto Ricans as nationals in the *Gonzales* ruling of 1904. In the World War I era, a new wave of petitions, strikes, and public appeals by Puerto Ricans focused attention in Washington on the question of citizenship. With the passage of the Jones Act in 1917, Congress granted Puerto Ricans U.S. citizenship, a legal status that entitled them to more rights than nationals but still fewer rights than full U.S. citizens. The confluence of events during World War I—including widespread protest on the island and growing concern in Washington over America's reputation abroad—made the condition of statelessness in Puerto Rico increasingly untenable.[5]

The place of statelessness in U.S. history has, until recently, been obscured by the conceit of American exceptionalism.[6] Defining the "stateless" as the "citizen's other," the legal historian Linda Kerber has brought attention to this long-overlooked subject, calling on U.S. historians to examine the history of those who lack secure citizenship.[7] Alongside this emerging work on statelessness has developed a rich literature on U.S. empire that adopts a nuanced understanding of power based on both contest and domination.[8] Christina Duffy Ponsa, for instance, has observed that the violence of empire should be understood in terms of the withholding—not just the extension—of national power. Both Kerber and Ponsa have done important work in locating examples of statelessness in the history of the U.S. empire. I build on this work by showing the ways that stateless people have worked to challenge and transform the legal status imposed on them by the metropole.

In the case of Puerto Rico, historians have traditionally emphasized external U.S. domination more than Puerto Rican agency in explaining the granting of U.S. citizenship with the Jones Act in 1917. Early explanations tied to Puerto Rican nationalist, or *independista*, politics maintained that citizenship was granted in order to conscript Puerto Rican soldiers into the World War I army, an interpretation that scholars have long debated.[9] Other explanations have emphasized U.S. national security concerns in the Caribbean.[10] Still others have argued that the granting of citizenship was a way for Congress to undercut the independence movement and reward Puerto Ricans' purported acceptance of U.S. rule.[11] While ultimately we cannot know the proximal cause of the Jones Act's passage, workers' agency should not be discounted.[12] In mobilizing island-wide strikes and petition drives during World War I, working-class Puerto Ricans contested the national status they had been ascribed since 1904 and helped focus attention in Congress on the question of U.S. citizenship.

White Regret over Black Suffrage

In the early years of U.S. rule, the perceived need for tutelage before citizenship could be granted was justified with reference to prevailing racial hierarchies and "white regret" over the lessons of recent U.S. post–Civil War history. Writing in the 1890s, at the height of the movement for black disenfranchisement in the South, the political scientist Goldwin Smith bemoaned the fact that the federal government had not established a program of tutelage for blacks in the American South before granting them citizenship with the Fifteenth Amendment.[13] Those who favored revoking the Fifteenth Amendment and tutoring southern blacks in citizenship gained support with the 1903 Supreme Court decision in *Giles v. Harris*.[14] In that decision, the court refused to allow federal tribunals, which were established to monitor southern voting laws, to bring Alabama's suffrage laws in line with the Fifteenth Amendment. Southern Democratic leaders heralded the Supreme Court's decision as a vindication of local control and a recognition that southern blacks were in fact unfit for suffrage.[15] Northern Republican newspapers like the *New York Sun* also celebrated the ruling, arguing that the decision to grant voting rights to southern blacks had been hasty in light of the fact that their capacity for citizenship was "exceedingly problematical in view of race characteristics."[16] These critics argued that tutelage was a better model than the immediate granting of citizenship because it could be both paternal and liberal.[17] As Dr. C. H. Parkhurst of New York put it, the authors of the Fifteenth Amendment had wrongly assumed that "altering the colored man's political status" would automatically "alter the colored man's intellectual and moral nature."[18]

If ideas of how best to train southern blacks in citizenship helped shape and justify colonial policy in Puerto Rico, the experience in Puerto Rico also shaped attitudes toward blacks in the United States. Critics of black suffrage in the United States, for example, pointed to U.S. policy toward Puerto Rico as justification for revoking the Fifteenth Amendment. Arguing that the "sociological problem" confronted by the United States in Puerto Rico was "identical with that which was encountered by our fathers in the

Reconstruction period," they claimed the U.S. decision to withhold citizenship in Puerto Rico resolved the problem "far more wisely."[19] According to a 1903 article in *Harper's Weekly*, the Supreme Court's decisions in the Insular Cases to withhold citizenship "revolutionized the attitude of many thoughtful men in the North with regard to the negro."[20]

In other ways, too, legal debates over citizenship in Puerto Rico reflected larger ideas of race and fitness for self-government at the turn of the twentieth century.[21] In 1901 the legal scholar Henry Brannon wrote: "We suppose that Puerto Ricans are entitled to naturalization, as they are of either Caucasian or African extraction."[22] Brannon's understanding of the Puerto Rican right to naturalize made sense in the context of 1901. Given the longstanding right of citizenship and naturalization for "free white persons," first established in 1793, white Puerto Ricans could naturalize. The extension of these rights to African Americans in the Fourteenth Amendment formally elevated blacks in the United States from a position of legal statelessness.[23] In the 1857 *Dred Scott* decision, the Supreme Court had ruled that freed slaves were not citizens nor were they aliens allowed to naturalize.[24] The contradiction of freedmen denied the right of naturalization and citizenship reached a breaking point after the Thirteenth Amendment granted slaves freedom but did nothing to establish secure citizenship. Written to address this situation, the Fourteenth Amendment effectively overturned *Dred Scott*, allowing blacks to attain citizenship.

After Congress amended the Nationality Act in 1870 to allow "persons of African nativity or ancestry" the right to naturalize, black Puerto Ricans joined white Spaniards (as white Puerto Ricans were identified) in applying for naturalization by first making a declaration of intent for citizenship in a U.S. court and then residing within the United States for a period of five years.[25] The difficulty of meeting these requirements, however, proved insurmountable for most island residents. Because there was no U.S. court with the authority to naturalize aliens on the island during the period of U.S. military occupation, residents would have had to travel to the mainland to declare their intent.[26] The case of Dr. Valeriano Asenjo reveals the challenges that Puerto Ricans faced. Asenjo wrote to Governor Davis in July 1899 asking to be naturalized. Born in Spain, Asenjo had lived in Puerto Rico for seventeen years. He had earned a medical degree at Long Island College Hospital in Brooklyn in 1895 and then returned to San Juan to practice. "My sympathies are entirely American," he wrote. "I speak and write English and I [am trying] as early as possible to become a citizen of the U.S."[27] But without a U.S. court on the island in 1899, Asenjo's only option was to travel back to the United States to make a declaration of intent. Though a physician like Asenjo might have been able to make such a trip to the mainland, most workers on the island could not afford to travel to the United States to declare their intent to become citizens.

After the U.S. District Court was established for San Juan under the terms of the 1900 Foraker Act, this first step toward citizenship became easier to satisfy. But when the Supreme Court defined Puerto Rico as an unincorporated territory in the 1901 *Downes v. Bidwell* decision—and thereby outside the protections of the U.S. Constitution—island residents would still have had to travel to the mainland to satisfy the additional requirement of residing for five years "within the United States."

The position of Puerto Ricans vis-à-vis naturalization law contrasted sharply with that of Native Americans and Filipinos. Native Americans who asserted their loyalty to a tribe or a nation could not be naturalized nor made U.S. citizens.[28] And because the Ninth Circuit Court in California declared in the landmark 1878 ruling *In re Ah Yup* that a Mongolian was not a white person, Filipinos, presumed to be of Asiatic mixed Mongolian and Malayan extraction, were not eligible for naturalization either.[29]

While the legal scholar Brannon was right to predict that black and white Puerto Ricans could legally naturalize in 1901, the advent of national status in 1904 would make naturalization a legal impossibility. In the 1904 *Gonzales v. Williams* case, the Supreme Court reevaluated Puerto Ricans' legal status and declared that they were neither aliens nor citizens, but rather nationals.[30] As Charles Tyler wrote in an article for *Harper's Weekly* entitled "Our Record in Porto Rico," nationals "cannot be naturalized and become citizens" because they are not aliens.[31] Thus national status effectively relegated Puerto Ricans to a legal status similar to that of Native American tribe members, Filipinos classified as nonwhite, and freed blacks defined as neither citizens nor aliens before the Fourteenth Amendment. In the early 1900s, when white and black immigrants from Europe and Latin America could legally pursue naturalization, national status placed Puerto Ricans in a legal backwater: Puerto Ricans, like Chinese immigrants, and others from Asia, were ineligible for citizenship.

The impossibility of naturalization after 1904 was particularly vexing to those who recognized the connections between citizenship status and economic opportunity. Puerto Ricans working at the U.S. naval station at Culebras, Puerto Rico, provide an especially telling example. The navy hired island-born men to work as carpenters and mechanics. Puerto Ricans attained entry-level positions by evading, or "blinking," the navy's requirement that all employees be citizens.[32] But when these employees sought promotions through the ranks, navy officials in Washington denied their requests on the grounds that they were not citizens. As nationals, without a means of naturalizing, they had no legal route to career advancement. In response to these exclusions, some working-class Puerto Ricans pressed for U.S. citizenship as a means of becoming eligible for U.S. government jobs.[33]

Leaders of the island's elite Republican Party expressed widespread concerns over the lack of U.S. citizenship in the early 1900s. The Republican Party was dominated by the professional class, including administrators of the sugar corporations, who supported annexation to the United States and did little to ameliorate the harsh conditions facing the working class.[34] These elites resented the lack of U.S. citizenship because it placed Puerto Rican migrants in an inferior legal position than that of emigrants from southern Europe arriving in large numbers on the mainland. In a speech before the Lake Mohonk Conference in 1907, George Arias, a U.S. citizenship advocate from the island, noted that "while Spaniards and foreigners may become American citizens in the United States or in Porto Rico by simply following the regulation of the law, the native of Porto Rico, who has been under the American flag for over nine years now, has no legal way of becoming a citizen of the United States."[35] In 1911, in the midst of massive emigration from southern Europe to the United States, Manuel Rossy of the Puerto Rican House of Delegates declared that "no opportunity has yet been given [Puerto Ricans] to become citizens . . . while during that time many thousands of foreigners, with, to say the least no better qualification than they, have immigrated to the U.S. and individually become citizens thereof."[36]

Various local government officials on the island supported citizenship in the hopes that it would contain growing social unrest. In the midst of labor strikes in 1905, for example, representatives of different municipalities met in San Juan to draft a petition to the U.S. Congress. Asking for full citizenship rights for Puerto Ricans, the petition named Congress as the "only power, which can save us in this supreme conflict."[37] The House of Delegates of Puerto Rico sent a memorial to Washington in early 1906 in recognition of the labor strikes of 1905, and of infringements by employers and the Insular Police on workers' right to peaceably assemble, a right protected by the First Amendment to the U.S. Constitution. Referring to the Foraker Act's withholding of U.S. citizenship from residents on the island, they said: "You are well aware of the fact that the privileges of your Constitution do not apply to our people."[38] Requesting that the Foraker Act be amended to extend the Constitution and the Bill of Rights to the island, the memorialists declared emphatically: "We love your liberties and wish for, and demand, ours."[39]

Some American officials contended that U.S. citizenship made sense, given the context of expanded citizenship rights under Spain in the years prior to 1898. Beekman Winthrop, the U.S. governor on the island from 1904 to 1907, argued that what was at stake for Puerto Ricans was their lack of representation in the U.S. Congress, especially since the island had several voting representatives in Madrid under Spanish rule. Winthrop asserted that the granting of U.S. citizenship was "exceedingly important."[40] In recommending citizenship in 1905 and again in 1906, Governor Winthrop spoke directly to the discrepancy between Spanish and U.S. rule, presumably to shame the United States: "Under the Spanish Regime Porto Ricans were classed as citizens of Spain, and it is naturally difficult for them to understand why citizenship should be denied them under the more free and liberal government in force in the United States."[41] Without voting representatives in Congress, a situation that U.S. citizenship would presumably remedy, Puerto Ricans held no legal power to influence U.S. trade laws shaping the island economy.

In a similar vein, U.S. Secretary of War Henry Stimson called for citizenship on the grounds that Puerto Rican statelessness could cause potential harm to the international reputation of the United States.[42] After visiting the island at the request of President Taft, Stimson recognized the need to improve Puerto Ricans' political status. Because they had held citizenship rights and representation in the Cortes under Spanish rule, Stimson informed Taft, Puerto Ricans regarded their national status as an affront, as a "badge of inferiority."[43] Noting how prevalent this concern was, Stimson recalled: "The one feature which impressed itself upon me most as essential to the future government of the island was this question of citizenship."[44] Such concern on the part of Puerto Ricans—represented by "innumerable petitions" Stimson received during his visit—justified, he reasoned, the granting of U.S. citizenship not only as a means of winning Puerto Ricans' loyalty to the United States, but, just as important, as a way to build support for the United States throughout the Americas.

Indeed, while traveling in the Caribbean, Stimson observed that various Latin American peoples "regarded this attitude of the U.S. toward Porto Rico as an evidence that we regarded not only the people there but Latin-American peoples in general, as of a different class from ourselves, and of an inferior class."[45] Thus granting citizenship to Puerto Ricans, Stimson contended, was a means of shoring up support for the Monroe Doctrine and

Roosevelt Corollary. Advocating a status for the island somewhere between unincorporated territory and state, Stimson recommended that the United States govern the island as Britain governed Canada and Australia—that is, as a self-governing colony.[46] Given the extent to which the island's economy was shaped by U.S. trade laws, he asserted, Puerto Ricans should be granted citizenship and full representation in Congress. "The island is," Stimson stressed, "very largely dependent upon our tariff on sugar."[47] "It would take only a few examples of that dependence," he continued, "to bring about an irresistible demand . . . for representation in the law-making body which has to do with the making of the tariff."[48]

But citizenship also had its detractors. Like those supporting citizenship, those opposing it justified their position by pointing to international concerns. In 1905, as early petitions from Puerto Ricans for citizenship arrived in Washington, Secretary Regis Post of the Puerto Rican Executive Council plainly stated his objections: "I believe that 90 percent of the people of Porto Rico lack the qualifications which we demand of foreigners who obtain citizenship of the U.S."[49] Thus, when Post compared the Puerto Rican status with that of other immigrant groups he found, contrary to his procitizenship opponents, justification for the status quo.

Elihu Root, a Republican senator from New York in 1912, also opposed citizenship. A key part of Root's assertion was the conviction that America's history of manifest destiny had come to a close: as he put it, "We have finished making states."[50] He regarded the 1898 annexation of Hawai'i as a mistake, one that would eventually have to be undone by making Hawai'i a separate, independent republic. He worried publicly that the precedent of extending U.S. citizenship overseas would, in his words, "involve us in political complications with Mexico, Central America, Cuba, Santo Domingo and all the other Caribbean countries."[51] While others saw granting citizenship to Puerto Ricans as a way of shoring up support for U.S. influence in Latin America, Root saw it as a liability that could serve to frustrate others, in a variety of imperial settings, who were interested in the same privilege.[52]

Root and others, including President Taft, also justified their opposition to citizenship in racialized terms. In an interview published in the *Observer*, Root remarked: "I am opposed and always have been, to the concession of citizenship. . . . [Puerto Ricans] are Latins, after all, and [their] conception of citizenship and of other fundamental principles is quite distinct from that of Saxons. . . . It is too much to ask that we so compromise ourselves for a country with a little over a million inhabitants of a race, civilization, and customs distinct from ours."[53] President Taft also objected to granting citizenship in

1912, but held out the possibility of doing so in the future if Puerto Ricans could prove their fitness for self-government. As Taft wrote in a letter to Santiago Iglesias, the AFL's lead organizer on the island, "As fast as the instinct and habit of self government is acquired by the people at large, and no faster, the fullest possible measure of local and fiscal self-government should be granted."[54] Such a statement combined a racialized conception of Puerto Rican inferiority with a promise of self-rule.

The elite Unionist Party of Puerto Rico joined Post, Root, and Taft in opposing U.S. citizenship, but for very different reasons. Unionists lobbied the U.S. Congress to delay the vote on citizenship in 1912 in order to first clarify the question of eventual statehood. Unionist Party leaders feared that citizenship without eventual statehood would lead to a permanently subordinate geopolitical position.[55] Luis Muñoz Rivera, resident commissioner of Puerto Rico and the leader of the Unionist Party, asserted: "What Puerto Rico wants is to be allowed to solve her problems alone—in other words, that they be decided upon by the insular Puerto Rican legislature and not by the Congress of the U.S." Muñoz Rivera and those in his party favored either citizenship with statehood or complete independence.[56] In this sense, the Union Party sought the very kind of autonomy from the United States that it had won from Spain in 1897.

As Puerto Rican citizenship was being debated in Washington, often in racialized terms, newspapers throughout the United States ran articles characterizing Puerto Ricans as backward and unfit for citizenship. Among this spate of articles attacking Puerto Ricans on racial grounds was a report in the *Los Angeles Times* titled "People of Porto Rico Eat Everything That Flies," likening Puerto Ricans to mongooses. Just as the "bloodthirsty little beast" devoured smaller birds nesting throughout the island, so Puerto Ricans, the author claimed, "formed the habit of eating any sort of birds they can get."[57] "Wherever there is a nest within reaching distance of a road or trail," the author continued, "it is robbed." The effect, according to Alexander Wetmore of the U.S. Biological Survey, was a deplorable decline in bird life. Because it was capable of such devastation, Wetmore maintained, the mongoose—and by implication Puerto Ricans—should be "rigorously excluded from the United States." Referring to the presumed backwardness of Puerto Ricans, he declared that "the chief hope lies in educating the rising generation through the public schools." He further compared Puerto Ricans to Italian immigrants in the United States: "This nest-robbing, bird-killing habit seems to be worst among the Italian laborers." Attributing violent qualities to Italians, and by extension, Puerto Ricans, Wetmore noted that police were reluctant to arrest Italian bird snatchers after two sheriffs had been killed in retaliation.[58] Such remarks reflected broader ideologies of racial inferiority that criticized the foodways of blacks, Chinese, and other nonwhite groups without accounting for dire poverty.

Resident Commissioner of Puerto Rico Tulio Larrinaga alleged that these articles were part of a campaign by U.S. officials in the Puerto Rican Executive Council—namely, Secretary William Willoughby, Attorney General Hoyt, and Auditor Ward—seeking to malign Puerto Ricans' capacity for self-government in an effort to protect their jobs.[59] "These gentlemen," Larrinaga charged, "have recently been flooding the press with the most disparaging literature about our people." "We are called," he continued, "a mongrel race," "a degenerate people," and, "a people incapable of governing ourselves."[60] Larrinaga quickly accumulated an immense pile of newspaper clippings from all over the country.[61]

Larrinaga asserted, in response to such diatribes, that because members of the Executive Council were worried about losing their offices should the appointed body be turned into an elected one, they fed U.S. newspapers exaggerated accounts of Puerto Rican backwardness. They could not be trusted, Larrinaga argued, to offer an unbiased view. Instead, he insisted, Congress should look to the Puerto Rican House of Delegates—which, unlike the Executive Council, was elected by the people of Puerto Rico, and which, by 1912, had passed numerous resolutions in support of citizenship—for a more accurate representation of Puerto Ricans' views.[62]

Claims for Economic and Political Citizenship

As efforts toward securing citizenship were continually stalled in Washington, supporters of the measure on the island drew on the few tools available to them—strikes, petitions, and public appeals—to make their voices heard. Kept outside the formal politics of U.S. national elections, working-class Puerto Ricans increasingly mobilized in the realm of informal politics to protest the *Downes v. Bidwell* decision and the condition of statelessness it imposed.

World War I marked a turning point in the global struggles of colonized peoples for self-determination.[63] In the case of Puerto Rico, the war prompted renewed concern over whether the Constitution should follow the flag. In the years just before World War I, when the U.S. Congress revised the tariff laws to encourage more competition among foreign sugar producers, the price of Puerto Rican sugar in U.S. markets fell precipitously. With Puerto Rican sugar tied to the price of sugar on the New York Coffee and Sugar Exchange—and mediated by U.S. tariff laws—sugar plantations laid off sugar workers in large numbers and reduced the wages of those they retained. Visiting the island in 1914, ten years after his first tour of the island, Samuel Gompers noted that "the deterioration in the condition of the people of Porto Rico was terrific."[64] By 1915, when European beet sugar producers were forced out of production by the war, demand for Puerto Rican sugar increased, and the price of sugar rose dramatically. It was within this context of rising sugar prices in the U.S. market after years of decline that Puerto Rican sugar workers seized the chance to call a general strike in 1915 and again in 1916.[65]

Spurred by increasing demand for Puerto Rican sugar in 1915, 40,000 workers throughout the sugar zone organized for higher wages in what would become the largest strike in the island's history.[66] Sugar workers in Bayamon first petitioned employers for a one-third increase in wages on January 1, 1915.[67] When this petition was rejected, the strike and the demand for increased wages soon spread across the island. But in striking for higher wages in the colonial export economy, Puerto Ricans also mobilized for basic labor rights. The myriad violations of the First Amendment right to peaceably assemble that came to light during and after the strike, served to bring the effects of Puerto Rican statelessness to the attention of officials in Washington.[68]

Throughout the 1915 strike, workers mobilized for higher wages and, in the face of violent suppression, for the right to organize unions in the first place. In the plantation town of Juncos, for example, the Insular Police and plantation owners used tactics of intimidation and force to suppress the strike. As residents of the town reported in sworn affidavits, plantation owners circulated a letter from Arthur Yager, the U.S. governor of Puerto Rico, among workers in order to "influence us in believing that no one had the right to go onto strike asking for better wages and more respect."[69] On February 4, 1915, the Insular Police of Puerto Rico forcibly disbanded a peaceful parade of striking sugar workers in Juncos. With revolver in hand, and insular policemen following quickly behind, an owner of a Juncos Sugar Mill led the ambush. "The flags which the strikers carried in the procession, even the American flag, were torn by the police from the hands of those who bore them."[70] Lucas E. Castro, a well-respected businessman from Juncos, deposed under oath that, while in Juncos during the February strike, he saw the Insular Police bringing to an end a meeting of workers "using their clubs and revolvers without justification at all." The violence of the police was so hostile toward the workers, he said, "that almost the whole town was compelled to close doors."[71] Twelve workers were wounded after being brutally clubbed by police, only to be arrested upon arriving at the hospital for treatment, and later sentenced in the Municipal Court of San Lorenzo without being given access to an attorney. The accused appealed to the District Court of Humanco which overturned the decision of the lower court, stating that the workers were all "innocent of the crimes imputed [to] them."[72] Other residents of Juncos who witnessed the violence also submitted affidavits. Luis Sanchez Ocana, Juan Roman, Jose Maria Pereira, and Juan Rivera, neighbors living close to the town center, reported that "the conduct of the strikers was of a high order; that assemblies of the strikers were clubbed in the streets, intimidated by the Insular police, and told to go to work in order to prevent being clubbed and imprisoned." Making reference to the First Amendment right of peaceable assembly, they claimed that "the constitutional rights of the strikers were violated by the Insular police of the island of Puerto Rico, and this permitted to be done under the flag of the Stars and Stripes."[73]

Sugar mill workers in Vieques, a small island off the southeastern coast of Puerto Rico, made a similar bid for higher wages and democratic freedoms in 1915. According to a series of sworn affidavits gathered by the attorney Rafael Lopez Landron, insular policemen Sergio Brignoni and Sotero Moreira were seen drinking rum at noon on February 16.[74] Witnesses asserted that they carried half-pint bottles of rum in their pockets as they rode out on the "Puerto Ferro" road to await the march of workers around 2:30 p.m. One witness deposed that he heard the police state, prior to their arrival at the scene of the strike, that they were ready to put an end to the strike that afternoon. Around 1:00 p.m., the police met some three hundred strikers and ordered them not to continue along the public road. When the workers refused, citing the inconvenience of turning back to the town center in order to start along another road, the policemen fired fifteen shots from carbines.[75] Violently dispersing the march, police left four workers dead and more than ten others wounded. Claiming self-defense, workers wounded two policemen with machetes. The police then quickly arrested all the strikers except those who swore not to offer evidence in court that might incriminate the police.[76] In total, one hundred workers were arrested by the Insular Police and charged by the Vieques Municipal Court with "carrying arms."[77] Upon appeal to the Superior Court of Puerto Rico, however, it was discovered that workers' so-called arms were actually "garrotes," or big sticks, from which they carried the American flag.[78] Of the one hundred arrested, all but six or seven were acquitted.[79] The pattern of false accusations fomented still further unrest. As Landron stated: "Such proceedings are influencing very much the minds of the laborers in Porto Rico, and all and every one of them are in a reign of terror."[80]

As in Juncos and Vieques, workers in Arecibo struggled against intimidation, false arrests, and violence. On February 16, Sofia Rivera, who was working for the Central Cambalache railroad crossing in Arecibo, moving a gate to block traffic along the road from Arecibo to San Juan when trains passed through, witnessed insular policemen disrupt a strikers' parade. Two policemen ordered the leaders to "abandon the autocar" in order to be searched.[81] When Rivera called out to a passerby to help the strikers, the police quickly arrested her. After a trial in the municipal court, she was sentenced to thirty days in prison for "disturbing the peace."[82] Strikers were also arrested and sentenced for "carrying working tools."[83] After twenty-eight days in prison, those who were charged won an appeal before the U.S. District Court, which ruled in favor of the workers and the crossing guard, dismissing all charges.[84]

As Puerto Rican workers argued that the Constitution should follow the flag to protect their right to unionize, the American flag itself became a fiercely contested symbol. While disbanding a meeting led by Santiago Iglesias in Arecibo, insular policemen accosted an elderly man holding an American flag, beating him with a club and tearing the flag from his hands.[85] In response, workers solicited the support of the mayor of Arecibo, E. Landron, who, on February 21, wrote a letter to Governor Yager asking that constitutional rights be restored in order to avoid weakening the "people's confidence in American principles of government."[86] Iglesias also appealed to Governor Yager for protection. When his request went unheeded, he concluded, "the wish of the police is secured, namely, that of breaking the strike of the poor country workers through fear and intimidation, through persecution and the 'stick.'"[87] Indeed, when Iglesias asked the chief of police for a meeting permit, the chief responded: "I never will permit you to speak anywhere. I will not permit ten peasants or five peasants, and this kind of demonstration will be prohibited."[88] In this and other instances of mass protest, Iglesias and island workers relied on a discourse that defined the United States as a nation of justice but one that had not yet fulfilled its promises in Puerto Rico. During this same period, however, the rights of workers to assemble and unionize on the U.S. mainland were far from secure. In one of the ironies of colonial labor conflicts, the assertion of contrasts between the colony and the metropole presented rights and identities in the United States as stable even when, in reality, they were not fully established or uncontested.[89]

Decrying the clear pattern of police violence against workers in Juncos, Vieques, and Arecibo, Santiago Iglesias alleged that the Insular Police of Puerto Rico sided with employers during the 1915 strike. On March 1, Iglesias spoke before a meeting of sugar workers in Ponce, the center of the southern sugar zone. At 7:30 that evening, Iglesias opened the meeting and spoke for more than an hour about how to best move forward in the strike effort. "The Police," he asserted, "could not be placed on an impartial and independent position while having their quarters in the premises of the sugar mills and plantations."[90] As Iglesias finished this sentence, shots rang out above the crowd. The police captain, Fernandez Nater, ordered Iglesias to step down from the podium, yelling out: "This meeting has finished."[91] The police fired shots into the crowd, killing one man and wounding several others. According to an affidavit signed by more than two hundred witnesses, the police "without motive or cause whatever attacked the defenseless masses that were then celebrating a meeting at the market place at Ponce."[92] Alberto Fernandez, a Ponce resident, witnessed the start of the police riot and then ran home down Leon Street. While passing Vives Street, he witnessed a policeman beating a worker with a stick resembling a stave; he heard the victim cry out "Don't hit me more," and then saw the policeman shoot the worker once and then a second time, killing him. The policeman, identified as Norberto Quiles, left the victim dead on Vives Street, and was indicted for voluntary homicide. In his defense, Quiles's attorney stated: "Admitting that Policeman Quiles was not very polite with the strikers . . . it is to be borne in mind that the conditions were extraordinary and that the police had to act arbitrarily to avoid disturbances."[93] In agreement with such arguments, the executive board appointed by the governor to conduct an investigation of the Ponce riot ruled that Quiles was innocent and allowed him to continue to serve in the Insular Police force.[94]

Hermenegildo Robledo, another spectator at the meeting, was chased down by police on his way home from the plaza. Upon apprehending Robledo, police beat him violently and shot him in his left arm and leg. After forty-five days of treatment at the Hospital Tricoche in Ponce, Robledo was left an invalid without the use of his left leg. As a sugar worker, who lived in a shack in the plantation zone around Ponce and earned forty cents a day, Robledo's injuries spelled ruin for his family. Robledo was also charged with a "breach of peace" by the district attorney of Ponce for the alleged crime of being present at the workers' meeting on March 1.[95] After the strike, the police moved to the Ponce office of the FLT, breaking locks in order to search and seize confidential strike committee papers.

As part of an investigation into the Ponce riot by the Puerto Rican House of Delegates—the elected body—Tous Soto, a member of the House and resident of Ponce, declared that the Ponce incident should "not be overlooked by the men who stand for the fundamental principles of the liberty we enjoy under the Constitution of the United States."[96] Soto proposed a motion condemning the violence committed by the Insular Police, but it failed to pass the House of Delegates by eight votes.[97] Iglesias also expressed his alarm: "If the federal authorities do not take rapid and energetic actions in favor of the American Constitution and on behalf of the Porto Rican laborers, we fear that the labor organizations may be swept from the island, and the workers revert to the old days of peonage under Spanish domination."[98] Residents of Ponce also protested against the violence, Iglesias reported, the second such incident in their city under U.S. rule: "The Ponce people, just thousands of people, have protested tremendously against such a brutal manner."[99]

Workers' agency in organizing strikes continually ran up against the power of employers and their supporters in the colonial government. For their part, plantation owners and government officials on the island maintained that the police had resorted to violence in order to defend themselves and the larger social order. In the case of Vieques, for example, Martín Travieso—a Puerto Rican–born graduate of Cornell Law School who served as U.S. secretary of Porto Rico, a member of the U.S.-appointed Executive Council, and a member of the Unionist Party—contended that the policemen acted out of self-defense when they fired into the marching crowd, killing four and seriously wounding five others.[100] Though agreeing that strikers should have a right to ask for a fair wage, Travieso faulted labor leaders Iglesias and Martinez for "trying to incite" the workers. In his words, Puerto Rican workers were, "peaceful but ignorant—you can take them either to church or to kill two policemen, if necessary, because of their ignorance."[101] Similarly, Travieso claimed that a Ponce worker had attacked one of the insular policemen, Corporal Ferrer, with a taper file, a steel tool with sharp teeth, after Police Chief Fernandez Nater ordered Iglesias down from the podium. It was only then, Travieso explained, that police fired into the crowd.[102]

Yet the workers' persistent protests spurred the colonial government to respond. By late February, mounting evidence of police violence prompted Governor Yager (1913–21) to reproach the Insular Police. In a letter dated

February 25, 1915, he explained: "It was not my intention that you should suppress peaceful meetings of the laborers who may gather . . . for the purpose of discussing in an orderly manner their grievances."[103] The fact that Governor Yager, an outspoken opponent of organized labor, sought to rein in police brutality lends further credence to the hundreds of worker affidavits citing examples of police abusing their power.[104]

Receiving news by telegraph of repression on the island, Samuel Gompers contacted Frank McIntyre, chief of the Bureau of Insular Affairs in Washington, to seek confirmation. McIntyre replied that he had not received any information regarding the murder of labor organizers or the infringement of civil liberties. Santiago Iglesias, it turned out, had attempted to send a cable to McIntyre reporting the violence: "Four workingmen killed . . . twenty-seven wounded . . . more than one hundred arrested."[105] His cable was intercepted, however, by Secretary Travieso of the Puerto Rican Executive Council, who declared that because, in his opinion, parts of the cable were "contrary to the facts," he could not allow the cable to be sent on to the chief of the Bureau of Insular Affairs.[106]

During and after the Sugar Strike of 1915, workers protested what they viewed as the coordinated effort of employers and the Executive Council to divest workers of their rights. In 1915, more than a thousand sugar workers in the U.S.-owned Fajardo Sugar Company filed formal complaints before a judge, arguing that the Labor Bureau chief served the interests of landowners. Bureau officials admitted as much. Indeed, in a bureau report, Chief J. C. Bills had declared: "The Bureau will not act in favor of any effort either of labor or those who claim to be working for the benefit of labor when such efforts are intended primarily to injure employers." In keeping with his pro-employer position, Bills removed a bureau inspector from Arecibo when a sugar plantation owner complained that the inspector maintained "good relations with the representatives of the Free Federation of Workingmen."[107]

The Sugar Strike of 1915 ended with the close of the grinding season in early June. In the wake of the strike, Iglesias reported to President Woodrow Wilson that "the position of the workers themselves is more wretched than it ever was before." Anticipating further strikes in the coming harvest season, Iglesias lamented that "the employers will understand that they can rely upon the force, upon the police and upon the Government to prevent the laborers from bettering their conditions." Indeed, when plantation owners cut their workers' wages by 40 percent in the months after the strike, the workers barely protested. As Iglesias reported to Samuel Gompers, the workers were so disillusioned by the use of government power against them in the 1915 Sugar Strike that they felt increasingly helpless. "The feeling now prevails," Iglesias wrote, "that all of the force and power of the government of the Island are being used to maintain and further the interests of the employers."[108]

Tensions between Colonialism and Democracy

Appealing to President Wilson at a time of war, when international attention was increasingly focused on America's democratic ideals and growing global reach, Iglesias declared, in a 1915 petition for citizenship rights, that "social crimes" had been committed against the Puerto Rican people that were "unknown to have occurred before."[109] Implying that basic citizenship rights had been better protected under Spanish rule, Iglesias forced a troubling comparison between old and new empires.

Officials in Washington took note of the suppression of labor organizing on the island, especially as Congress and President Wilson had just established the first federal laws to govern the conditions of labor. With the passage of the 1914 Clayton Antitrust Act, which replaced the Sherman Antitrust Act of 1890, Congress passed what Samuel Gompers called organized labor's Magna Carta.[110] The Clayton Act protected the basic right of workers to organize by exempting unions from the legal charge of "conspiracies in restraint of trade," a charge that had been levied against unions in the United States under the terms of the Sherman Act and against Puerto Rican workers under the terms of both Spanish law and U.S. colonial law.

The protest of Puerto Rican workers as registered through strikes, petitions, and official testimony prompted President Wilson and the U.S. Congress to investigate. Alarmed by the scale of unrest on the island, and the way that protests were violently suppressed, Congress undertook a series of hearings in 1915 and 1916 to investigate conditions on the island. In one of his first acts as president, Wilson appointed the Commission on Industrial Relations to conduct congressional investigations into the causes of labor unrest. Headed by Frank Walsh, a supporter of organized labor, the commission held hearings on labor conditions throughout the United States, bringing before the public and officials in Washington the conditions of what Walsh termed "industrial feudalism."[111] The commission's investigations in Puerto Rico made clear to congressional leaders in Washington that the 1915 strike was but one manifestation of a deeper economic and political crisis. Surveying hundreds of people on the island, the commission collected evidence of economic privation, political statelessness, and the connections between the two.

As part of this investigation, Manuel Rodriguez Serra, a leader of the elite Puerto Rican Unionist Party, testified before Congress as to the effects of U.S. trade laws on the Puerto Rican economy. Because the 1900 Foraker Act had made no provisions for protecting Puerto Rican coffee in the U.S. market, Serra insisted, "we were compelled to look to tobacco and sugar, the best-protected articles, and as great capital was required to considerably increase the production, and we had not it, gradually all the best sugar and tobacco land and factories became the property of great foreign corporations."[112] But, Serra explained, "When the balance of trade of last year showed about $15,000,000 in favor of the island, there were people within the sugar zone almost starving."[113]

Serra argued that these economic changes occurred under U.S. rule in part because Puerto Rico lacked representation in Congress. In this sense, Serra maintained, the Foraker Act, which denied Puerto Ricans the right to vote in national elections or elect a voting representative to Congress, was a dramatic setback from the 1897 Autonomy Charter with Spain, which had granted Puerto Ricans the right to full representation in Madrid. Without the right to vote on legislation in Washington affecting the island's economic tariffs and trade agreements, Serra argued, the effects of the Foraker Act "have been disastrous on our collective life. We are now under a practical agricultural feudalism."[114]

Like Serra, Luis Muñoz Morales, chairman of the Porto Rico Bar Association, also argued before Congress that a kind of feudalism had gripped the island under U.S. rule. Though generally unresponsive to the demands of the working class, Muñoz expressed sympathy for the plight of small farmers. He asserted that the growing power of foreign corporations—and the attendant displacement of small coffee farmers—amounted to an "agricultural feudalism dangerous and fatal to the general prosperity of the country."[115] The five hundred-acre clause of the Foraker Act had set a legal limit on each corporation's landholdings on the island. But because the United States did not enforce the law, sugar and tobacco corporations looking to expand their holdings routinely evaded the statute. Thus the Foraker Act, despite the intent of the five hundred-acre limit, had the effect of allowing large U.S. corporate plantations to buy up the land of small farmers. As Representative Cay Coll Cuchi, a Unionist Party member of the Puerto Rican House of Delegates, lamented: "We had the island very well divided up into a great number of small parts, but American corporations came down, and foreigners came down, and they hold today all of our valuable property."[116]

Samuel Gompers echoed the claims of elite Puerto Ricans like Serra, Muñoz, and Coll Cuchi, testifying that the Foraker Act severely limited both economic opportunity and political expression on the island. Gompers claimed that "the conditions of trustification and corporation have gone on in connection with the island's development to such a degree that there is little, if any, avenue left for the workers to find expression. They find expression only through the AFL."[117]

AFL leaders remained wary of government efforts to belittle their struggle for basic rights. When Governor Yager tried to discredit the AFL on the island by stating that it was "in the hands of a few interested leaders" and that "the workers had not expressed themselves," workers quickly repudiated such claims and called on Congress to undertake an investigation of the island economy. Gompers asked Congress to examine the extent to which U.S. corporations—and the laws that permitted their practice—had "converted the country into a factory worked by slaves and peons."[118]

Congressional investigations further revealed that the situation of Puerto Rican workers, marked by low wages, an effective prohibition on unions, and a lack of representation in government, was exacerbated by the rising cost of living. As one prolabor observer noted, workers on the island were "employed at wages which are inadequate to furnish proper food and clothing."[119] Indeed, because tariff policies were set in Washington for the primary benefit of the U.S. states, they protected woolens, coal, and machinery that residents on the tropical, agricultural island had little use for. At the same time, staples of the island like rice, beans, and beef that were mass-produced on the mainland were heavily taxed. "Everything that they really need," Gompers explained, "is taxed highly under our laws. Everything that they really do not want is either on the free list or on a low-tariff basis." In Gompers's view, U.S. tariff policies—affecting prices on the most basic food staples—amounted to nothing less than "the undoing of the people of Porto Rico."[120]

In the Senate hearings, it emerged that the Foraker Act constrained the economic life of the island in other ways as well. Because it made only one of the Puerto Rican houses of government, the House of Delegates, elective, and left the other, the Executive Council, to be appointed by the U.S. president, laws favored by a majority of island residents were routinely struck down by Executive Council members. In one example, a proposal for a Puerto Rican bank designed to provide loans to small farmers, was repeatedly voted down by the Executive Council. When proponents on the island appealed to the U.S. Congress, it was turned down again.[121]

It was the 1915 strike, and the subsequent congressional hearings in which Puerto Ricans testified, that exposed the breadth of the political and economic crisis on the island and made the question of citizenship in Puerto Rico a legislative priority in Washington. Bills granting U.S. citizenship to Puerto Ricans had been introduced in each Congress since 1900, but none had passed. By 1912 a bipartisan consensus had developed in support of the bill but it was not brought for a vote in the Senate until 1917. In that year, Congress passed the bill and President Wilson signed it into law.[122] In the context of a war to "make the world safe for democracy," and widespread protest on the island that could draw international attention to U.S. colonial practices, officials in Washington brought the citizenship bill up for a vote.

President Wilson, in fact, had urged Congress to back an earlier version of the Jones bill, in December of 1915, after much of the Senate committee's hearings had been completed. Recognizing how unrest in Puerto Rico could compromise America's international reputation, Wilson called for Congress to act on the Puerto Rico bill. In his annual message to Congress Wilson stated: "Our treatment of them [Puerto Rico and the Philippines] and their attitude toward us are manifestly of the first consequence in the development of our duties in the world and in getting a free hand to perform those duties." Wilson called on the United States to free itself "from any unnecessary burden or embarrassment."[123] Like woman suffrage activists picketing at the White House gates during the war, Puerto Ricans protesting their treatment under the American flag had exposed the hypocrisy of Wilson's stated war aim to "make the world safe for democracy."[124] Wilson recognized that the problem of statelessness in Puerto Rico—and the contradiction between democratic ideals and colonial practices that it revealed—could well prove to be a political liability.

As the war in Europe continued to rage into 1916, the island's procitizenship leaders, along with supporters of the Puerto Rican labor movement, appealed for the rights they understood to be almost two decades overdue. During the Senate committee hearings on the Pacific Islands and Porto Rico, Willis Sweet of Puerto Rico stated that Puerto Ricans "do not understand why they may not be citizens in the full sense of the word—an appeal to the fundamental law of the U.S. that protects all citizens."[125] Sweet, like thousands of others before him, urged officials in Washington to allow the Constitution to follow the flag.

Samuel Gompers also lent his support to the citizenship cause throughout this period. Claiming that a sense of American superiority had delayed action for too long, American corporations on the island, he lamented, had shown Puerto Ricans little regard, to the point of becoming "anti-Porto Rican." When Senator James Vardaman, a Democrat from Mississippi, queried, "Isn't that characteristic of the Anglo Saxon dealing with another race?" Gompers replied that, while Americans generally regarded themselves as superior to foreigners, "We have not been so indifferent, nor so cruel, nor so unjust to the people in the Philippine Islands as we have to the people of Porto Rico."[126] Referring to the fact that Puerto Ricans were no longer represented in the metropole government as they had been under Spain, Gompers stated: "There is scarcely within my range of reading and observation an instance of darker pages of tragedy and wrong doing and injustice and brutality than the pages of the history of the people of Porto Rico since they have become part of the United States."[127]

Congress held extensive hearings from 1915 to 1916 and into 1917. Yet, even as support for citizenship grew in Washington, several groups opposed it. Racialized concerns about Puerto Rican fitness for citizenship persisted among some representatives in Congress. At a time when Jim Crow laws prevailed in the South, southern senators openly worried about giving Puerto Rican blacks the vote.[128] "What percentage of the population," Senator Vardaman pointedly asked Gompers in early 1916, "do you know are colored—negroes?"[129] Others worried that Puerto Ricans were largely unfit for democracy because they were so easily persuaded to vote for one candidate over another at the urging of their plantation owner. Gompers retorted that the same phenomenon occurred in the United States. In both the elections of 1896 and 1900, he claimed, the AFL had routinely removed broadsides from U.S. factories that owners had placed there to intimidate workers into voting for particular candidates.[130]

Increasingly, the citizenship cause was opposed by island elites. Indeed, members of the elite Unionist Party on the island objected to the granting of U.S. citizenship without statehood. Continuing the work of autonomists in the late nineteenth century, and earlier unionist efforts in 1912, the Unionist Party sought the largest measure of self-rule possible, either as a kind of commonwealth of the United States or as an independent country. Unionists, dominated by large landowners, held power from 1904 to 1924 with a platform that supported low corporate taxes and opposed expansion of public education.[131] Unionists controlled all seats in the Puerto Rican House of Delegates and accounted for some 110,000 of the 150,000 votes cast in the island's 1912 election.[132] Given that universal manhood suffrage had been in place in Puerto Rico since 1904, workers who struck periodically and voters electing the unionists were overlapping groups.[133] Expressing the sentiment of many unionists, Manuel Rodriguez Serra, representing the Civic Association of Porto Rico, asked rhetorically what made Puerto Ricans deserve the punishment of "being foreigners in the land which keeps the ashes of more than 12 generations of our forefathers?"[134] Because he viewed statehood as unlikely, Serra worried presciently that U.S. citizenship would always be a kind of second-class citizenship. "We, of course, could not willingly accept a political status in which we might be within the nation an inferior kind or class of citizen."[135] In a similar vein, Cay Coll Cuchi, a Union Party member of the Puerto Rican House of Delegates, called on Congress to make a decision on statehood at the same time that it decided the citizenship question. Predicting that if the United States decided at some future date to establish a government on the island in the form of a protectorate like that in Cuba or Panama, "they would be confronted with the very serious problem of unmaking 1,500,000 citizens of the U.S., which is a more serious problem than making them citizens."[136] Muñoz Rivera, as leader of the Unionist Party, asked Congress to allow a plebiscite on the island, a request Congress ignored.[137]

Unionist opposition to U.S. citizenship had hardened in the years after the election of President Wilson in 1912, as Unionist Party leaders became disillusioned with inaction in Washington on the question of the island's status. As Muñoz stated in 1914, "The Union [Party] had in its program two supreme solutions: statehood and independence. It became convinced one fine day that statehood was impossible. And it erased [statehood] from its program, and left standing, alone and dignified [the option] of independence."[138] Muñoz stated as early as 1913 that the ideal of the Unionist Party was "a free fatherland."[139]

Some leaders of the Unionist Party even drew on the U.S. colonial discourse of Puerto Rican inferiority to advance their own cause. In claiming Puerto Ricans would not likely assimilate, Cay Coll Cuchi, in a presumably disingenuous statement, asserted: "I can not be an Anglo-Saxon."[140] Puerto Rico, he stated, "can not be assimilated by the U.S." Senator Broussard pushed back, citing the example of Louisiana, which though originally a territory of French- and Spanish-speaking residents, later became fully a part of the United States. "Isn't that an example in American history of creating a loyal state out of a people of your own race?"[141] Coll Cuchi responded that such a trajectory was unlikely on the island. Because of its high population and distance from the mainland, he predicted, intermarriage with Americans—thought to be a primary engine of assimilation—would remain uncommon.[142] Opposing U.S. citizenship, Serra maintained that U.S. officials in Washington had "taken for granted that we were an inferior people or race, always in want of tutorship."[143]

But despite the concerns of those in Washington and on the island who were opposed to citizenship, Congress brought the Jones bill to a vote in 1917. First introduced in 1916 by Democratic Congressman William Jones of Virginia, a leading anti-imperialist, bill H.R. 9533 gradually won support in the House and Senate from both anti-imperialist Democrats and a smaller number of liberal Republicans.[144] The Jones bill, which became law on March 2, 1917 turned the island's U.S.-appointed Executive Council into an elected Senate, and declared all residents of the island citizens of the United States.[145] This was not full citizenship, however. Representation in Washington was still withheld, as the bill did not grant residents the right to vote for president of the United States and did not grant the island's resident commissioner in the U.S. House of Representatives the right to vote on legislation.[146]

When the Jones Act went into effect in March of 1917, provisions were made for those on the island who chose to refuse American citizenship. Of the island's over one million residents, only 288 opted out of the Jones Act, choosing instead to retain Spanish citizenship.[147] Yet even those who retained Spanish citizenship were subject to the U.S. military draft under the Selective Service Act.[148] Scholars have pointed to this fact when challenging conventional narratives of the Jones Act as simply an effort to conscript soldiers into the World War I army.[149]

That large-scale unrest on the island, petitions to the U.S. Congress from a broad swath of the Puerto Rican public, and subsequent congressional hearings could, in part, move officials in Washington to action suggests a more dynamic and contested exercise of imperial power than common top-down models would imply. When forty thousand Puerto Rican sugar workers throughout the island walked out in protest of low wages in 1915, they mounted a larger struggle for the right to strike in the first place and, more broadly, the right to have the Constitution follow the flag. In response to workers' protests, Congress began a series of investigations under the auspices of the Commission on Industrial Relations and the Senate Committee on Pacific Islands and Porto Rico. Presenting overwhelming evidence of labor unrest and infringements on civil liberties, these investigations alerted members of Congress and President Wilson to a developing crisis, as Puerto Ricans were increasingly willing to risk their lives for citizenship on the island. U.S. leaders realized that the crisis reverberated throughout the Caribbean and Latin America. In the context of World War I, when Wilson proclaimed America was fighting to "make the world safe for democracy," and when unrest on the island stood to compromise the reputation of the United States abroad, the conflict between statelessness on the island and America's democratic ideals proved increasingly untenable. The successful drive for citizenship was possible in the context of the separation of the legal status of Puerto Rico from that of the Philippines and the stripping, since the 1890s, of the guarantee that citizenship included fundamental rights—two developments that reduced the perceived threat of Puerto Rican citizenship. This history of citizenship and statelessness suggests the role of working-class strikes and petition drives as well as the efforts of selected members of the political elite on the island in bringing the question of U.S. citizenship before lawmakers in Washington. It offers an example of working-class agency within a colonial system where, as the historian Paul Kramer has observed, "bottom-up and mid-range claims-making was no less typical (if always less welcome) than top-down command."[150] Migrants traveling to the U.S. mainland would soon test the guarantees of the Jones Act as they sought employment opportunities in the metropole.

Chapter 5

"Working People Going North"

In April of 1917, just one month after the passage of the Jones Act, Arthur Yager, governor of Puerto Rico, wrote an urgent missive to Frank McIntyre, chief of the Bureau of Insular Affairs (BIA) in Washington: "I look forward to the dead season this summer with great anxiety. The cost of food has increased so rapidly and largely in Porto Rico that I am sure there will be much suffering."[1] Predicting that the prices of food imported from the mainland would only rise with the U.S. entry into the World War, Yager recommended dramatic action to alleviate poverty on the island: he called for the transport of large numbers of unemployed Puerto Ricans to the mainland. As war industries began to demand laborers to replace those drafted into service, and as Congress had just granted Puerto Ricans U.S. citizenship, American colonial officials in Puerto Rico argued that "working people going north" could simultaneously earn a living and "render patriotic service."[2]

In this chapter, I examine how the granting of U.S. citizenship to Puerto Ricans in 1917 shaped migration patterns to the U.S. mainland during World War I and after. I show how citizenship made Puerto Ricans more broadly eligible for employment, thereby drawing them further into the mainland economy. Previously unauthorized to hire Puerto Rican nationals, the U.S.

Department of Labor in 1918 recruited 12,000 Puerto Ricans—now U.S. citizens—to the mainland to work in army camps. Similarly, U.S. employers, looking to secure cheap labor during a period of immigration restriction, took advantage of the fact that U.S. citizenship permitted Puerto Ricans to enter the mainland while other groups were excluded.

Puerto Ricans were recruited as part of a broader project of U.S. employers and the state to import laborers from different sites of U.S. empire during periods of wartime demand and immigration restriction. Historians have explored various labor migrations of this period such as the recruitment of Filipino nationals and Mexican migrants to work in Western agriculture in the 1920s.[3] Though included as laborers in the American economy, these groups were routinely excluded from the polity. In a process the historian Mae Ngai describes as "imported colonialism," employers and the colonial state recruited colonial and semicolonial migrants only to later render them invisible through political exclusion and deportation from the U.S. mainland.[4]

Unlike Mexican and Filipino migrant laborers, however, Puerto Rican migrants became a core concern of the U.S. colonial state because they posed a fundamental challenge to colonial law. Marking a departure from previous colonial policy, the Jones Act of 1917 had extended U.S. citizenship to Puerto Ricans on the island. In response to growing unrest in Puerto Rico, the colonial state sought to trumpet the benefits of U.S. citizenship and contract labor programs. Yet, at the same time, the Jones Act limited the extension of U.S. citizenship by tying it to the territorial status of the island. Colonial officials often declined to issue passports or identity cards as a means of confining U.S. citizenship to the island and limiting migration to the mainland. Puerto Ricans who did move to the United States tested the guarantees of the Jones Act and the delicate balance of colonial policy it had made law. Puerto Rican challenges to colonial policy and racial nationalism built on the practice of labor activism they had honed on the island during the first two decades of U.S. rule. When mainland courts and employers refused to recognize their citizenship, conflicts over the legal status of Puerto Rican migrants became a federal issue. Precisely because Puerto Ricans moving to the mainland could become residents of an incorporated territory or state and, potentially, gain full U.S. citizenship, migration proved to be a central conflict for the U.S. colonial regime after 1917. At a time when many in Washington sought to obscure the remnants of America's colonial project, migrants from Puerto Rico made questions of colonialism and citizenship increasingly visible.

Wartime Labor Demands and Colonial Migrants

Shortly after the United States entered World War I in April 1917, Department of Labor officials in Washington fretted about the problem of increasing demand for labor. With the institution of the draft in May of that year, employers throughout the United States reported difficulties in replacing workers going off to war. As the demand for labor grew, employers began seeking employees from far afield by advertising in out-of-state newspapers. Some newspapers declined to publish these advertisements, however, on the grounds that local employers could not afford to lose their own laborers. When the New York City–based Kiernan & Co. submitted advertisements for ironworkers and helpers to newspapers in Connecticut, for example, the *Post and Telegram* of Bridgeport, Connecticut, stated: "We have deemed it policy to discontinue the insertion of advertisements which would take labor away from the Bridgeport shops."[5] Several employers framed the problem as a labor shortage. The Norfolk and Western Railway, dependent on agriculture for much of its business, reported an "increasing shortage of labor" on farms using its lines throughout the western states.[6]

While the draft clearly increased the demand for labor, not everyone agreed with the assertion of employers that the result was necessarily a shortage.[7] American Federation of Labor president Samuel Gompers insisted that there was no labor scarcity at all by citing reports from Missouri, Oklahoma, Kansas, and other midwestern states claiming to have no shortage of workers. Gompers argued that the talk of scarcity and shortage was, in fact, born of war hysteria and "the desire of employers to profit" by importing cheap labor.[8] J. W. Sullivan, head of the Division of Labor, U.S. Food Administration, agreed with Gompers. "The problem," he wrote, "is a mal-adjustment of supply rather than a total absence of needed labor." Reports from throughout the country supported Sullivan's claim. As the commissioner of labor in California wrote in June 1917, the supply of labor was sufficient but needed "organization to meet the requirements of gathering the crops."[9] Recognizing the increased demand for labor, especially temporary farm labor, Sullivan recommended that the secretary of labor create a federal employment agency for the purpose of connecting employers with laborers within the United States.[10]

Yet southern planters vigorously opposed the Department of Labor's plan to redistribute the domestic labor supply. Because its purview was broad enough to include industrial and agricultural labor, southern planters feared losing their own workers to western farms and northern factories. The U.S.

Department of Agriculture (USDA), heavily influenced by southern farmers, objected to the Department of Labor's plan to simply move workers within the country from areas of lesser need to areas of greater need. Siding with the opposition from the USDA and southern planters, the Department of Labor began recruiting workers from outside the mainland United States.[11]

Thus, despite the arguments of Food Administration official Sullivan and AFL president Gompers that workers within the United States could meet wartime labor demands, and the established practice of private industries such as the railroads of recruiting southern blacks, the Department of Labor began recruiting foreign workers from Mexico in 1917.[12] Congress passed the Burnett Immigration Law, over President Wilson's veto, in February 1917.[13] By order of the secretary of labor on May 23 of that year, the United States made Mexican immigrants exempt from the literacy requirement of the Burnett Law in order to recruit thousands of Mexicans to work for U.S. employers, primarily on farms and ranches in the Southwest.[14]

Nativists and labor leaders promptly registered their objections. Eugenics had gained legitimacy and influence in the United States in the early 1900s and fearful predictions of white race suicide began appearing in American newspapers.[15] By the 1910s, proponents of the new race science wielded considerable influence in Congress. John C. Box of Texas and Albert Johnson of Washington, for example, were members of both the U.S. Congress and the American Eugenics Society.[16] Supporters of the literacy requirement in 1917 and the immigration restriction laws of the early 1920s, eugenicists in Congress became increasingly frustrated with the "Mexican loophole."[17]

The speedy nullification of the literacy requirement in the Mexican case came as a particular shock to AFL leaders who had vigorously lobbied for two decades to protect American workers from what Gompers described as "unnecessary and harmful competition" with the "lower standards of life and work of illiterate foreign workers."[18] Gompers objected to what he called the "temporary entrance of illiterate Mexicans into this country."[19] He explained that the Burnett Immigration Law, which, for the first time, had established literacy requirements for immigrants over the age of sixteen entering the United States, was now willfully violated by the Department of Labor and large-scale agricultural growers throughout the Southwest who stood to gain from the recruitment of Mexican workers.[20]

The AFL's strenuous protest of the Department of Labor's decision to admit workers from Mexico may have prompted the department to pursue recruitment from Puerto Rico more actively. Gompers and the AFL could stand on legal principle when protesting the department's decision to allow illiterate Mexicans workers into the United States. But the legal position of Puerto Ricans was different. While Mexicans could be cast as immigrants subject to restriction, Puerto Ricans had just been declared citizens of the United States with the passage of the Jones Act on March 2, 1917. As such, they were officially exempt from the literacy requirement and all other immigration restrictions. Puerto Ricans and Mexicans, in the eyes of employers and government officials, had overnight become legally distinct.

It was in this socio-legal context, in which American workers called on Immigration Service officials to enforce the literacy law, that the Department of Labor turned its attention from Mexico to Puerto Rico. As early as June 1917, William B. Wilson, U.S. secretary of labor, recommended that railroad companies recruit Puerto Ricans to work in the Southwest. In consultation with representatives of the railroad and agricultural interests, he suggested that the railroads hire Puerto Ricans for track work for part of the year, allowing them to work for growers in the Southwest during the harvest season.[21] Such calls for temporary employment were consistent with the need expressed by labor officials in the Southwest. As Simon J. Lubin, commissioner of housing and immigration for the state of California, stated, there is a "demand for large numbers of men and women whose services will be required for only brief periods."[22] Wilson's proposal to recruit Puerto Ricans to serve as temporary workers in the U.S. Southwest, a region thousands of miles from Puerto Rico, but adjacent to Mexico, appears strange until we recognize the changing legal landscape of immigration exclusion.

As early as November 1917, F. C. Roberts, representing the U.S. Department of Labor in San Juan, recruited several thousand workers for U.S. railroads and other corporations. Given the seasonal cycles of employment and unemployment among sugar workers on the island, Roberts found an "abundance of labor available after grinding season."[23] In May of 1918, the U.S. Department of Labor recruited laborers from the island "for the purpose of supplying the need of common labor in the United States."[24] Roberts organized the recruitment effort and carefully selected those who were older than draft age but still physically fit: the fathers of those who had, in fact, been drafted into the war.

Camp Jackson

In one of the largest of these government-sponsored recruitment efforts, the U.S. Department of Labor also recruited 12,000 Puerto Rican workers to numerous army camps and navy yards throughout the U.S. South to work in construction, shipbuilding, and supply manufacture during World War I. In September and October of 1918, 1,241 men were transported from Puerto Rico to the New Orleans Army Supply Base; 1,735 to Camp Bragg, North Carolina; 2,954 to the Picric Acid Plant in Brunswick, Georgia; 1,859 to North Camp Jackson, South Carolina; 901 to the Picric Acid Plant in Little Rock, Arkansas; and 1,678 to Camp Jackson, South Carolina. An additional 2,611 men were transported to the United States in October of 1918 only to be returned to Puerto Rico, for reasons that are unclear, before even disembarking.[25]

At Camp Jackson, outside Columbia, South Carolina, to take one example, the U.S. Army Quartermaster's Office solicited the help of the U.S. Department of Labor in securing construction workers for the camp in 1918. In October of that year, the labor secretary notified officials at Camp Jackson that they had arranged for 1,769 Puerto Ricans to be shipped to South Carolina. Two commissioned officers met the Puerto Ricans at the port of Charleston when they arrived in early November. The officers boarded the ship to record each man's name and distribute buttons displaying each man's "working number." The Puerto Ricans were then transferred to train cars of the Southern and Atlantic Coast Line Railway en route to Camp Jackson.

From the start, camp administrators expressed prejudicial views of Puerto Ricans. Upon arrival, the Puerto Ricans were escorted to what became known as "the Porto Rican area," an area made up of bunkhouses, mess halls, and latrines that was segregated from both the black and white sections of the camp. In one example, P. K. Holjes, charged with managing the seven segregated mess halls serving the Puerto Rican workers at Camp Jackson, replaced American cooks and kitchen help with a number of the new Puerto Rican workers in order to "provide meals such as they had had in their native homes." But untrained in preparing food for such large numbers, the Puerto Rican workers-turned-cooks inevitably wasted food in the process. Army officers took this waste as evidence of inferiority. As the quartermaster asserted, "These Porto Ricans were of the very lowest type of laborers, and they had no sense of decency or economy in the handling of their foodstuffs."[26]

Camp Jackson officers naturalized differences between themselves and Puerto Ricans by continually casting Puerto Ricans as inferior to mainland workers. Puerto Ricans were described as "naturally out of place," "dressed in their native clothes," and barefoot. According to the quartermaster's report, the recruited Puerto Ricans "proved to be a failure in the way

Figure 5.1. "Mess Halls at Porto Rican Camp." A Puerto Rican recruit stands in front of a mess hall in the Puerto Rican section of Camp Jackson, South Carolina, 1918. Box 137, RG 165, NACP.

of labor at this camp."[27] Camp officials were, in fact, so dissatisfied that they continually petitioned the Department of Labor for replacement workers. The department proved to be unable to secure other sources of labor, however, as both American workers and proponents of race science continued to press for enforcement of the 1917 Literacy Act and restriction of Mexican immigration.

When an influenza epidemic broke out at Camp Jackson in 1918, it disproportionately affected the Puerto Rican population in the camp, a fact that further fed the racialized arguments of white officers about Puerto Rican inferiority. Hundreds of Puerto Ricans were stricken so that an average of 400 to 500 Puerto Rican men were in the base hospital at any one time. The high rate of Puerto Rican sickness and death was understood in racial terms: "Naturally, on account of their low vitality, they were not able to overcome this disease as well as the average American."[28] In making such racialized claims of low vitality, camp officials ignored the fact that infection spread quickly among Puerto Ricans because the army had accommodated them so poorly. Segregated in "the Puerto Rican area," they lived in 18 bunkhouses,

Figure 5.2. Photograph of Teodosio Castillo, who worked for the U.S. Shipping Board in 1920. Box 312, folder 1493–238, RG 350, NACP.

each 24' x 120', that were built quickly in the five days before their arrival to sleep 100 men each.[29]

While some died of influenza, most of those recruited to work in U.S. army camps and navy yards returned to Puerto Rico, often with little cash in hand to show for their expedition north. When the war ended in 1919, the Department of Labor shipped 1,392 of the 1,769 Puerto Ricans who had been recruited to Camp Jackson back to the island. Many of the remaining 377 had either died of influenza or were too sick to make the trip.[30]

Those who stayed on the mainland often faced continued hardship. A small number remained in the United States, moving from Camp Jackson to other jobs along the East Coast. Teodosio Castillo, for example, who had left Puerto Rico in October 1918 at the age of eighteen to work as a laborer at Camp Jackson, later traveled north to work at the U.S. Navy Yard, Labor Camp No. 2, in Norfolk, Virginia. He then worked for the U.S. Shipping Board, Division of Operations, traveling to Brazil on board the steamship *Chebaulip* and returning to New York City in October 1920.[31] Family members reported that mail they sent to his address at 38 South Street, New York City, was repeatedly returned.[32] In October 1920, his father, Gaspar Castillo, having not heard from him for nearly three years, wrote to the governor of Puerto Rico asking for help. "The fact of my having not received any news as to my son's death," he wrote, "leads me to believe that he is alive."[33] But by the end of June 1923, after searching for his whereabouts with the United States and Brazil Steamship Line, the U.S. Navy, the U.S. Shipping Board, and the City of New York, the Bureau of Insular Affairs pronounced him officially missing.[34] The case of Teodosio Castillo reflected the frustrated expectations of many on the island that labor migration to the mainland would lead to economic betterment for families on the island.

Still others found themselves stranded on the mainland, without the means to make a living in the United States or return to the island.[35] In 1922 three hundred Puerto Ricans who had migrated to the United States during World War I to work in the Construction Division of the U.S. Army were without work in New Orleans, Louisiana. When they sought help from Dr. Charles Paz, a Spanish-speaking dentist living in the city, Paz wrote to the U.S. secretary of war on their behalf to ask if the government could provide them free transport back to Puerto Rico.[36] In response, Charles Walcutt of the Bureau of Insular Affairs recommended that the workers either seek relief from the Red Cross or offer to work on a steamship in order to pay their way back to the island. "In view of the present unemployment situation in both continental United States and Porto Rico, [the government is] unable to offer any further advice."[37]

Family members on the island, in fact, often paid a tragic price for the migration of their sons, brothers, and husbands. Basilio Maldonado, who left Fajardo, Puerto Rico, for Camp Jackson, South Carolina, in 1918, left his wife behind on the island. Shortly after arriving in the United States, Maldonado died of unknown causes. After receiving word of Maldonado's death by way of the U.S. Employment Service, his widow, Concha Garcia, petitioned the U.S. military for compensation. In a letter dated August 14, 1922, Garcia stated that without an income from her husband she had "been subjected to terrible conditions in the struggle for life." She asked for "commensurate compensation for the death of my husband" in order to "seek relief in my misfortune."[38] In a similar case, Diego Pagan, while working in an army camp near Columbia, South Carolina, "was caught in the current of a river and perished by drowning." His father, Felix Pagan Merly, petitioned for compensation, writing, "now my only bread is tears."[39] The Bureau of Insular Affairs responded that, because Pagan had worked for the Wateree Power Company, a private company that had contracted with the U.S. Army, the government could not offer him "financial aid."[40]

Second-Class Citizenship

Even as Puerto Ricans were recruited to work in the U.S. economy, they continued to be excluded in legal and racial terms from full citizenship. Though federal immigration law imagined only national boundaries—especially after the Supreme Court ruled in 1875 that states did not have the authority to control immigration—citizenship was often shaped, and even diminished, at the level of states.[41]

This second-class citizenship was reflected in debates over the need for identification cards for Puerto Ricans. When an identity document for Puerto Ricans was first considered in 1917, the Bureau of Insular Affairs declared that such a document was unnecessary. Richard Campbell, commissioner of naturalization, wrote, as late as April 1919: "I incline to the opinion that the class of persons referred to, are citizens of the United States, but I fail to see anything which I can do to definitely settle their status."[42]

Puerto Ricans' requests for legal recognition began immediately after the Jones Act and mounted toward the end of the war. Puerto Ricans enlisted in the U.S. Navy filed numerous complaints with Resident Commissioner Félix Córdova Dávila in Washington, claiming the navy had misclassified them as aliens.[43] As such, they were routinely paid less than other Americans working the same jobs.[44] As increasing numbers of Puerto Ricans called for recognition of their status during the war demobilization of 1919, the Bureau of Insular Affairs considered different ways of publicizing Puerto Ricans' U.S. citizenship status.[45] Arthur Yager, the governor of Puerto Rico during the Wilson administration, wrote in 1919 to the Bureau of Insular Affairs to recommend that officials in Washington be authorized to distribute a certificate to Puerto Ricans in the United States in order to protect Puerto Ricans from infringements on their rights as citizens. This would serve, Yager reasoned, to "give publicity to the real facts about which so many people in the United States seem to be confused and misinformed."[46]

Part of the confusion within the U.S. military and the public at large derived from the fact that Puerto Ricans traveling from the island to the United States were not issued American passports. As William Phillip, assistant secretary of state, wrote in a letter to the Bureau of Insular Affairs, passports could only be issued to Puerto Ricans leaving the island for foreign countries. "It is a well-established practice," Phillip wrote, "to issue passports solely to accredit the American citizenship of persons purposing to travel abroad."[47] Despite the passage of the Jones Act, the State Department still relied on the 1901 *Downes v. Bidwell* decision defining Puerto Rico as an unincorporated territory of the United States, and thereby "foreign in a domestic sense." The State Department did not consider travel from Puerto Rico to the United States to be travel abroad. With such restrictions on issuing passports, Assistant Secretary of State William Phillip recommended, instead, "the more extensive publication of the laws conferring American citizenship upon Porto Ricans."[48]

Questions about the reach of the Jones Act also contributed to the confusion. A small number of residents of the island renounced U.S. citizenship in the months following the passage of the Jones Act in 1917 in an attempt to escape conscription into the U.S. Army. In a telegram dated April 20, 1917, Arthur Yager asked officials in Washington to rule on the question of whether or not renunciation would release Puerto Ricans from compulsory military service. He asked for a quick reply, "so as to avoid a campaign for renunciations among the people."[49] The Bureau of Insular Affairs responded that Puerto Ricans who renounced U.S. citizenship were citizens of Puerto Rico "entitled to the protection of the United States." "Being entitled to such protection," the bureau declared, "they should be required to render service to the government of the United States."[50]

Such a policy was in line with the U.S. Army's practice of drafting noncitizens in World War I from Mexico and other locations of U.S. empire. In the first round of the draft in June of 1917, more than half of the 123,277 immigrants drafted had not yet filed "first papers" to become U.S. citizens.[51] In Texas, the U.S. Army drafted immigrants in large numbers, often by force as Anglos rounded up Mexicans in order to register them. Though the Selective Service Act specified that aliens could be conscripted only if they had initiated the naturalization process, local draft boards sidestepped this stipulation to draft more than 70,000 nondeclarant aliens in 1917. In this context, the only way immigrants could be exempted from military service was by proving foreign citizenship. For Mexicans, this was a nearly impossible task given the large number of birth certificates destroyed in the course of the Mexican Revolution. While some nondeclarant aliens accepted the draft, many others fled the country. As the historian Benjamin Heber Johnson has observed, the drafting of so many noncitizen immigrants by local draft boards in Texas and other states qualified as a form of coerced labor recruitment.[52] In the moment when the United States mobilized to make the world safe for democracy, large numbers of noncitizens fled the country if they could, with many in the Southwest crossing to safety in Mexico.

In the colonial context of Puerto Rico, the policy of drafting noncitizens was put to the test in 1918 when Jose Lopez Garcia protested his conscription before the U.S. Draft Board in San Juan.[53] Claiming Spanish citizenship, Garcia stated that his father, Joaquin Lopez Cortes, had elected to retain Spanish citizenship in 1900, in accordance with the allowances made in Article IX of the Treaty of Paris between Spain and the United States.[54] In June 1917, one month before turning twenty-five, the legal age of majority under Spanish law, Jose Lopez Garcia declared himself a Spanish citizen by registering with the Spanish Consulate in San Juan.[55] Garcia renewed his registration with the Spanish Consulate in June of 1918. When ordered to appear before the board on June 24, 1918, Garcia issued a formal protest. Stating, "I am a subject of the King of Spain," Garcia objected to "being compelled to serve in the military forces of the United States."[56] Ruling on the case in the U.S. District Court in San Juan, Judge Peter Hamilton declared that Garcia had not effectively renounced his U.S. citizenship because he had failed to do so before turning twenty-one, the legal age of majority under U.S. law.[57] The court thus denied him an exemption from military service, ruling that he was a U.S. citizen under the terms of the Treaty of Paris. Garcia later filed an appeal with the U.S. Supreme Court in 1918, but the court declined to hear the case.[58] Jose Garcia's case highlights the inconsistent application of U.S. citizenship to Puerto Ricans: for purposes of military service, even those who sought to retain Spanish citizenship were defined as U.S. citizens; yet, for purposes of laying off workers during war demobilization, U.S. citizens from the island could be redefined as aliens. Unlike Mexicans who could escape conscription by seeking refuge within the sovereignty of their home country, Puerto Ricans had nowhere to escape to within U.S. colonial borders.

The case of Jose Garcia, and others like it, generated some confusion in Puerto Rico and on the mainland as to the citizenship status of Puerto Ricans after the Jones Act. But the number of those who retained Spanish citizenship remained comparatively very small. With an island population of around one million, only 4,889 retained their Spanish citizenship in 1900.[59] Garcia was one of only 40 Puerto Ricans of draft age who were registered with the Spanish Consulate in 1918.

In the midst of such contradictions, and mounting complaints by Puerto Ricans that they were not able to exercise citizenship rights even after the Jones Act, the Bureau of Insular Affairs issued a broadside aimed at publicizing the fact that Puerto Ricans were U.S. citizens. Released on October 12, 1920, the broadside titled "Porto Ricans are American Citizens" stated: "The ties binding Porto Rico to the Continental United States will be strengthened by a wider knowledge among the people of the mainland that the Porto Ricans are their 'fellow citizens.'"[60] Yet, despite this conceit of broadening the U.S. public's knowledge, the broadside obscured as much as it clarified. Though the title implied few limits to American citizenship for those on the island or mainland, the text itself specified citizenship rights only for "inhabitants of Porto Rico," thereby constraining citizenship to the island or "by locality." Listing three broad groups—U.S. citizens, citizens of Porto Rico, and aliens—it left the reader without the tools to determine who exactly was a citizen and who was an alien. In failing to clarify the status of specific individuals applying for jobs—as an identity card would have done—the broadside did little to protect Puerto Ricans' rights of citizenship. It thus highlighted the reluctance of the colonial state to clarify that citizens of a territory could seek fuller citizenship on the mainland. It also showed the broader legal morass caused by the contradiction between democracy and colonialism.

The lack of individualized identity documents heightened Puerto Ricans' vulnerability. Because traveling from colony to metropole was not considered "travel to a foreign country," they were denied passports. Because national status presented legal obstacles to applying for citizenship,

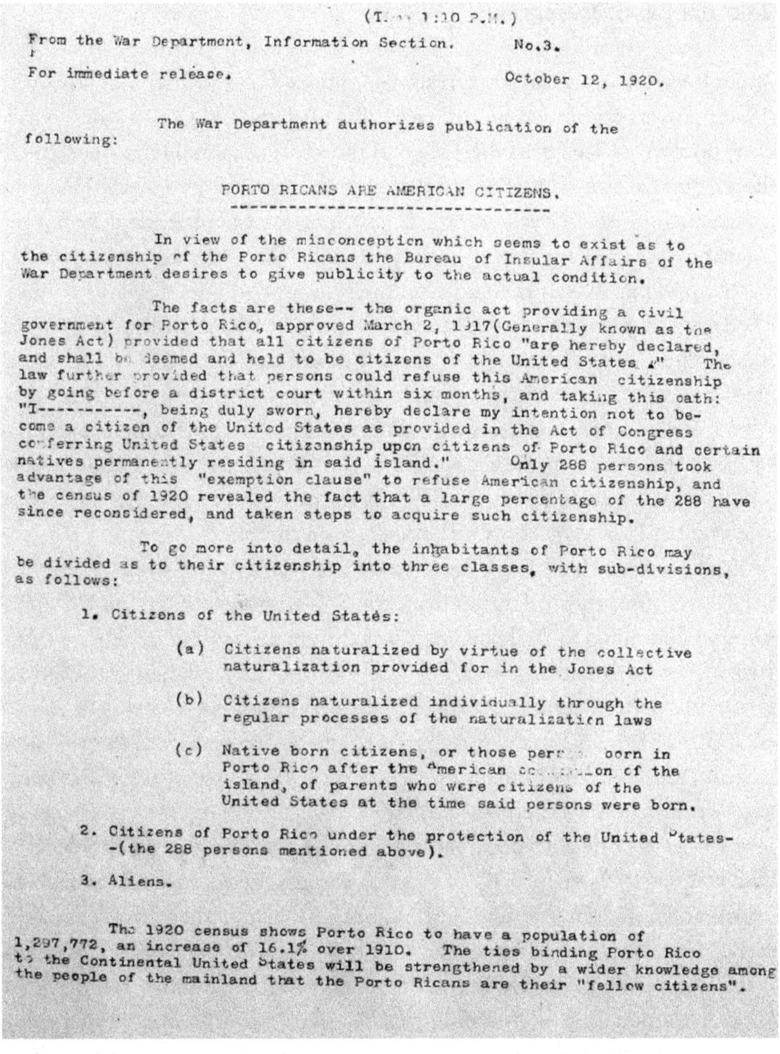

(T[illegible] 1:10 P.M.)

From the War Department, Information Section. No.3.

For immediate release. October 12, 1920.

The War Department authorizes publication of the following:

PORTO RICANS ARE AMERICAN CITIZENS.

In view of the misconception which seems to exist as to the citizenship of the Porto Ricans the Bureau of Insular Affairs of the War Department desires to give publicity to the actual condition.

The facts are these-- the organic act providing a civil government for Porto Rico, approved March 2, 1917(Generally known as the Jones Act) provided that all citizens of Porto Rico "are hereby declared, and shall be deemed and held to be citizens of the United States." The law further provided that persons could refuse this American citizenship by going before a district court within six months, and taking this oath: "I----------, being duly sworn, hereby declare my intention not to become a citizen of the United States as provided in the Act of Congress conferring United States citizenship upon citizens of Porto Rico and certain natives permanently residing in said island." Only 288 persons took advantage of this "exemption clause" to refuse American citizenship, and the census of 1920 revealed the fact that a large percentage of the 288 have since reconsidered, and taken steps to acquire such citizenship.

To go more into detail, the inhabitants of Porto Rico may be divided as to their citizenship into three classes, with sub-divisions, as follows:

1. Citizens of the United States:

   (a) Citizens naturalized by virtue of the collective naturalization provided for in the Jones Act

   (b) Citizens naturalized individually through the regular processes of the naturalization laws

   (c) Native born citizens, or those per[illegible] born in Porto Rico after the American [illegible]on of the island, of parents who were citizens of the United States at the time said persons were born.

2. Citizens of Porto Rico under the protection of the United States--(the 288 persons mentioned above).

3. Aliens.

The 1920 census shows Porto Rico to have a population of 1,297,772, an increase of 16.1% over 1910. The ties binding Porto Rico to the Continental United States will be strengthened by a wider knowledge among the people of the mainland that the Porto Ricans are their "fellow citizens".

Figure 5.3. "Porto Ricans are American Citizens." Broadside issued by the Bureau of Insular Affairs, War Department, October 12, 1920. Box 180, folder 1390, AGPR.

they were often denied naturalization papers. And because the Bureau of Insular Affairs ultimately rejected the proposed identity document, they were denied legal papers of any kind certifying their U.S. citizenship status, even after 1917.[61]

Colonial Labor Reserves

While Puerto Ricans' citizenship status remained undocumented, however, U.S. employers continued recruitment efforts on the island. They drew on a labor pool made legally vulnerable and thereby cheap and continued these efforts after the war.[62] One Puerto Rican originally employed by the U.S. government in the army camp in North Carolina, for example, stayed on after the war to work for a private company, the T. H. Gill Company in Greenville, North Carolina. When the Gill Company sought additional laborers, they asked their employee from the island for names of friends he thought would be interested. With the names of "about a dozen friends there," Gill wrote to Chief McIntyre of the Bureau of Insular Affairs to begin the formal process of recruiting contract laborers from Puerto Rico.[63] In this example, and others like it, laborers who were brought to the United States for public, emergency purposes, later served as the basis for private corporations' efforts to recruit other low-wage contract laborers from the island.

In response to the Great Migration during World War I, when thousands of African Americans migrated from the South to the North, the U.S. government continued to facilitate large-scale migrations of Puerto Ricans from the island to the mainland South. While most blacks remained in the South during this period, Senator Joseph Ransdell of Louisiana wrote in 1923 that sugar growers in his state were anxious to secure laborers from Puerto Rico because "the colored population of several of the southern states has been largely transferred to the northern cities."[64] In a letter to Ransdell, Horace Towner—a Republican from Illinois who served as governor of Puerto Rico from 1923 to 1929—approved of sending Puerto Ricans to work on Louisiana sugar plantations. He advised Senator Ransdell that these workers could likely be hired cheaply: "Wages [in Puerto Rico] have been very small, comparatively speaking, largely because of the excess of labor, so the expectations of the laboring men would not be very great."[65] After talking with sugar planters throughout Louisiana who were eager to secure cheap labor, Senator Ransdell requested that the U.S. Department of War provide for the transport of Puerto Ricans from the island to Louisiana.[66] The War Department arranged for a special voyage to be made from Puerto Rico to New Orleans at a cost to the Louisiana growers of $18,700.[67]

The largest of these post–World War I recruitment efforts focused on bringing thousands of Puerto Rican families to pick cotton on ranches owned by the Arizona Cotton Growers' Association.[68] Growers throughout the Salt River and Gila valley regions of Arizona founded the Cotton Association in

1915 in order to coordinate efforts to secure a sufficiently inexpensive labor supply for each harvest season. The Cotton Association, serving farms totaling 370,000 acres, comprised mostly cotton ranches, and, to a lesser extent, lettuce and cantaloupe farms.[69]

After years of acquiring adequate labor from Mexico, the Cotton Association claimed, in the mid- to late 1920s, that its members faced a shortage of unskilled and agricultural labor that was annually becoming more acute. The immediate cause of the perceived shortage was the passage of the 1924 Johnson-Reed Act.[70] This law imposed numerical caps on immigration from each country outside of the Western Hemisphere. Though exempting Mexican immigrants from numerical quotas, the law imposed other new requirements on Mexican immigration: it required that Mexicans obtain visas at U.S. consulates, pay head taxes, and submit to physical exams at U.S. immigration stations. The act did significantly more than just establish these new entry requirements; it also allocated funds for their enforcement. It created the U.S. Border Patrol as the enforcement arm of the U.S. Immigration Service along the U.S.-Mexico border. E. J. Walker, labor agent for the Cotton Association, claimed such requirements imposed "restrictions upon Mexico as to make it practically impossible for families of the desired class of people to enter the United States."[71] While the Johnson-Reed Act hardened the U.S.-Mexico border, the claim that this law made it impossible for Arizona farmers to import Mexican laborers was surely an exaggeration. When the Border Patrol first began policing the border and enforcing the act's new requirements in the harvest season of 1925, growers claimed an acute shortage of labor such that many were unable to harvest their cotton and produce.[72] Yet Mexican immigration boomed in the years between the Johnson-Reed Act and the Great Depression.[73] In fact, the growing number of Mexicans entering the United States in the 1920s dismayed eugenicists who viewed the Johnson-Reed Act's exemption of Mexicans from numerical quotas as a grave mistake.[74] As Samuel Gompers and other labor leaders had long contended, the perceived shortage was not of labor per se, but only of workers willing to accept starvation wages.

As Mexicans already living in the Southwest began organizing for higher wages, in fact, Mexican labor became less cheap. A series of significant strikes in Arizona, including the Clifton-Morenci strike in 1903 and the Cananea strike in 1907, established Mexican demands for higher wages. In the Bispee strike of 1917, Mexicans calling for an end to racially tiered wage levels in Arizona's copper mines were silenced through deportation.[75] But by the mid-1920s, with Mexican migration on the rise after the passage of the Johnson-Reed Act, labor organizers again called for living wages. As one observer noted in 1926, "In recent years the Cotton Growers of Arizona have enjoyed the cheapest kind of Mexican labor but the Mexicans have become more independent and demanded fair treatment and fair prices."[76] With Mexican labor becoming more expensive, growers in the Southwest looked to Puerto Rico for alternative sources of cheap labor.

At the same time as Mexicans organized for higher wages in the Southwest, the Bureau of Immigration cracked down on those deemed illegal or undocumented. Though the Department of Labor had authorized large numbers of Mexicans to enter the United States in 1917, these workers were seen as early guest workers who would eventually return to Mexico.[77] Yet many remained in the United States. After Michigan sugar-beet farmers recruited one thousand Mexican workers through contract labor agents in San Antonio, Texas, in 1918, for instance, some stayed north of the Rio Grande, migrating between the Midwest's cities and beet fields. With the Immigration Acts of 1921 and 1924, Bureau of Immigration officials apprehended Mexicans suspected of overstaying wartime contracts. Those who were unable to show a contract or legal basis for entry prior to 1921 were arrested and deported.[78]

Migrant workers, however, increasingly contested their exploitation in U.S. courts during and after World War I. In the war period, the U.S. Employment Service, an arm of the Department of Labor, guaranteed written labor contracts for seasonal workers. The growing number of such documents, after a period of mostly spoken contracts, gave rise to a number of court challenges when employers broke the terms of these contracts. Court challenges demonstrate the agency of U.S. workers as well as the ways that laws in favor of business interests pitted workers against each other. In 1922 three African American laborers filed complaints against Roman Gonzalez, a Mexican American labor agent, after their contracted employer refused to hire them as mule skinners near Kingman, Arizona. The El Paso judge in this case ruled against Gonzalez, stating that he should refund the laborers the fees they had paid him for securing them employment. Given long-established racial requirements for citizenship to be restricted to whites and blacks, African Americans in this era of Jim Crow could sometimes find legal redress in the courts. As the historian Gunther Peck has argued, such cases reveal the strategic ways that migrant workers attempted to use the law and citizenship to contest the power of labor agents and employers in the 1920s.[79] Mexicans, in contrast, found little protection in the courts. As Juan Castillo, a migrant cotton picker in Texas, stated in 1927, "There is a law for the Americans but none for the Mexicans."[80]

In the midst of these conflicts between African American workers and labor agents and between Mexican laborers and low-wage employers, the Cotton Association sent its labor agent, E. J. Walker, to San Juan in February 1926 to explore the possibility of recruiting workers from the island. Walker reported favorably on the prospect of recruiting Puerto Ricans, positioning them within a racial hierarchy above blacks and roughly equivalent to Mexicans. As he stated, Puerto Ricans "are of Spanish blood, and are not negroes as is commonly believed. They will compare favorably with the interior Mexican that has been used here during the previous periods of labor shortages."[81] Walker's views squared with those held by organizers of the Puerto Rican exhibit at the 1926 Philadelphia Exposition. As *Porto Rico Progress*, published in San Juan, reported on September 8, 1926, the Puerto Rican "Department of Agriculture and Labor has dedicated itself to proclaiming Porto Rico as a great mart for cheap laborers" at the Philadelphia Exposition. There, advertisements claimed that Puerto Rico was "a seedbed of laborers as cheap as the Chinese."[82]

While in San Juan, Walker was assisted by BIA chief Frank McIntyre, in making contacts with officials on the island.[83] McIntyre took particular interest in recruiting labor from Puerto Rico. Migration to the mainland, he predicted, would prove to be a means of Americanizing residents of the island. In describing how earlier generations of Americans had moved west to find economic opportunity, he called on Puerto Ricans to "adopt this American custom."[84]

When the first steamship arrived in San Juan to transport Puerto Ricans to Arizona in 1926, more than six thousand people gathered at the dock with the hope of gaining passage to the United States. As Walker reported, several immigration officers and insular policemen worked through the night to remove those from the ship who were not listed as contract laborers for the Arizona cotton ranches. Yet, even after officers searched the ship, thirty-three stowaways were found on board after leaving San Juan, a reflection of how desperately many on the island sought passage to the United States.[85]

Jaime Bague, assistant commissioner of agriculture and labor in Puerto Rico, oversaw the transport, sailing with the Puerto Rican families from San Juan to Galveston, Texas, on board the S.S. *Munsorleans*. By order of a 1919 law passed by the Puerto Rican legislature, Bague, as the commissioner of agriculture and labor, was required to travel with the recruits to the United States in order to "look after the interests of laborers leaving the island under contract."[86]

But despite the best efforts of Bague, and the intentions of the Puerto Rican legislature, conflicts between laborers and recruiters quickly developed. On the first day of the trip, several Puerto Ricans protested the lunch served. Claiming that the rice, beans, and cod were poorly prepared, the passengers threw their forks and plates into the ocean in protest. Upon arrival in Galveston, they protested again when they were compelled to undergo medical and immigration inspection. As citizens of the United States, they were officially exempt from such examinations. But as dark-skinned, Spanish-speaking families entering the mainland by way of Texas, they became suspect in the eyes of U.S. immigration inspectors who were wary of illegal Mexican immigration after the passage of the Johnson-Reed Act. After the exam, the recruits were loaded onto fifteen train cars of the Southern Pacific Company headed toward Phoenix, Arizona. There, members of the Cotton Association met the train to take the Puerto Rican families to ranches throughout the region.[87]

On the cotton ranches, protests continued. The Puerto Ricans were insulted by the fact that the houses constructed for them had dirt floors. Though cotton growers countered that Mexicans who had worked for them before preferred to sleep on the bare ground as they considered it cooler, the Puerto Ricans, accustomed to tropical rains that always left the ground damp, insisted that floors be installed in each of the houses.[88] The Cotton Association allotted the funds to meet this request.

Shortly after arriving on the ranches, another conflict emerged between some twenty families and the ranchers they worked for. The Puerto Ricans, many of whom had been skilled tradesmen on the island, asked to be paid the wage of two dollars a day that was specified in their contracts. According to Bague's report, a "swift-tongued Mexican laborer" had appeared on the scene and incited the families to protest. But the pattern of protest established from the first day of the expedition north suggests that the role of an outside agitator alone could not explain this conflict.

Indeed, labor migrants from the island brought with them a strong, indigenous tradition of labor activism. Many crossing to the mainland in this period had been artisans in the island's cities. Skilled in trades such as carpentry, shoemaking, and tobacco rolling, they had traversed the island in search of better opportunities before crossing to the United States. On the island, *tobaqueros*, along with other artisans, led the formation of the Federación Libre de Trabajadores and helped found the Socialist Party in Puerto Rico.[89] On the mainland, labor migrants in Arizona and other parts of the United

States carried forward a tradition of labor activism through appeals to colonial officials and organized labor.

Widespread conflict over wages on Arizona's cotton ranches soon caught the interest of national labor leaders who were concerned that colonial migration would lower the wages of the U.S.-born. Puerto Rican migrants protesting in Arizona wrote Santiago Iglesias, then Spanish-language secretary for the Pan-American Federation of Labor, to complain that they were making less than originally promised, and not "enough to buy groceries." Iglesias, in turn, took their concerns to BIA chief Frank McIntyre in Washington, DC.[90] McIntyre responded that by his estimate, two dollars a day—the rate promised in the labor contracts signed in San Juan—was more or less equivalent to the rate of a dollar and twenty-five cents per pound of picked cotton being paid on the ranches.[91]

Dissatisfied with the response from Washington, the Puerto Ricans in Arizona took their complaints to the local AFL affiliate in Phoenix, which in turn brought national attention to the issue. On September 27, 1926, the Associated Press reported that eighty Puerto Rican men, women, and children were "living in State Fair Grounds lacking shelter and food" and "refusing to work under conditions imposed by the Cotton Growers Association."[92] The Associated Press report was later confirmed by several other sources, including urgent cables from labor leaders in Arizona to the AFL headquarters in Washington. In a September 1926 cable, the Phoenix Central Trades Council, an affiliate of the AFL, reported that it was "caring for over 100 men, women and children."[93] Other telegrams claimed that a "great number" of the Puerto Ricans recruited by the Cotton Growers were being "guarded by officers to prevent them from running away."[94]

Given the desperate situation of these workers and the failure of the Cotton Growers Association to meet their contracts, the Central Labor Council of Phoenix passed a resolution calling on the American Federation of Labor to lobby in Washington "against further importation of any Porto Ricans into Arizona."[95] Consistent with long-standing AFL fears of immigrants driving down wages, the council stated: "Those already here will minimize the scale of wages and lower the living conditions."[96]

Yet, recognizing that Puerto Ricans, as U.S. citizens, could not be legally excluded from entering the mainland, AFL president William Green, responded, "The Department of Labor can do nothing to stop people from coming from Porto Rico."[97] Instead, Green recommended that organized labor, along with the Department of Labor, work to monitor and enforce labor contracts and prevent employers in the United States from "obtaining Porto Ricans under false pretenses."[98]

By November 1926, the AFL had succeeded in negotiating "effective restrictions" on Puerto Ricans entering the United States. Given the Arizona crisis, and evidence of increasing numbers of impoverished Puerto Ricans entering the United States, the AFL negotiated with the Pan-American Federation of Labor—an international labor congress founded in 1918 by Samuel Gompers and representatives from several Latin American countries including Mexico, Puerto Rico, El Salvador, and Guatemala—to limit the further recruitment of Puerto Rican laborers to the American Southwest.[99] Their agreement resulted in an "effective limitation upon the movement of nonemployed from Porto Rico to the United States to enter into competition with the higher priced American workers."[100] At their national convention in 1926, the AFL voted in support of two related resolutions: the first recommended the establishment of a full civil government in Puerto Rico (including a locally elected governor) to replace the current government under the U.S. War Department; the second called on Congress to "investigate conditions into the island possession."[101] In approving both of these resolutions, the AFL signaled an understanding that the desperate political and economic conditions on the island had sparked migration patterns to the mainland.

E.J. Walker, the labor agent and general manager of the Arizona Cotton Growers Association, sought to explain the failure of the migration to Arizona in terms of Puerto Ricans' racial inferiority and outside agitators. He reported that the comportment of these Puerto Ricans was "not what I would call satisfactory." "They do not fit," Walker continued, "into our Arizona life in a way that would encourage more to come." Walker reported mutual disdain among whites and Puerto Ricans in and around Phoenix: "What they think of Arizona undoubtedly is not favorable, and what Arizona thinks of them as a whole, is likewise."[102]

Walker further claimed that the failure was primarily caused by labor leaders in Arizona who prodded the workers into protesting their conditions for the self-interested purpose of discouraging the "importation of these people."[103] In his report, Walker wrote: "It appears that certain individuals interested in supposedly helping the cause of organized labor objected to the importation of the Porto Rican cotton pickers, even when they knew that there was a shortage of labor throughout the entire Southwestern part of the United States."[104] Walker asserted that labor organizers traveled from ranch to ranch, urging Puerto Ricans to quit and move to

Figure 5.4. Photograph of E. J. Walker standing behind Puerto Ricans picking cotton in Arizona, *Arizona Republican*, August 1, 1926. Box 312, folder 1493-A, RG 350, NACP.

Phoenix. He wrote that the "Porto Ricans are recognized as being rather temperamental and quite easily influenced, particularly under such conditions as existed, which placed them in a position to be easy prey, owing to their unsuspecting natures."[105]

Puerto Rican workers' letters to AFL officials told a different story. Manolo Hernandez, working in Arizona, wrote to his father Don Salomon Hernandez in January of 1927. Hernandez stated that because the rains kept the ranch hands from working, he had to spend what he had earned. Without work or money, and "suffering each day more in seeing his children go without necessities," he wrote that he was in "the most sorrowful situation in his life."[106] Bacilo Rivera, picking cotton at Litchfield Camp 51, Arizona, protested low pay and poor housing by calling on the U.S. government to honor Puerto Ricans' service in World War I: "I think that the protection of the American flag belongs to us . . . because we Porto Ricans have shed our blood for it."[107]

For its part, the Cotton Growers Association continued to maintain that such protests were merely the result of labor agitators who sought to make the situation "as odious as possible and arouse public sentiment against the Porto Ricans so that further importation would be stopped." They claimed that the Cotton Growers Association took only a "friendly and helping attitude toward the Porto Ricans."[108] Despite such claims, the AFL succeeded in negotiating restrictions on Puerto Rican immigration. And by 1928, most of the original recruits had moved on to other jobs around Phoenix—in restaurants, for city public works, or on streetcar and railroad track repair.[109]

According to the *Silver Belt*, a prolabor newspaper based in Miami, Arizona, some had faulted the Mexican community in Arizona for stirring up conflict between Puerto Ricans and business owners. One Mexican union allegedly tried to agitate among Puerto Ricans as a means of making Mexican labor more attractive to employers. But, the *Silver Belt* reported, the "evidence does not bear out this accusation." "The Union men," it continued, "while not enthusiastic over the horde of cheap labor imported into their midst, acted only from a humanitarian standpoint."[110] The source of the problem, the *Belt* concluded, was the failure of the Cotton Growers Association to meet the promises made to the workers they recruited and the simultaneous failure of many Puerto Ricans to "become proficient" in their new work. The cause of this failure, of course, was more likely tied to Puerto Ricans' refusal to acquiesce to conditions on the ranches than any inherent inability to do the work of cotton picking.

Even as some Puerto Ricans in Arizona attempted to return to the island, critics decried the unrestricted entry of colonial migrants on racist grounds. In June 1929, six Puerto Rican families became stranded and destitute in Galveston, Texas. Originally part of the Arizona migration in 1926, these families were attempting to make their way back to the island after their three-year contract expired. But without money to buy steamship tickets, they could not leave Galveston. In an article titled "Immigrants Who Are Not Immigrants," the editor of the *Galveston News* publicly worried that if other employers adopted the same practice as the Arizona Cotton Growers Association, "a problem of considerable proportions" would develop. Puerto Ricans, as U.S. citizens, the article noted, could not be excluded from entering the United States. But, given that Puerto Ricans "are alien in every practical sense of the word, and apparently do not offer promising material for assimilation," the editor called on the government to discourage employers from importing Puerto Ricans to the United States.[111]

Migration Schemes in Florida and Hawai'i

Despite the conflicts in Arizona and labor leaders' subsequent call for restrictions on Puerto Rican immigration, employers throughout the South sought workers from the island in the period of immigration restriction after World War I. In 1927, for example, agricultural growers outside Miami, Florida, telegrammed BIA chief Frank McIntyre to seek his approval for their plan to recruit Puerto Rican laborers. McIntyre forwarded their request to Puerto Rican governor Horace Towner, who rejected the proposal outright. In Towner's words, the "Government here cannot give its official approval of any emigration plan."[112]

In 1933 Florida citrus growers, interested in cheap labor, tried again to win support for recruiting as many as fifty thousand Puerto Rican families to the United States. When Robert H. Gore, a journalist and businessman with business interests in Florida, was appointed governor of Puerto Rico, he backed the migration plan. Wary of potential opposition, he proposed importing one family as a trial run before bringing Puerto Ricans in large numbers.[113] Interested in developing sugarcane as a new crop, Florida growers called on officials in Washington for support in creating a "colony of Puerto Ricans in Florida."[114]

But officials in Puerto Rico remained dubious. Conscious of the Arizona conflict of 1926, Prudencio Rivera Martinez, commissioner of labor for Puerto Rico, stated that he could support the Florida plan only if the migrants were "treated as human beings, where they will be given enough land, a decent home for each family, agricultural implements, work animals, seeds and all the necessary means, economic and others." Ultimately, Martinez rejected the proposal, stating that he was unwilling to send Puerto Ricans to the United States merely to "work as salaried slaves for a corporation or individual without hope of emancipation for them or for their children."[115]

The largest of these migration schemes was the proposed recruitment of 100,000 Puerto Ricans to Hawai'i. Since the early 1920s, U.S. government officials in Washington and sugar growers in Hawai'i had explored, for different reasons, the possibility of recruiting Puerto Rican laborers to Hawai'i. The 1920 census showed, for the first time, that the Japanese had become the largest immigration group in Hawai'i. Of a total population of 255,912 in Hawai'i, 109,274 were Japanese, 25,507 Chinese, 27,002 Portuguese, 21,051 Filipinos, and 5,602 Puerto Rican.[116] As in U.S. corporate enclaves in the banana, rubber, and sugar regions of Latin America, plantation owners in Hawai'i recruited members of these different groups in the late nineteenth and early twentieth centuries in order to segment their labor forces along racial lines.[117] In this context, Washington officials grew concerned about potential Japanese political power in Hawai'i. Many feared the growing number of Japanese born in Hawai'i, who by virtue of being born in the United States were American citizens and entitled to vote.[118] As Irvine Lenroot, U.S. senator from Wisconsin, stated after visiting Hawai'i, "There can be no evading the possibility of the Japanese possibly coming into control through the franchise."[119] As one observer wrote, the high Japanese concentration in Hawai'i represented "a difficult race and political problem menacing the Territory."[120] In the context of the racial nativism of the 1920s, the prospect of Asiatic political control over a U.S. territory helped prompt calls in Washington for immigration restriction.

In 1923, before Japanese exclusion was legislated through the 1924 Johnson-Reed Act, some in Washington saw recruiting Puerto Ricans to Hawai'i as a solution to the problem of growing Japanese political influence. By transporting thousands of people from the island—perhaps even tens of thousands—Puerto Ricans, by then U.S. citizens, could outnumber the votes of the U.S.-born Japanese. In response to the concerns of Senator Lenroot and others, BIA chief Frank McIntyre suggested transporting as many as a hundred thousand people from Puerto Rico to Hawai'i in order to "meet the situation which Senator Lenroot, in common with most Americans who have visited Hawai'i, has noted."[121] Racial ideologies positioning Puerto Ricans as Latins above Japanese Asiatics lent support to such a proposal. But after Congress passed the 1924 Johnson-Reed Act, which excluded Japanese immigrants from entering the United States, concern in Washington over Japanese political influence in Hawai'i dissipated.

In 1925, however, the U.S. War Department had another reason for supporting Puerto Rican migration to Hawai'i. In a confidential report entitled "A General Staff Study: Importation of Porto Ricans as an Asset to the Military Manpower of Hawai'i," E. M. Lewis, major general commanding, argued that the Japanese and Filipinos would not be dependable sources of military strength in the event of a future military draft. As he stated, "The defense of Oahu largely depends upon the quality and availability of the local man power for military purposes."[122] With Filipino nationals and first-generation Japanese ineligible to citizenship, Lewis maintained that neither group could be relied on to defend Hawai'i from enemy attack. "The Department of War," Lewis continued, "therefore should interest itself in securing additions to the population from people owing allegiance and who could be depended upon in any emergency." Given this shortage of loyal manpower, Lewis called for Puerto Ricans to move to Hawai'i. He predicted that the transfer of large numbers of Puerto Ricans to Hawai'i would "remove any doubt as to the loyalty of a majority of the population under any circumstances."[123] Yet such moments of enthusiasm for recruiting Puerto Ricans had no sustained benefits for the status of Puerto Ricans already resident in the United States. Racial nationalists, furthermore, found reasons to object to various immigrant groups and their reasons proved inconsistent—depending on the particular argument they sought to make—for preferring one over the other.

Indeed, the recommendation to recruit Puerto Ricans in 1925 was surprising given the earlier history of Puerto Ricans in Hawai'i. Of those first recruited to Hawai'i in 1901, an estimated two thousand remained on the islands by 1918.[124] After the Jones Act was signed into law in 1917, Puerto Ricans in Hawai'i had expected to enjoy the new benefits of U.S. citizenship. But many wound up organizing protests and desertions because, in the words of Pedro Guzman, Hawai'ian officials routinely "usurp[ed] our civil rights."[125] Toward the end of World War I, Puerto Ricans living in Hawai'i sent a petition to Washington asking for help in returning to Puerto Rico. By stating that "we prefer to earn a peseta in Porto Rico than 92 centavos in Hawai'i," they made clear their preference for returning to the island even though that would mean earning lower wages.[126] In response to this petition, the Puerto Rican House of Delegates passed a resolution calling on the resident commissioner from Puerto Rico in Washington to thoroughly investigate conditions in Hawai'i in order to ensure that Puerto Ricans living there were "respected in their rights."[127]

Puerto Ricans had also protested publicly that they were denied the most basic citizenship rights. When Manuel Olivieri Sanchez attempted to vote in Honolulu, in 1918, David Kalauokalani, county clerk, refused to register him on the voting rolls. Kalauokalani claimed that "Porto Ricans of Hawai'i are not American citizens under the Jones Bill."[128] With the support of Joseph Lightfoot, a local attorney, Sanchez took his case to court. The Supreme Court of Hawai'i in *Sanchez vs. Kalauokalani*, declared: "Manuel Olivieri Sanchez and all Porto Ricans residing in Hawai'i are as much citizens of the U.S. as those who have resided or do reside in Porto Rico."[129] This ruling granted the same level of citizenship to Puerto Ricans in Hawai'i as to those living in Puerto Rico.[130] But given Hawai'i's status as an incorporated territory of the United States, Puerto Ricans residing there should have been entitled to a fuller citizenship than those living in the unincorporated territory of Puerto Rico. This was because the Jones Act limited Puerto Ricans' citizenship through territoriality, and Hawai'i's territorial status was advantaged compared with that of Puerto Rico.

Thus the ruling in the *Sanchez* case and other challenges to the perceived alien citizenship of Puerto Ricans also point to the reasons why migration was a crucial concern for the American colonial regime after 1917. In the *Sanchez* case, Manuel Sanchez, a Puerto Rican labor migrant, won the right to vote in the United States. Through migration Puerto Ricans could become citizens of an incorporated territory or a state and, theoretically at least, free themselves of their compromised citizenship as residents of an unincorporated territory.

The Lewis Report of 1925, which expressed concern about the rise of Japanese power in Hawai'i, in fact painted a complex portrait of Puerto Ricans, one that emphasized an inherent racial inferiority alongside a capacity for national loyalty. While recommending Puerto Ricans as more loyal than Asians, the report also racialized Puerto Ricans as inferior in some ways to the Japanese and Chinese. Puerto Ricans, Lewis wrote, "lack the industry, energy and ambition of the Japanese, and the thrift and cleanliness of the Chinese."[131] Though Puerto Ricans' purported lack in skill or hygiene would not stand in the way of military service, disloyalty would. That is why it is surprising that Lewis further characterized Puerto Ricans as "lacking truthfulness." Lewis reasoned that this negative trait was "an inheritance from their ancestors." Still, he stated, Puerto Ricans possessed a kind of moral sense that enabled them to improve on their inheritance. "This moral sense," he wrote, "is sufficient to enable them to develop the feelings of patriotism and military duty to a satisfactory degree."[132]

U.S. government fears about national military security soon converged with the demands of agribusiness for ever-cheaper labor. With support for Filipino exclusion building in Congress in the late 1920s and early 1930s, the Hawai'ian Sugar Planters Association showed renewed interest in recruiting laborers from Puerto Rico.[133] In hearings of the House Committee on Immigration and Naturalization in April and May 1930, U.S. representatives debated the merits of a bill introduced by Richard Welch, a Republican from California, to "exclude certain citizens of the Philippine Islands from the United States."[134] Recognizing that congressional Republicans were threatening to bar Filipinos from entering the United States, the Hawaiian

Association ordered Montague Lord, its chief labor agent in Manila, to travel to Puerto Rico to survey the possibility of large-scale recruitment.[135] Walter F. Dillingham, president of the Oahu Railway and Land Company and a prominent business leader in Honolulu, who also visited Puerto Rico in 1931, recommended that the recruitment of Puerto Ricans to Hawai'i would be "to the advantage of both American outposts."[136] Noting the strong possibility that Congress would grant the Philippines independence in the next Congress, Dillingham anticipated the need for employers in Hawai'i "to look for a labor supply within a shorter time than we expect."[137] And, in a measure of the growing interest in the proposal, President Hoover also visited San Juan in 1931 to examine what he viewed as the overpopulation problem on the island, and the possibility of "wholesale immigration of Porto Rican laborers to Hawai'i."[138] Having issued a temporary ban on Filipino migration after a meningitis outbreak in 1929, Hoover approached Puerto Rican labor as perhaps a better alternative.[139] As the proposal to recruit Puerto Ricans to Hawai'i illustrates, U.S. policy makers and employers tried to sort out competing demands between labor recruitment and national security. In doing so, they modified their operating racial hierarchy, which, in this case, placed Puerto Rican citizens above Asian alien citizens and noncitizens.

As it turned out, fears about a loss of Filipino workers in Hawai'i were not borne out. In late 1931, Congress voted to allow Filipinos to continue to enter Hawai'i and the mainland United States for the time being.[140] That same year, Prudencio Rivera Martinez, commissioner of labor for Puerto Rico, spoke out against the Hawai'i plan: after receiving word of bread lines and destitution in New York at the height of the Depression, he recommended that Puerto Ricans not head for the United States.[141] In response to these developments, the Hawai'ian Sugar Planters Association and the U.S. War Department backed away from their plan to recruit workers from Puerto Rico.[142]

The extension of American citizenship to Puerto Ricans through the 1917 Jones Act profoundly influenced migration patterns to the United States during and after World War I. Citizenship made Puerto Ricans more broadly eligible for employment on the U.S. mainland. Prior to 1917, the U.S. government had officially refused to hire Puerto Ricans then defined as nationals. But after 1917, the U.S. government recruited twelve thousand workers from the island to work in army camps and navy yards throughout the U.S. South. At a time of immigration restriction, when labor leaders and racial nationalists sought to exclude Mexicans and Asians,

U.S. employers from Arizona to Hawai'i looked to Puerto Rico as a legal source of imported labor. Throughout this period, Puerto Rican migration was a core concern of the American colonial regime precisely because of the possibility that migrants could become citizens of an incorporated territory or state. Migrants to Hawai'i, Arizona, and the U.S. South tested the limits of the Jones Act when they protested deplorable living conditions, low wages, and racial discrimination. Ultimately, because they were denied passports, naturalization records, and identification cards by the colonial state, Puerto Ricans struggled to be recognized as citizens long after the granting of citizenship in 1917.

Chapter 6

Colonial Migrants in New York

It was a cold January morning in 1921 when Charles Aran, a seven-year-old living in a tenement in the 7800 block of Third Avenue, Brooklyn, New York, knocked on the door of a downstairs neighbor, Morris Englebardt. So weakened by hunger that he could barely stand, Charles gestured desperately for help. Englebardt ran upstairs to find the boy's family lying on a mattress, "suffering intensely" in a room with no fire. Charles's older sister, Lola, age sixteen, explained that they had sold some of Charles's toys the day before in order to buy food but all they could afford was some tinned meat and a single can of sour milk. Englebardt immediately called for the police and an ambulance. New York City patrolman Alexander H. Quinlan arrived shortly thereafter and bought the family "$2 worth of food."[1] The doctor who examined the Arans declared that the entire family was suffering from ptomaine poisoning, a kind of food poisoning then thought to be caused by bacteria in meat and dairy.[2]

Pedro Aran, his wife, Marcoes, and their four children, Charles, Lola, twenty-year-old Carmine, and eight-year-old Rosa, had moved to Brooklyn from Puerto Rico just two months earlier. Once a prosperous midsize coffee grower in Mayagüez, Puerto Rico, Pedro Aran had seen his fortunes steadily decline under U.S. colonial trade policies that favored coffee imported from

Figure 6.1. Photograph of Pedro Aran and Family. "Family on Verge of Starvation—Police to Rescue," *New York Daily News*, January 15, 1921.

Brazil. As the market for Puerto Rican coffee all but disappeared, Aran had looked to sell his coffee farm, known as the Estancia Josefa. After one lone buyer pulled out, Aran went into debt and lost the land. Dispirited, he took up gambling before deciding, in an act of desperation, to use the last of his savings to bring his family to New York City.[3] But after months without finding work in New York, the Arans ran out of money to buy food and firewood.

The Aran story came to national and international attention when the *New York Times* and the *New York Daily News* reported how the family was found "on the verge of starvation." On January 15, 1921, R. A. Sierra, export manager for Colonial Cycle Supply Co. in New York, mailed clippings of the articles to Félix Córdova Dávila, resident commissioner for Puerto Rico (1917–32) in the U.S. House of Representatives in Washington. Writing "on behalf of a Porto-Rican member of our staff," he asked Córdova Dávila to "do anything within your power to relieve the sufferings of this family."[4] In San Juan, Governor Arthur Yager also read reports of the Aran family and cabled the Bureau of Insular Affairs the following week to ask that an investigation be undertaken of all those Puerto Ricans who were "destitute and suffering in the streets of New York."[5]

Pedro Aran was but one of many Puerto Rican migrants who struggled to be included in the mainland economy and polity in the 1920s and 1930s. With growing numbers of Puerto Ricans impoverished by the colonial economy arriving in New York, the Asociación Portorriqueña, a mutual aid society of the Puerto Rican community in New York City, appealed to the federal government for assistance.[6] In letters on behalf of those suffering, the asociación asked the U.S. government to provide free transport back to the island. Though relief for the poor was the domain of private charities and local governments in the pre–New Deal period, Puerto Ricans drew on their colonial position within the United States to make claims on the federal government for free transport. Since the early twentieth century, Puerto Ricans in Hawai'i and on the mainland—both those who had migrated voluntarily and those who had been coerced by labor recruiters—had asked the federal government for return passage to the island. Many of those who had migrated to the United States in search of work found conditions to be so intolerable that they sought to return home to family and friends on the island, even if it meant a continued life of penury.

In the midst of the economic downturn of 1921, Gonzalo O'Neill, president of the Asociación, wrote to Newton Baker, secretary of war, to ask that Puerto Ricans in New York—those "in an almost starving condition"—be allowed to board government ships sailing south.[7] As head of the Asociación, O'Neill was part of a network of working-class Puerto Rican activists in New York that included Bernardo Vega, Jesús Colón, and Victor Fiol Ramós and his close friend Erasmo Vando, a poet and activist who supported anti-imperialist causes.[8] O'Neill was a playwright who later won critical acclaim for "Under Only One Flag" (1928), which explored the status question facing the island and possible political solutions. In the 1920s, O'Neill also served as president of the Liga Puertorriqueña e Hispana, a coalition of working-class groups, and led efforts in the *colonia*, the Puerto Rican community in New York City, to engage in Democratic Party politics.[9] At the same time as O'Neill issued his request to the secretary of war, Victor Fiol Ramós, who later became secretary of the Liga Puertorriqueña e Hispana, petitioned John Francis Hylan, mayor of New York, suggesting the use of federal ships to transport those who were suffering in New York back to the island. Ramos wrote: "I understand that people of all different nationalities are suffering the same effects of this economic crisis, but the majority of foreigners in New York can look to their consulates for help," which Puerto Ricans could not.[10] Taken together, the petitions of Ramos and O'Neill asked that the federal government take on the role, in effect, of a foreign consulate for Puerto Ricans.

In response to these requests, the Bureau of Insular Affairs asserted that Puerto Ricans were no different from other immigrant groups and thus could not be granted free transport home. BIA chief Frank McIntyre responded that reports of such suffering in New York echoed the experiences of countless other immigrant groups before them. As he wrote, the situation of Puerto Ricans in New York is one "which many of the immigrants in New York are in each winter." McIntyre declined to offer free transport back to Puerto Rico, stating that the government had no appropriation for "the transportation of private parties who voluntarily leave their country." The presumed voluntary nature of Puerto Rican migration served as the official justification for refusing government transport. Such a practice, he wrote, would set a precedent whereby other immigrant groups in New York could also seek government transport back home.[11] If Puerto Ricans in New York were granted free transport, went the argument, so too could other groups in New York. Even Commissioner Córdova Dávila agreed with this line of reasoning: "Our compatriots thoughtlessly ventured to come to this country, and now they are suffering the consequences of their rashness."[12]

Such an understanding of Puerto Ricans as just another immigrant group seeking refuge in the United States ignored the myriad ways in which Puerto Ricans were actually migrants moving within a unified field of U.S. empire. Characterizations of Puerto Ricans as a people who "voluntarily [left] their country" and "thoughtlessly ventured to come to this country," constructed Puerto Ricans as foreigners entering the United States from a fully separate economy and polity. Despite colonial ties between the island and the mainland going back to the War of 1898—from American capital penetration to trade regulations and the granting of U.S. citizenship—many Americans in the 1920s and 1930s continued to look upon Puerto Ricans as just another immigrant group coming from a distant and separate country. This conception shored up ideas of American liberal democracy, both by seeing the United States as always a promised land for immigrants in need of rescue from foreign lands, and by obscuring the history of colonialism and the challenge it posed to the ideals of the American republic.

At the same time, Puerto Ricans often contested the label of foreign by pointing to the role of the United States in spurring their migrations from the island. They justified their rights to immigration and citizenship with the recognition that U.S. colonial policy had led to economic dislocation on the island. As in the case of Pedro Aran, it was largely the U.S. categorization of the island as coastwise that led to the collapse of the coffee market and widespread unemployment. The refusal of the United States to extend disaster relief after Hurricane San Ciriaco, meanwhile, stemmed from government reluctance to spend resources on a colony. The extension of citizenship under the Jones Act of 1917 further encouraged migration to the mainland. Part of a larger colonial process that the historian Paul Kramer has described as "empire's role" in "selectively promoting, sponsoring, channeling and disciplining migrations in pursuit of labor power," Puerto Ricans increasingly made their way to the United States.[13] The contradictions they faced upon arriving in the metropole in the 1920s and 1930s—that of being labeled foreign immigrants despite the granting of U.S. citizenship through the Jones Act—underscored the asymmetries of power that had long marked colonial migrations. Yet, in asserting claims to citizenship in the state of New York and electing their first voting representative to the U.S. House in 1934, Puerto Ricans challenged the imperial boundaries that limited citizenship through territorial status.

Defining Puerto Ricans as Foreign

Conceptions of Puerto Ricans as immigrants from a foreign country had a long history. Shortly after the War of 1898 and U.S. takeover of the island, U.S. immigration officials argued in the case of Jorge Cruz that Puerto Ricans were aliens like immigrants from Russia or any other foreign country. In the 1904 *Gonzales* case, the Supreme Court revised such ideas at the level of immigration law by defining Puerto Ricans as nationals exempt from immigration restrictions. And in the 1917 Jones Act, the decision of Congress—partly in response to Puerto Rican pressure—to grant U.S. citizenship to the island brought Puerto Ricans further into the American polity. While tensions between colonial migrants and racial nationalists mounted in the rural areas of the U.S. South, Arizona, and Hawai'i, migrants faced similar challenges when arriving in New York City, a critical urban center in the circuit of imperial migration that was home to the largest Puerto Rican community on the U.S. mainland and soon became known as the "island's metropolis."[14]

Even after Puerto Ricans were legally defined as U.S. citizens, ideas of Puerto Rican foreignness persisted in urban centers, much like in rural areas. The charity boards in New York, for example, defined Puerto Ricans as foreign to justify repatriations and thereby shrink their relief budget. In the midst of the economic downturn of 1921, several in New York City listed unemployed and destitute Puerto Ricans on their doles: the New York State Board of Charities reported in 1921 that it was handling 16 cases of

Puerto Rican poverty in the city, involving 35 people; the Charity Organization in Manhattan reported handling 25 similar cases; the Department of Public Welfare in Brooklyn, 8 cases; and the Brooklyn Bureau of Charities, 13 cases.[15] In an effort to reduce its case list, the New York State Board of Charities drew on funds earmarked "for returning destitute and helpless foreigners to their own country" to send Puerto Rican families back to San Juan. Charity workers often justified repatriations by a nativist logic in which foreigners were undeserving of being on the dole.[16] In the case of Mexicans and other foreign nationals, nativists resented those who had not renounced their allegiance to their homeland by naturalizing as U.S. citizens.[17] In the case of Puerto Ricans, however, such fears of foreign allegiance were largely misplaced as Puerto Ricans faced difficulties in naturalizing until the federal court ruling *In re Giralde* (1915) defined them as white aliens for the purposes of naturalization.[18] In the economic downturn of 1921, then, definitions of Puerto Ricans as foreign could be used to either counter or justify repatriation efforts. Such contradictory readings of Puerto Ricans' position in New York underscored the specific legal challenges that had defined colonial migrations as different from the international and domestic migrations of Italians, Jews, and African Americans.

In response to the contradictory rulings of a federal government that defined Puerto Ricans as foreign to counter repatriation requests, and a New York State board that relied on the same definition of foreign to fund repatriations, Puerto Ricans in New York and on the island sought new ways to address the needs of their community on their own. In order to support those in New York who either wished to stay or return to the island, the asociación began its own fundraising campaign to collect money for Puerto Ricans without work. Among their efforts was a ball held on March 4, 1921, with the hope of raising two thousand dollars. The New York Asociación Portorriqueña recognized that even if they raised such a sum it would not be enough as "there are so many needy people."[19] Victor Fiol Ramós agreed. In a 1921 letter published in the elite Puerto Rican newspaper *La Democracia*, he lamented that the economic crisis "has affected cruelly the poor classes on the East Side in the city." Charitable work that is "as a rule done by the rich Italian colony for the poor Italians, by the rich Jews for the poor Jews, rich negroes for poor negroes, etc., does not," he maintained, "extend to thousands and thousands of Porto Ricans who . . . are suffering greatly."[20]

Like New York charity boards and BIA officials, intellectuals of the 1920s routinely defined Puerto Ricans as foreign and just another immigrant group in an attempt to restrict migration from the island. Robert F. Foerster, a professor of economics at Princeton University, was typical of the period. In 1925 he wrote a report for the U.S. Department of Labor entitled "The Racial Problems Involved in Immigration from Latin America and the West Indies to the United States." In the report he included Puerto Rico in a survey of "countries south of the United States," without making any mention of Puerto Rico's status as an unincorporated territory of the United States, or its residents' status as U.S. citizens exempt from immigration restrictions.[21] By grouping Puerto Rico with other Latin American countries, Foerster obscured the colonial ties that had, since 1898, brought the island within the sphere of America's economic and political power.

Foerster believed race was a determinant of behavior and strongly opposed the immigration of nonwhite people. He described Puerto Ricans as white, black, and mulatto, defining the latter as the "offspring of unions of European and African stocks."[22] According to the U.S. census of 1920, the island population was 25 percent mulatto, 4 percent black, and 71 percent white. Foerster made no objection to white residents of the island entering the United States, even though they were, as he put it, of a Spanish Mediterranean race, and not the Northern European Nordic or Teutonic races that had been largely preferred in the 1924 Johnson-Reed Act. On blacks from the West Indies and Brazil, he exclaimed disparagingly, "None other of the great primary races of mankind has had so slender a history of achievement."[23]

But it was the phenomenon of racial mixing that Foerster, and other proponents of eugenics in the 1920s, found most worrisome. Admitting explicitly that there was no scientific proof of the adverse effects of miscegenation, he wrote that, nevertheless, it had been "universally observed" that mulattoes were generally inferior to whites but superior to blacks. Such observations made sense, he reasoned, in light of the Mendelian theory that the traits of offspring were a "general average between parental stocks." Assuming that environment as well as heredity shaped racial traits, Foerster concluded: "Where a race is in a position to maintain its purity it is best that it should not breed with what appears to be an inferior or distant race." For Foerster, the policy implications were clear: while science might someday determine Latin Americans to be of high racial stock, the United States should limit their entry for the time being.[24]

Racial nationalists' ideologies vis-à-vis immigration developed new attributes in this period. With the passage of the Johnson-Reed Act in 1924, the one-drop rule became dominant, so much so that the category of mulatto was removed from the census in 1930. As Melissa Nobles has written, it was at this time that "science, law, and the census had converged to accept the one-drop rule of nonwhite racial membership."[25] That same year, the census added the category Mexican, but then removed it shortly thereafter in response to allegations that it was discriminatory because it facilitated the large-scale deportation and repatriation of Mexicans in the United States.[26]

Over the course of the late 1920s, the white-black binary came to supersede concerns that different white ethnicities were racially unequal to each other.[27] Italians, for example, were increasingly defined as an ethnic, rather than a racial group, with racial classifications reserved for Caucasians, Negroes, and Orientals.[28] Such a shift in racial thought can partly be explained in terms of the success of the Johnson-Reed Act in restricting the immigration of southern and eastern Europeans as well as the African American Great Migration and early civil rights struggles, which brought the politics of Jim Crow to the national stage. Yet still another reason may have been Americans' imperial encounters abroad. As the historian Matthew Frye Jacobson has observed, "The manufacture and maintenance of 'Caucasian' whiteness depended in part . . . upon national encounters with 'barbarian dominions' even more problematic than the immigrants themselves."[29] But what happened when nonwhite peoples from those foreign dominions became migrants entering the metropole? Though Forester believed mulattoes were superior to blacks, he still preferred that nonwhite Puerto Ricans stay on the island.

Foerster rejected the long-standing U.S. law that allowed numerically unrestricted immigration from Latin America. Congress exempted the countries of Latin America from the country quotas established in the Immigration Act of 1924. This decision was shaped by the labor demands of U.S. employers in search of cheap, seasonal workers as well as the objectives of the State Department to support diplomatic relations within the Western Hemisphere.[30] In an appeal to immigration restrictionists, Foerster wrote in a tone of alarm, "The entire lands to the south of the United States are sources of future immigration." Arguing for extending quotas to Latin America, he rejected the argument that U.S. relations with Latin American countries required open borders. "The neighborliness of countries does not require that their peoples should cross their borders with the same freedom that is allowed to movement within one country." In this discussion, Foerster grouped Puerto Ricans, despite their U.S. citizenship status, with immigrants from foreign countries.[31]

In the context of racial nativism in the 1920s, Foerster asked rhetorically why the 1924 Johnson-Reed Act had made immigrants from Latin America exempt from its restrictions. "In blood," he wrote, "the people of the United States are mainly European and white." In contrast, "the people of Latin America and the West Indies are mainly Asiatic (Indian) or African, mainly brown or black." Foerster urged the United States to only admit immigrants from Latin America who met racial standards of fitness for citizenship—who are "at least equal, if they do not excel, the average of its own citizens in fitness for government, including self-government and industry. No good grounds exist for supposing that the immigrants of countries to the south of the United States would meet the requirements of this criterion," he argued. Given that, in the first year of the Johnson-Reed Act, immigrants from Mexico alone equaled a large percentage of the quota established for all countries, Foerster hoped to extend immigration restriction to Latin America. Why, he asked, should Latin Americans be granted special privileges denied to Europeans and other groups?[32]

Challenging Foreign Status

While academics like Foerster, New York charity boards, and BIA officials defined Puerto Ricans as foreign for the purposes of restricting immigration, reducing relief rolls, or denying free government transport, Puerto Ricans recognized the ambiguous and fluid nature of their legal status. Some may have accentuated their foreignness in an effort to avoid association with U.S. blacks. Scholars have long recognized how Puerto Ricans of color used the Spanish language to differentiate themselves from African Americans in the decades before the civil rights movements.[33] As Lawrence Chenault has written of Puerto Ricans in New York in the 1920s and 1930s, "the darker the person from the West Indies is, the more intense is his desire to speak only Spanish and to do so in a louder voice."[34]

Yet there is evidence to suggest that this was not the only pattern of self-identification in this period.[35] Many Puerto Ricans sought full recognition as U.S. citizens. R.J. Marquez, a Puerto Rican resident of New York City, wrote a letter to the editor of the *New York Times* in 1923 calling for full recognition of Puerto Ricans as U.S. citizens. When purchasing a steamship ticket in New York to travel to Puerto Rico, Marquez was informed that Puerto Ricans and aliens departing from the United States "should appear before the Collector or Revenue Agent," in order to "satisfy all income tax obligations" and then obtain a "tax clearance" from the Custom House.[36] Claiming that an American citizen was not required to "waste half a day or sometimes more waiting for his turn at the Custom House," Marquez asked: "If Porto Ricans are citizens of the United States by act of Congress and supposedly have the same rights enjoyed by Continental citizens, why this discrimination? What is more bitter, he is put on a parity with aliens."[37] Marquez called for an end to such practices in order to strengthen relations between the "mother country and the small insular dominion."[38] A year later, Commissioner Córdova Dávila echoed Marquez's call that Puerto Ricans be "considered the same as other 'American citizens,'" as part of a bid for residents of the island to be able to elect their own governor.[39]

In the variety of ways Puerto Ricans negotiated and debated their legal status, many made claims to citizenship while also constructing a relationship with their home country. Some maintained that as citizens they should be able to move freely between the island and the mainland. Given the seasonal nature of the island's sugar economy and their need to seek employment on the mainland, some Puerto Ricans called for more affordable steamship fares between San Juan and New York. American steamship companies' monopoly on transport from Puerto Rico to the United States had developed after President McKinley first extended coastwise shipping laws to the island during the War of 1898. These laws eliminated the competition of non-U.S. carriers that would have otherwise driven down fares. The lack of affordable transport left many stranded in San Juan, Ponce, New York, San Francisco, Honolulu, and scattered other points in between in the 1920s and 1930s as more workers had gone north. In 1923 a union of telegraph operators in Ponce petitioned the U.S. government to make available low-cost steamship fares between the island and the United States. With steady work in the Bureau of Insular Telegraph, a branch of the U.S. colonial government that was based in Ponce, telegraph operators were not subject to the seasonal employment cycle of the sugar industry that drove much of the island population to migrate to the United States. But in transmitting cablegrams, their daily work put them in contact with the often-painful stories of others on the island who were struggling to make their way to the mainland and back home again. Based in Ponce, the southern capital of the sugar zone, they typed out the urgent pleas of those in Ponce seeking U.S. government transport to the mainland. They also relayed the desperate calls for help from Puerto Ricans in the tenements of New York, the sugar fields of Hawai'i, and the cotton ranches of Arizona who were unable to get back home to the island. Subsidized steamship travel would, they predicted, offer an enormous opportunity for the poor classes to travel to and from the north.[40]

Others also saw the potential benefits of subsidized steamship travel, especially for laborers in need of seasonal work. F. Vall Spinoza, a journalist who wrote under the pseudonym Fred Armstrong for *La Democracia*, called for a "bridge to New York," in the form of affordable steamship fares.[41] In a letter dated June 25, 1923, he wrote that such a service would be a tremendous benefit to the "thousands and thousands" of Puerto Ricans who were "anxious, desirous, dreaming of the day they can go 'to the States.'"[42] This bridge, he claimed, could be more easily crossed in both directions, so that Puerto Ricans could migrate to New York for work and back to the island to visit family. Spinoza suggested that the bridge could also benefit U.S. employers, enabling the easy movement of a kind of reserve labor force. As he put it, "If a New York contractor needed 300 men for a month, they could be furnished and they could return when work was finished." While employers had been recruiting Puerto Ricans to work in the United States for years, an Insular Transport Service, he contended, would allow these laborers to return to the United States.[43] Such a bridge, he argued, would represent a vast improvement over previous contract labor arrangements carried out by private steamship companies in collaboration with U.S. employers. And Puerto Ricans deserved a reasonable chance to work in the United States given their status as "full fledged American citizens entitled to all the privileges that go with that great honor."[44] Spinoza and the Ponce Telegraph Workers Union thus claimed that the government should facilitate independent, voluntary circulation back and forth.

Such calls for a bridge to New York suggest emerging views of citizenship and mobility that took hold in the early 1920s in a range of imperial settings. Particularly for those of the working classes, the very meaning of citizenship was bound up in the practical right of mobility. Beginning in 1919, Marcus Garvey, the leader of the Universal Negro Improvement Association, formed the Black Star Steamship Company to facilitate the movement of West Indian workers migrating between U.S. business enclaves in Central America and the Caribbean.[45] As in Puerto Rico, such efforts to provide migrant workers greater access to steamship travel served as a challenge to various forms of corporate and colonial power within the U.S. empire.

Though the Insular Transport Service was never established, Puerto Ricans continued migrating to the United States in the 1920s. Santiago Iglesias, the island's most prominent labor leader, stated in 1926 that the economic effects of U.S. colonial rule on the island compelled Puerto Ricans to migrate to the United States in ever larger numbers. Despite the Foraker Act's official prohibition on corporate land ownership in excess of five hundred acres, Iglesias maintained, U.S. sugar corporations had converted the island's workers into "colonial serfs."[46] Of a total population of approximately 1.5 million people, 300,000 labored as peons in the sugar fields, working only four months a year for 50 to 80 centavos a day.[47] Faced with such limited and seasonal opportunities for work on the island, many found migrating to the United States their only means of earning a living. Keenly aware of the links between the island and mainland economies, Santiago Iglesias wrote that the recent migration of Puerto Rican workers to New York and other parts of the mainland was only the most recent and severe "indictment of the colonial system that has dizzily developed on the island."[48] Migrants' complaints of poor working conditions and low wages in the post-1917 period of citizenship echoed those of earlier migrants who had entered the U.S. as aliens or nationals.

Mainland labor leaders also recognized that workers traveled along imperial circuits to the mainland. At the same time that Iglesias noted the increasing migration to New York, the mainland AFL sought to restrict Puerto Rican migration to the cotton-growing regions of the U.S. Southwest. Negotiations between the AFL Executive Council and the Pan-American Federation of Labor resulted in an "understanding on the basis of effective limitation upon the movement of non-employed from Porto Rico to the United States to enter into competition with the higher paid American workers."[49] But in a split with AFL leaders, Iglesias responded that such attempts to limit migration to the U.S. Southwest did nothing to address the still worsening unemployment problems on the island and in the mainland cities. "While some believe that we should halt immigration from Puerto Rico to New York," he wrote pointedly, "others believe that we should extend to them all types of assistance and facilitate their employment not only in New York but in all the large cities of the nation."[50]

Indeed, by June 1, 1927, officials on the island estimated that a hundred people or more left Puerto Rico each week on steamships headed for the United States. Though no official record was kept of all of those who left the island, the Bureau of Labor and Agriculture of Puerto Rico pulled together the available numbers of those buying tickets on passenger ships, those working in exchange for passage on freight ships, and those found as stowaways after leaving the island. There was, Governor Horace Towner reported, "a constant stream of emigration which is leaving the Island."[51] According to Jaime Bague, acting commissioner of the Puerto Rican Bureau of Labor, those who left mostly settled "around New York City."[52]

Countering Nativism with Claims of Citizenship

With their numbers increasing, Puerto Ricans faced growing hostility from New Yorkers who were wary of immigrants competing with them for jobs, undercutting their wages, or filling the relief rolls. In response, Puerto Ricans increasingly challenged U.S. colonial practices as they asserted their right to enter the mainland. They focused not merely on the untenable status of the island but also on U.S. domestic politics, or what became known as the "politics of here." In the summer of 1926, violent conflicts arose between Jews and Puerto Ricans in East Harlem. Details on the origins of this conflict are scarce but writers in *La Prensa*, a newspaper published by Puerto Ricans in New York, pointed to an intensifying rivalry between these two groups as Puerto Ricans came to predominate in the commercial development of the neighborhood as shopkeepers.[53] Coming just two years after the Johnson-Reed Act of 1924 limited Jewish migration from Eastern Europe, what Puerto Ricans came to call the *Choques* (clashes) may have reflected the disparity in immigration law that limited Jewish immigration but continued to allow migration from Puerto Rico. The incident served to focus Puerto Ricans' attention on the limits of U.S. citizenship on the mainland.

Whatever might have prompted the incident, the Choques provoked spirited exchanges in *La Prensa* over strategies for defending the best interests of the growing Puerto Rican community in the 1920s. In an editorial published shortly after the incident, *La Prensa*'s editors called on Puerto Ricans to stand strong, just as other immigrants had done before them in New York. In response, J. M. Vivaldi, a Democratic activist in colonia politics, wrote a pointed letter to the editor criticizing *La Prensa* for lumping together Puerto Ricans and immigrants from other nations, and thereby implying that Puerto Ricans were foreigners the same as Mexicans or Russians.[54] "The 'bill' Jones," Vivaldi wrote, "converted Puerto Ricans into American citizens with the same rights and duties as those born in this land." Vivaldi sought to highlight the distinct legal position of Puerto Ricans relative to other immigrants, proclaiming "Puerto Ricans are not foreigners."[55]

In response to the violence, the Liga Puertoriqueña e Hispana was formed to bring together Latinos throughout the city for the purposes of mutual aid and protection. Attending their first meetings were a number of those wounded in the Choques. An editorial hailing the newfound unity among Latinos in New York, stated that the liga responded to the "bloody tumult" by vowing to strengthen "la raza."[56] The historian Lorrin Thomas has observed that the Choques of 1926 marked a turning point in the political culture of the colonia, as Puerto Ricans became increasingly aware of the "limitations of their American citizenship."[57] Whereas much of colonia politics in the pre-1926 period had focused primarily on the status of the island, Puerto Ricans after the Choques expanded their political work to include "political empowerment to achieve recognition as equal citizens."[58] They thus expanded their focus on electoral politics in the United States.

Puerto Ricans were not, of course, the only Latino group entering New York from sites of American empire. Cubans and Dominicans also came from countries whose economies had been substantially damaged by American interventions. The U.S. military occupation of the Dominican Republic from 1916 to 1924 had devastated the island economy but restrictive immigration policies kept migration numbers to the U.S. mainland comparatively small until the 1960s.[59] The United States intervened extensively in Cuba at the turn of the century even after Cuba became an independent nation in 1904. Cuban migration to the U.S. mainland was significant in the early decades of the twentieth century. After Puerto Ricans, Cubans and Dominicans were the most populous Latino groups in New York City in those years.[60] According to census figures from 1930, 40.7 percent of New York's Hispanic population was Puerto Rican and 17.9 percent was Cuban and Dominican. (The remaining 40.4 percent of Hispanics were predominantly from Spain; Mexicans did not migrate to New York in large numbers until decades later).[61] A history of U.S. intervention in their home country, however, did not grant such migrants non-alien status in New York. Despite their countries' ties to the United States, Dominicans and Cubans, marked by color and the Spanish language, often struggled to be recognized as citizens once they naturalized.

As the largest Latino group in New York, Puerto Ricans came under increasing scrutiny as the Depression wore on. The *New York American*, a news daily published by William Randolph Hearst, stated in early 1931 that the most miserable of all those suffering in the Depression were the "residents of color" and the "immigrants from Puerto Rico."[62] The paper also claimed that Puerto Ricans in New York were "incapacitados nativos," or unintelligent natives. Newspapers based in Puerto Rico quickly combated the insult. A *La Democracia* editorial noted that if anyone should be ashamed, it should not be Puerto Ricans on the mainland "but rather those who arrived on our shores claiming to be the redeemer of subjugated peoples . . . and who in time re-subjugated this great and generous people."[63] In this way, *La Democracia* rejected the accusation of incapacity for citizenship by pointing to the citizenship enjoyed by Puerto Ricans in the last days of Spanish rule that was then revoked by the Foraker Act of 1900. More than three decades after the United States acquired the island, Puerto Ricans in the colonial metropole drew on the history of U.S. imperialism to repudiate claims that they were foreign immigrants unfit for citizenship.

Repatriation Debates of the 1930s

In April of 1930, the Welfare Council of New York City called an emergency meeting of government officials, public health experts, and welfare agencies. With what newspaper reports called "the influx of thousands of undernourished, impoverished and frequently diseased Porto Ricans," the Welfare Council met to study the scope of a situation that was deemed critical.[64] In a report stating that 16,000 Puerto Ricans had arrived in New York over the previous year, the State Board of Social Welfare claimed that "Porto Ricans who settle here seldom return to their Island voluntarily, as conditions there are much worse than here."[65]

Shortly after this meeting, the New York State Board of Charities accelerated its repatriation program, paying for scores of Puerto Ricans in New York to travel back to the island on commercial steamships. In early January 1931, twenty-six Puerto Ricans in New York who relied on state aid boarded the steamship *Carabodo*, operated by the Red D. Line Steamship Company, heading for San Juan. New York charities worked in cooperation with the American Red Cross in Puerto Rico to coordinate the relocation of some eighty Puerto Ricans that winter.[66] Yet these repatriations directly affected a small number of Puerto Ricans. New York was home to 158,000 Puerto Ricans in 1931 according to a study of the New York office of the Bureau of Commerce and Industry. Given that this number exceeded the population of Ponce and San Juan, *Porto Rico Progress*, a pro-American island paper, claimed that "New York may now be considered the island's metropolis."[67]

The history of Puerto Rican repatriation debates is little known and has not been discussed by historians, perhaps because they unfolded on a local rather than a federal stage.[68] International repatriations were usually collaborations between consulates and local welfare offices. Welfare offices, for their part, often deemed it more cost effective to pay the cost of one-way railroad tickets than to pay regular welfare payments.[69] In the case of Mexican repatriations from the U.S. Southwest, consulates supported voluntary repatriations but opposed involuntary ones. Immigrants from Jamaica, Haiti, and other countries in the Caribbean relied on consulates in New York for assistance in naturalization, employment, and for support in contending with discrimination against black foreigners.[70]

Puerto Ricans in New York envied their immigrant neighbors who could turn to their consulates for help in voluntarily repatriating.[71] Indeed, Mexicans who were denied relief in the United States routinely requested help from their local consulate. Mexicans living in Rockdale, Illinois, for example, petitioned the Chicago Mexican Consulate in 1930: "We hope His Excellency will act on our behalf, offer us repatriation and collaborate towards the enrichment of our beloved nation."[72] The Puerto Ricans' case was different from both Mexican and other Caribbean immigrants because there were no consuls to work on their behalf on the mainland United States. A column in *Grafico*, a working-class weekly in New York City of which Jesús Colón was a founding editor, stated in 1927: "Truly it seems a paradox that, being American citizens, we should be the most defenseless. While the citizens of other countries have their consulates and diplomats to represent them, the children of Borinquen have not one."[73] Though Puerto Ricans sometimes expected the federal government to take on this role, it did not, in fact, accept any responsibility for Puerto Ricans on the mainland.

Even foreign citizens with consulates to support them sometimes struggled to resist involuntary repatriations, however. In Detroit, a special Mexican Bureau, staffed by American officials, was set up by the Department of Public Assistance to facilitate repatriations among both Mexican nationals and those who were U.S. citizens through birth or naturalization. People with legal U.S. citizenship were often pressed to repatriate against their will because of the "dependency of their family."[74] In one case, a Mexican Bureau caseworker insisted that a fifteen-year-old girl born in Michigan who "did not wish to return to Mexico" be repatriated.[75] Puerto Ricans, then, were not the only citizens who were treated as noncitizens in the repatriation debates of the early 1930s. Instead, their experiences were sometimes similar to those of U.S.-born Mexicans, Filipinos, and others who were both U.S. citizens and members of national groups presumed to be entirely alien.

Debates about Puerto Rican migration, repatriation, and legal status in the 1920s and 1930s were bound up in larger policy discussions about immigrants from quota-exempt nations. Efforts in Congress to curtail Mexican immigration, for instance, were vehemently opposed by employers in the Southwest who claimed that they would need to recruit Filipinos or Puerto Ricans as replacement laborers. When the Box bill, designed to exclude Mexican immigrants, was under consideration by the House Immigration Committee, agribusiness owners in the Southwest railed against it, claiming that whites refused to work the "stoop and knee" crops. As the U.S. Border Patrol worked to enforce visa requirements at the U.S.-Mexico border, employers noted in 1930 that Mexican immigration had declined. Racial nationalists, meanwhile, pointed to the Watsonville, California, riots as a harbinger of what was to come as Filipino laborers moved in to fill the jobs formerly held by Mexicans only to become the object of racial hatred. Should the Box bill become law, employers in the Southwest predicted increased racial conflict as Filipinos or an "even less desirable social element, Porto Rican negroes," would move in.[76] As the *Los Angeles Times* stated in an editorial opposing the Box bill, "those who attempt to close the door against Mexican migration at the same time force open another which cannot so easily be closed."[77] Given that Filipinos were still considered to be U.S. nationals in this period and Puerto Ricans were U.S. citizens, neither group could be excluded by federal law in the way that the Chinese had been since the exclusion laws of the 1880s. For racial nativists who were wary of unlimited immigration from the colonies, Mexican migration offered a way to keep these groups out: "If Filipinos and Porto Ricans are to be kept out, the Mexicans must be let in."[78]

Yet, as the Depression worsened, increasing numbers of Mexicans returned to Mexico out of fear of deportation. Shortly after William Doak took office as the U.S. secretary of labor in late 1930, he promised to remove some four hundred thousand illegal aliens. An appointee of President Hoover, Doak sought to support the Republican Party's efforts to address the expanding economic crisis. In particular, he charged the Immigration Bureau with the task of removing illegal aliens who he claimed were stealing American jobs.[79] With involuntary repatriations and deportations on the rise in the early 1930s, then, many people decided to return to Mexico on their own. In what the *Los Angeles Times* reported as "The Great Migration Back to Mexico," more than ten thousand Mexican families crossed the border each month in early 1931.[80] Their decision to leave, in turn, prompted anxieties among employers who relied on Mexican labor to work the fields or repair the train tracks. Officials of the Southern Pacific Railroad, for instance, considered importing "Porto Rican Negroes" but worried that "Porto Ricans would be a constant burden to the railroads, for they would not be as assimilable as Mexicans in other jobs when railroad work is short."[81]

The Citizenship Racket

Even as Puerto Ricans chafed against the ambiguities surrounding their own legal status, other Latin Americans sometimes tried to assume a Puerto Rican identity through false documents. In the context of Doak's deportation campaign and the ongoing requirements of the Johnson-Reed Act, some Mexicans and other Latin Americans attempted to pass as Puerto Rican in order to enter the mainland without restrictions, stay in the United States beyond their visas, or avoid deportation. Immigrants from throughout Latin America sought entry to the U.S. mainland through Puerto Rico. As Representative Johnson, chair of the House Committee on Immigration, asserted in 1927, "hundreds of Latin-American negroes are admitted via Porto Rico." Johnson claimed that his research documented a hundred thousand fake Puerto Ricans in New York with more than three hundred arriving each month. Those claiming to be Puerto Rican held "faked birth certificates or other forged papers."[82] With heightened enforcement of visa requirements, large-scale deportations, and anti-Filipino violence, some Mexicans sought ways to legally pass as Puerto Ricans who had been granted citizenship. In what New York police named the "citizenship racket," fraudulent Puerto Rican birth certificates and baptismal papers were sold for a hundred dollars apiece to Mexicans looking to overstay their visas.

In April 1931, Benigno Bonilla and Alfred Perez were arrested in New York on a federal charge of forgery. Bonilla, a thirty-eight-year-old Puerto Rican who worked in Brooklyn as a notary public, and Perez, a Spanish seaman also living in Brooklyn, were accused of selling fraudulent Puerto Rican birth certificates and baptismal certificates to "hundreds of Mexicans" and "other Spanish-speaking aliens" over a period of two years.[83] The two were arrested while traveling from New York to Philadelphia with a foreigner said to be a prospective client.[84]

The New York police investigation of the citizenship racket was part of a larger effort in the early 1930s to identify and deport illegal aliens. In 1931 New York police began systematically tracking alien criminals after the appointment of Captain McDermott as head of a special detail charged with collecting information on every arrest in the city. All of those arrested were forced to prove U.S. citizenship or provide information on the date of their arrival and the ship they traveled on.[85] McDermott explained: "Heretofore, there has been too much leniency. Anyone could go to court, swear he was an American citizen and that was the end of it. Now, criminals have to prove it to me or face deportation."[86] U.S. Secretary of Labor William Doak sent a "flying squad" of twenty agents to assist McDermott. When in the process of McDermott's investigations aliens were discovered who had not committed a crime, the flying squad took over the investigation, looking for those who had attempted to sidestep the Johnson-Reed Act. In the context of immigration restriction and the Depression, immigrant families already established in the United States expressed frustration over the quotas and waiting lists involved in bringing over remaining family members legally. It was these families with "personal grudges," McDermott explained, who provided tips to the police. They were "bitter" when they saw immigrants come in illegally through Canada or as stowaways on ships only to "take the places which their own might otherwise have." "They send one anonymous letter after another to us and to the immigration authorities."[87] In the first four months of 1931, police and immigration officials in New York arrested 683 aliens and deported almost all of them. In the case of Spanish-speaking immigrants from Latin America, however, many claimed to be Puerto Rican. As one immigration official stated, "South Americans were bothersome because they maintained they were natives of Porto Rico and therefore were not liable to the immigration laws. Now they must furnish birth certificates."[88] Thus, as deportations increased in New York, so too did the market for false papers, especially those showing Puerto Rican birth.

As the worsening Depression gave rise to the citizenship racket, it also created new challenges for Puerto Ricans looking to secure a measure of economic security, despite their ambiguous legal status. Indeed, as the number of Puerto Ricans in New York surpassed a hundred thousand in the early 1930s, racialized conceptions of Puerto Ricans as nonwhite foreigners only hardened.[89] In response, Puerto Ricans of color sometimes avoided association with African Americans out of fear of being mistaken as another kind of second-class citizen. As one African American newspaper noted, the "already difficult" situation in New York City was made more complex by the fact that Puerto Ricans were a mixed racial group. "White Porto Ricans mix with the whites in the United States, but the colored Porto Ricans do not mix with the American Negro."[90] Yet, little is known about the complex dynamics between Puerto Ricans and African Americans in this period. In the depths of the Depression, in fact, countervailing evidence suggests that some Afro-Puerto Ricans identified with African Americans. In pursuit of higher education in a racially segregated college system in 1932, for example, six Puerto Rican students enrolled at Howard University, a historically black college. Along with students from Haiti, Cuba, Africa, and the British West Indies, these students were soon targeted for deportation and listed as foreign students instead of as American citizens. In an effort to reduce job competition among students supporting themselves in college, the U.S. Department of Labor ordered that foreign students be deported if they worked for wages. In the wake of this ruling, the educational opportunities for these black Puerto Ricans were sharply curtailed once they were labeled as foreign students and slated for deportation.[91]

Contesting the Limits of Locality

The contradictions surrounding Puerto Ricans' foreign or domestic status—and the various ways that racial nationalists and Puerto Ricans themselves privileged one status over another at different moments—illustrate the asymmetries of power that marked imperial migrations as different from transnational ones. In *Balzac v. Porto Rico* (1922), five years after the Jones Act granted citizenship, the U.S. Supreme Court held that it was locality rather than the citizenship status of the inhabitants in Puerto Rico that determined the application of the Constitution. Chief Justice William Howard Taft stated that, even after the Jones Act, the full rights of U.S. citizenship did not apply to a "territory belonging to the United States which has not been incorporated into the Union" as a state.[92] Yet in the decades after the Jones Act, Puerto Ricans' migration to the metropole and claims for full citizenship there challenged the imperial boundaries that had served to limit citizenship through locality and territorial status.

Such tensions and contradictions continued into the 1930s, with BIA officials leaning on racial justifications to define Puerto Ricans as aliens unfit for citizenship, and Puerto Ricans in New York contesting such labels with efforts to mobilize their votes collectively for greater political influence. In a memorandum to the secretary of war, F. Parker, the acting chief of the Bureau of Insular Affairs, grouped Puerto Ricans with other "alien races." Given the "troublesome problems" that resulted from Chinese, Japanese, and Filipino immigration in the West and Mexican immigration in the Southwest, he warned against large-scale recruitment of Puerto Rican labor for East Coast employers.[93] Puerto Ricans, he claimed, were as alien as Asians and Mexicans, given their "decidedly lower scale" of productivity and living standards, tendency to "resist Americanization," and "large admixture of negro blood." In grouping together Puerto Ricans with the Chinese, Japanese and Filipino, Parker evoked the exclusion laws that had barred the Chinese beginning with the Exclusion Acts of the 1880s and the Japanese through the "Gentleman's Agreement" of the early 1900s. Filipinos also became the subject of exclusion debates in the 1920s and 1930s. Each of these groups included natural-born citizens who could not be easily excluded from the U.S. polity yet were deemed racially alien by nativists. In this sense, there was a similarity between Puerto Ricans and U.S.-born Filipino, Japanese, and Chinese Americans, groups that the historian Mae Ngai has termed "impossible subjects."[94] Yet the anxieties of Parker and other nativists were likely heightened in the case of Puerto Ricans, a group they deemed as unfit for citizenship as Asian immigrants, but one that could not be legally excluded because of the granting of citizenship in 1917. Thus, while some nativists saw a distinction between Latin- and Afro-Puerto Ricans, others saw mixture and Latinness as indistinguishable; still others saw mixed and Latin populations as unsuitable for incorporation into the U.S. racial body. In discussions of these different racialized perceptions of Puerto Rico from the period of the U.S. takeover through the 1930s, there was a clear parallel in the language of incorporation used to debate, on the one hand, extending suffrage to the island, and on the other, regulating migration to the states, such as New York, where they would enjoy suffrage.

The objections of BIA officials like Parker can be read as concern that migration would turn colonial citizens, whose suffrage had been limited through law—territorial status, the Insular Cases, and the ruling of locality in *Balzac*—into mainland citizens with the full rights of participation in the polity. As part of his memorandum to the secretary of war, Parker pointed with concern to the political influence Puerto Ricans were already wielding in New York City. Puerto Ricans in New York, he asserted, are a "controlling factor in local elections that determine membership in the United States House of Representatives as well as the State Legislature." Such political participation, he reasoned, followed predictable patterns of immigrant voting, whereby voters were "swayed more by the special interests of their particular group or the locality of their nativity than by the general welfare of their adopted state or that of the nation as a whole."[95] Such anti–Puerto Rican sentiment reflected broader Republican critiques of urban politics and of immigration. Democrats embraced the growing Puerto Rican community in New York and used political clubs in the city to strengthen its immigrant and working-class base.[96] As immigration generally fueled Democratic power in northeastern cities, Republicans had led the successful efforts to restrict immigration in the 1920s. Yet Puerto Ricans, as U.S. citizens, would be exempted from the Johnson-Reed quotas.

Elite intellectuals and colonial officials like Foerster and Parker were not alone in their view of Puerto Ricans as foreign immigrants; working-class nativists made similar claims. In a 1933 letter to President Roosevelt, one working-class New Yorker described his new Puerto Rican neighbors with contempt. Puerto Ricans in New York, he claimed, were a "terrible set of diseased people." By using "hospitals such as Mt. Sinai," he claimed, they became a "charge upon the City." "There must be a way," he urged Roosevelt, "of keeping these people in Porto Rico."[97] With unemployment skyrocketing in New York, Theodore Roosevelt Jr., the governor of Puerto Rico and eldest son of President Theodore Roosevelt, made a public announcement in January 1931, urging residents of the island not to embark for the United States, "particularly for the city of New York."[98] Such calls by academics, working-class nativists, and government officials for restricting the movement of Puerto Ricans to the mainland reflected most North Americans' understanding of immigration as a process fully distinct from U.S. foreign policy even as the legal and economic effects of U.S. colonial power on the island assured only continued migration to the metropole.

Such racist and exclusionary responses to Puerto Ricans who migrated to U.S. states serve as essential, if largely overlooked, evidence regarding the nature of Puerto Rican citizenship. After the Jones Act was passed in 1917, Puerto Ricans who migrated to the mainland and met local residence requirements (in New York this was a minimum duration of six months) held the right to vote. A high percentage of residents of the Puerto Rican colonia in New York participated in elections in the late 1910s, with almost 50 percent voting by some accounts in the 1918 election when Al Smith was the Democratic candidate for New York governor.[99] But the state of New York passed an English-language literacy requirement for voters in 1921, causing voting rates to fall precipitously.[100] Estimates of Puerto Rican voter participation vary in this period but stay well below 50 percent. Jesús Colón and other Puerto Rican leaders in New York estimated that only 15 percent of Puerto Ricans of voting age managed to vote in the period of the English literacy laws from 1921 up to 1965, when the federal Voting Rights Act overturned the law.[101]

The New York law required that voters present a diploma from an elementary school where instruction was in English or pass an English language exam. Migrants from the island expected their diplomas to satisfy the first requirement as the colonial education system was based in English. Yet many Puerto Ricans in New York City charged that local election officials refused to validate their diplomas.[102] As colonia activist Homero Rosado recounted, "Officials submitted the aspirant to an interrogation with the purpose of frightening them and making them abandon their original political persuasions. This only served to keep Puerto Ricans away from the polls."[103] The law stipulated that diplomas from Puerto Rican schools would be permissible where instruction was "carried on predominantly in English."[104] Yet opponents to Puerto Rican voters contended that, because the federal government sometimes allowed Spanish to be used in the colonial schools, not all diplomas necessarily demonstrated English literacy. The resulting ambiguity surrounding the law and its enforcement contributed in part to the low voter turnout in this period.[105]

As New York state officials worked to enforce the English literacy law over the next several decades, a small fraction of Puerto Ricans in New York City managed to cast their votes in the 1920s and 1930s, either because they could prove literacy in English or because the law was not always enforced. Editors of *La Prensa*, in an early effort to improve voter turnout, called readers' attention in 1924 to the potentially decisive influence of their votes: "Many districts of [New York] are controlled by [Puerto Ricans], in the sense that, with their votes, they can decide an election."[106]

Even as editorials in *La Prensa* throughout the 1920s urged Puerto Ricans to vote in New York, they did not discuss the legal impediments to voting. In language typical of these calls to vote, the editors argued that Puerto Ricans "must vote in a systematic and collective way," that "Puerto Ricans are an enormous potential force in New York," and that they must "use the vote with the maximum efficiency and intelligence in defense of their compatriots, of their nation, and of their own race."[107] The editors chose to lament a lack of political unity and savvy among voters rather than discuss the English literacy law and the local decisions of election officials as to what was acceptable proof of primary school graduation. The editors of *La Prensa* rejected claims of anti–Puerto Rican discrimination, urging Puerto Ricans instead to avoid a self-defeating attitude. This could explain why editorials in *La Prensa* made no mention of obstacles to voting during the period of the English literacy law. In 1926 José Comprubí, the paper's chief editor, called charges of discrimination "absolutely false" and warned that "our people who believe themselves to be persecuted, hated and despised here, will never succeed in developing themselves as they should and could."[108]

La Prensa's editors worried that a large percentage of Puerto Ricans in New York declined to vote because of their anti-American sentiment.[109] Keenly aware of how concerns about the injustice of the island's political status led some to abstain from participating in mainland politics, the editors maintained that "abstaining from the vote is neither useful nor patriotic."[110] Building political influence in New York was the key, they insisted, to having a voice in Washington and improving conditions on the island: "In this North American democracy of which Puerto Rico forms a part, the only effective, decisive, and useful weapon is the vote."[111] *La Prensa* editorials stressed the importance of engaging in the local politics of New York and then "extending their radius of influence" to Washington and San Juan. This constituted "the most patriotic service Puerto Ricans on the mainland could render the *patria.*"[112]

In March of 1927, Resident Commissioner Félix Córdova Dávila echoed this strategy when he visited New York to meet with Puerto Rican groups, including the Liga Portorriqueña e Hispana and the Caribe Democratic Club. Addressing an assembly of members of the colonia, he declared that "with your 40,000 voters you are a respectable force that the national politics will need to take into account." Notably, Dávila remarked that Puerto Ricans' votes were potentially more effective than his own presence in Washington since he did not have a vote in Congress.[113] Other Puerto Rican leaders in New York City also recognized migrants' votes in states as the key to challenging colonialism on the island. Carlos Tapia, a leader of the Brooklyn colonia in the 1920s and 1930s, stated that "the only way for our island to get political recognition is through the Puerto Ricans here in New York and in other states of the Union. Someday the Puerto Ricans in New York and in many other states of the United States, will by their political power get what our brothers on the island will never get: congressmen who in exchange for our help to elect them will have to help our beloved Puerto Rico."[114]

In their focus on the homeland, Puerto Rican political mobilizations in New York were similar to those of other immigrant groups such as the Irish and the Italians, groups that, in the words of the historian Donna Gabaccia, typically sought "change in the countries they had left."[115] But while immigrant politics tended to influence foreign nations more than the United States, Puerto Rican political mobilizations in the colonial metropole directly challenged U.S. imperial policy. Theirs was a form of diaspora nationalism, like that of Filipinos, Cubans, and Mexicans, that proved threatening to the United States.[116] Over the course of the 1920s and into the 1930s, as Puerto Ricans in New York City struggled with repatriations, the Choques of 1926, and the onset of the Depression in 1929, they increasingly embraced "the politics of here." Puerto Ricans in New York sought to assert their citizenship rights to make demands of the federal, state, and municipal governments while simultaneously seeking to advance island sovereignty, a strategy that culminated in the election of Vito Marcantonio as the representative from East Harlem in the U.S. House of Representatives in 1934.[117] An Italian American who was sympathetic to Puerto Rican concerns, Marcantonio was the first voting member of Congress to represent Puerto Ricans. Puerto Rican migration to U.S. states, then, reveals an increasingly complex relationship between migration and colonialism. Not only did colonialism spur migration to the metropole but migrants in various ways threatened to undermine colonial rule through claims of full citizenship in New York, the Empire State. As Puerto Ricans gained political power on the U.S. mainland, however, racial nationalist responses took on ever newer forms. The impulse behind defining Pedro Aran as a foreign immigrant in 1921 and blaming him for his rashness in coming to New York later took the form of racialized attitudes toward Puerto Ricans in New York in the 1930s and beyond.

Conclusion

U.S. Empire and the Boundaries of the Nation

In May of 1937, the Kiwanis Club of New York met for a luncheon at the McAlpin Hotel on the corner of Broadway and 34th Street in Manhattan, one of the most luxurious hotels in the city, replete with a Turkish bath on the twenty-fourth floor and a small hospital offering the latest in medical care exclusively for guests. The topic for discussion was immigration and the invited speaker was Rudolph Reimer, district commissioner of immigration and naturalization at Ellis Island. Reimer, who was active in Democratic politics and known as a friend to immigrants, had been honored two years earlier by the Hebrew Sheltering and Immigrant Aid Society for his support of Jewish immigrants passing through Ellis Island. On this occasion, he spoke about Puerto Rican immigration.[1] Reimer explained that Puerto Ricans entering New York represented one of the chief challenges for immigration officials at Ellis Island because, as U.S. citizens, they were free to enter without restriction. The effect, he claimed, was a "slum condition in the city." He stated that "the Puerto Rican was unable to perform ordinary labor because of climatic conditions, his physique, and his susceptibility to ailments, and therefore usually turned to casual labor or menial jobs."[2]

Reminiscent of earlier claims of Puerto Rican racial incapacity for citizenship, Reimer called for curbs on Puerto Rican migration through required examinations before entering Ellis Island. Such a racial nationalist response to colonial migration echoed those of nativists in other imperial centers, notably London. As the historian Laura Tabili has shown, British nativists ignored Britain's imperial past when responding to colonial subjects entering England. "Discounting the imperial experience when examining British race relations," Tabili argues, "perpetuates the view of Black British subjects as outsiders to the system, rather than recognizing them as a section of Britain's global workforce kept structurally separate to ensure their enhanced exploitability."[3] Racial nativists like Reimer, who supported Jewish immigration but sought to limit Puerto Rican immigration, all but erased the history of U.S. colonialism and located the source of Puerto Rican poverty and unassimilability in perceived faults of ethnicity and race.[4]

In November of 1937, just six months after Reimer's speech at the McAlpin Hotel, Puerto Ricans of various political stripes joined forces in East Harlem to elect Oscar García Rivera to a seat in the New York State Assembly representing the 17th district in Manhattan.[5] The first Puerto Rican to hold elected office in the United States, García Rivera was a Republican who stood in opposition to a Democratic Party that increasingly disregarded Puerto Ricans, and dismissed Vito Marcantonio—who had been elected to the U.S. House in 1934 to represent Puerto Ricans in East Harlem—as too radical. Though elected by a wide margin of voters, including many who crossed over from the Democratic Party, García Rivera would lose a reelection bid in 1939 when the New York County Republican Committee pulled their support because of allegations that he had communist leanings.[6]

This fleeting victory highlighted both the agency of Puerto Rican migrants and the persistent challenges they faced. Almost four decades after the United States invaded Puerto Rico, migrants successfully mobilized in Harlem to overcome a litany of historical obstacles to full citizenship—from restrictive voting laws on the island to New York State's English literacy law—and to place a Puerto Rican in elected office. García Rivera's election marked a triumph of political representation. Yet his quick defeat, coupled with the increasing marginalization of Vito Marcantonio, meant that Puerto Ricans' political demands in the colonial metropole went largely unheeded. It would not be until after World War II, when commercial air travel made migration to the mainland more affordable, that the growing Puerto Rican community in the United States demanded anew the attention of elected leaders. Still, the struggle for political representation would continue to be hampered by both an unwillingness of Americans to acknowledge what Marcantonio called "our ruthless imperialism" and by persistent ideas of

Puerto Rican incapacity for citizenship that began with the U.S. takeover of the island in 1898 and continued through Commissioner Reimer's remarks in New York City in the late 1930s.[7] The dynamic cycle of U.S. imperialism, followed by migration to the metropole, racial nationalist backlash, and Puerto Rican claims for full citizenship, continued well into the twentieth century. While others have explored in depth the post–World War II history of Puerto Rican migration, I have focused on the early roots of this migration and how it was shaped by the forces of American empire and migrants' own agency.[8]

By situating Puerto Rican migration within the larger context of U.S. empire in Latin America, the Philippines, and beyond, I have demonstrated how U.S. policy channeled and disciplined migration to the mainland and how Puerto Ricans, in contesting their own colonial subjugation, transformed the colonial state. In tracking the movement of people between the island and the mainland, this book contributes to the emerging literature on the relationship between empire and migration, and to the larger project of transcending nationalist constraints in order to internationalize the study of American history.

In this book, I have challenged the traditional paradigms of immigration history, which assume that the political and economic forces pushing immigrants toward the United States are unconnected to U.S. foreign policy. If such a framework accurately describes much of European immigration to the United States through the late nineteenth century, it fails to describe the movement of migrants since then from Latin America, Asia, and the Middle East who have often migrated precisely because of the effects of U.S. policies in their home countries. In focusing on the case of Puerto Rico, I have shown how specific foreign policy decisions made in Washington—from coastwise shipping to the Jones Act—structured migration from the island to the mainland.

In the early 1900s, for instance, when thousands of unemployed laborers from Ponce traveled by rail and steamship to Hawai'i, they were responding to the pull of U.S. contract labor agents as well as the push of U.S. trade and shipping policies that had devastated Puerto Rico's coffee economy. And in the early 1920s, when Pedro Aran and his family moved from the island to New York, they responded to still-worsening conditions in Puerto Rico's coffee sector as U.S. policy made what had been the island's primary export unprofitable. Rather than moving between two separate economies, Puerto Ricans migrating to the mainland moved within one integrated economy and polity. With these and other examples, this history anticipates a broader twentieth-century phenomenon of mass migration from countries that were fundamentally reshaped by American military, economic, and political interventions.

Even as Puerto Ricans were drawn into the mainland economy, various groups of racial nativists, from union rank and file to congressional representatives, defined them as foreign immigrants unfit for citizenship. In the early 1900s, immigration officials at Ellis Island equated Puerto Rican migrants like Jorge Cruz and Isabel González with foreigners from another country, the same as immigrants from Russia. During this early period, 1898–1904, Puerto Ricans were regularly detained in the Port of New York under charges of violating the prohibition on foreign contract labor.

Yet colonial power is not the whole story here. I have shown how Puerto Ricans were protagonists in their own struggle to secure the basic rights of mobility, employment, and political representation. In response to attempts to exclude them from the U.S. mainland, Puerto Ricans seeking to flee an island economy in crisis challenged ideas of their own foreignness by arguing that residents of a colony of the United States could not be legally defined as aliens. In bringing her case before the U.S. Supreme Court in 1904, Isabel González prompted a change in U.S. immigration law when the court defined Puerto Ricans, and by extension Filipinos, as U.S. nationals exempt from immigration restrictions. Thus trade policy decisions made in Washington, which led to the decline of the coffee sector on the island, spurred migrants to enter the mainland in search of work. These migrants, in turn, forced changes in U.S. immigration law, which opened mainland ports to increasing numbers of both Puerto Rican and Filipino migrants.

Puerto Ricans contested and sometimes transformed U.S. colonial policy in other ways as well. In the World War I period, workers on the island striking for better wages and petitioning for U.S. citizenship played a pivotal role in bringing Congress to vote on the Jones bill. In the context of a war fought "to make the world safe for democracy," President Wilson called on Congress to rid the nation of what he called the embarrassment made plain by the protests of Puerto Rican colonial subjects in the American republic. The advent of U.S. citizenship status spurred even greater labor mobility than national status had a decade earlier, as U.S. employers proved to be more likely to hire Puerto Ricans who were defined unambiguously as U.S. citizens.

The difference citizenship made could be seen most readily in the increased work opportunities for Puerto Ricans on the mainland. In 1905 Juan Rodríguez, a U.S. national from Puerto Rico, was denied the opportunity to apply for employment at the U.S. Navy Yard in Washington, DC. While allowing that nationals could freely enter the mainland, the U.S. Supreme Court upheld the navy's ruling that nationals—as people who were not U.S. citizens—were ineligible for employment by the U.S. government. After citizenship was granted in the Jones Act of 1917, however, the U.S. Department of Labor recruited some 12,000 Puerto Ricans to work in army camps and navy yards throughout the U.S. South to help with the war effort. U.S. citizenship would make possible one of the largest migrations of the twentieth century, with more Puerto Ricans living on the mainland than on the island by the early 2000s.[9]

Yet, even after the granting of citizenship in 1917, ideas of Puerto Rican foreignness persisted. During the demobilization of war industries in 1919, for instance, many employers defined Puerto Rican employees as aliens in order to justify their dismissal. In the late 1910s and early 1920s, municipal officials throughout the United States regularly denied Puerto Ricans the right to vote, claiming that Puerto Ricans were not U.S. citizens. And in the 1930s, charity boards interested in shrinking their relief rolls claimed that Puerto Ricans were foreigners who could be repatriated to their home country. Puerto Ricans who protested such actions before U.S. courts were required to show documentation proving their citizenship status. But because they were routinely denied naturalization papers, visas, and passports by the colonial state, Puerto Ricans had few ways of proving their legal status.

Such evidence challenges the notion that the categories of citizen and noncitizen immigrant have always been legally distinct and historically opposite. We expect citizens to have more rights than noncitizens. But as I have shown, racial nationalists in the United States constructed Puerto Ricans as noncitizen immigrants, even after the Jones Act of 1917. As citizens of the United States from a colonial territory, Puerto Ricans on the mainland lacked the documents necessary to prove their citizenship status before courts, employers, and charity boards. In this sense, they were made more vulnerable to discrimination than immigrants from other countries who possessed naturalization papers. By highlighting how a sociocultural reality of noncitizenship could accompany the formal political status of citizenship, I have demonstrated that citizenship has long been an unstable category—one that has permitted, in specific historical moments, the exclusion of various groups from full participation in the polity.

As in the early twentieth century, Americans in the early twenty-first century are again embroiled in intense public debate over immigration.

Amid debates over extreme vetting of refugees, Muslim bans, a border wall with Mexico, and a new wave of Puerto Rican migrants fleeing an acute economic crisis on the island that was exacerbated by the catastrophic destruction caused by Hurricane Maria in September 2017, few acknowledge the long history of American involvement overseas. This book contributes to a historical understanding of newer immigrants entering American society from a variety of U.S. imperial settings. While American political culture has long assumed that immigrants come from a world set apart, this book reframes our understanding of immigrants by illustrating how many are actually migrants responding to the exercise of U.S. power abroad and moving within the domain of America's global reach. As in the case of migrants from U.S. corporate enclaves in Latin America and from U.S. war zones in Asia and the Middle East, the history of migration from Puerto Rico makes clear how U.S. interventions overseas have not only affected the histories of foreign nations but also fundamentally changed American history itself.

Notes

Introduction

1. Puerto Rico was officially spelled "Porto Rico" in the Treaty of Paris after the War of 1898 and not changed until 1932 when Congress restored the correct spelling. A variety of Americans and Puerto Ricans used the incorrect spelling in the period in between. See Article II of "A Treaty of Peace between the United States and Spain," S. Doc. No. 62, pt. 1 (Washington, DC: Government Printing Office, 1899), 5–11.

2. Petition of Arcadio Santiago, Secretary General, Porto Rican Club of San Francisco, San Francisco, California, to the Resident Commissioner for Porto Rico, Washington, DC, March 19, 1919, box 180, folder 1390, Fortaleza Collection, Correspondence, Archivo General de Puerto Rico (hereafter cited as AGPR).

3. Mae M. Ngai, *Impossible Subjects: Illegal Aliens and the Making of Modern America* (Princeton, NJ: Princeton University Press, 2004), 2, 8, 170, 175.

4. Eiichiro Azuma, "Racial Struggle, Immigrant Nationalism, and Ethnic Identity: Japanese and Filipinos in the California Delta," *Pacific Historical Review* 67, no. 2 (1998): 166–73.

5. Petition of Arcadio Santiago, Secretary General, Porto Rican Club of San Francisco.

6. Ibid.

7. For studies of the construction of American borders, see Rachel St. John, *Line in the Sand: A History of the Western U.S.-Mexico Border* (Princeton, NJ: Princeton University Press, 2011); Adam M. McKeown, *Melancholy Order: Asian Migration and the Globalization of Borders* (New York: Columbia University Press, 2008); Ngai, *Impossible Subjects*; Daniel S. Margolies, *Spaces of Law in American Foreign Relations: Extradition and Extraterritoriality in the Borderlands and Beyond, 1877–1898* (Athens: University of Georgia Press, 2011); Mary Dudziak and Leti Volpp, eds., introduction

to "Legal Borderlands: Law and the Construction of American Borders," special issue, *American Quarterly* 57, no. 3 (September 2005): 593–610.

8. The historian Laura Tabili argues, in the British imperial context, that "labor migration itself must be understood as a form of agency and resistance to global economic imbalance." *"We Ask for British Justice": Workers and Racial Difference in Late Imperial Britain* (Ithaca, NY: Cornell University Press, 1994), 183.

9. Though excluded from Spanish constitutional rights since 1837, Puerto Rico did win suffrage for taxpayers and literate classes as well as representation in the Spanish parliament in 1873, the same year Spain abolished slavery on the island. Puerto Rican reformers failed to win additional rights as the liberal government in Madrid gave way to a monarchical regime in 1874. See César J. Ayala and Rafael Bernabe, *Puerto Rico in the American Century: A History since 1898* (Chapel Hill: University of North Carolina Press, 2007), 21.

10. Saskia Sassen theorized this linkage in the 1980s: *Mobility of Labor and Capital* (Cambridge: Cambridge University Press, 1988), 15. See also Lucie Cheng, ed., *Immigration under Capitalism: Asian Workers in the United States before World War II* (Berkeley: University of California Press, 1984).

11. For calls to bring together the study of empire and immigration, see Paul A. Kramer, "Power and Connection: Imperial Histories of the United States in the World," *American Historical Review* 116, no. 5 (December 2011): 1382. Julie Greene has also called for new research to "determine how colonial relationships shaped the migratory experience and the reception those migrants received in the United States." Julie Greene, "The Labor of Empire: Recent Scholarship on U.S. History and Imperialism," *Labor: Studies in Working-Class History of the Americas* 1, no. 2 (2004): 129. See also George J. Sanchez, "Race, Nation, and Culture in Recent Immigration Studies," *Journal of American Ethnic History* 18, no. 4 (1999): 66–84; Julie Greene, "Movable Empire: Labor, Migration, and U.S. Global Power during the Gilded Age and Progressive Era," *Journal of the Gilded Age and Progressive Era* 15, no. 1 (2016): 4–20.

12. Christina Duffy Burnett (now Ponsa) and Burke Marshall, eds., *Foreign in a Domestic Sense: Puerto Rico, American Expansion, and the Constitution* (Durham, NC: Duke University Press, 2001); Efrén Rivera Ramos, *The Legal Construction of Identity: The Judicial and Social Legacy of American Colonialism in Puerto Rico* (Washington, DC: American Psychological Association, 2001); Bartholomew H. Sparrow, *The Insular Cases and the Emergence of American Empire* (Lawrence: University of Kansas Press, 2006); José A. Cabranes, *Citizenship and the American Empire: Notes on the Legislative History of the United States Citizenship of Puerto Ricans* (New Haven, CT: Yale University Press, 1979).

13. Legal historians Sam Erman and Christina Duffy Ponsa have done important recent work on imperial law and the exclusion of colonial subjects from citizenship. I build on this work by focusing on colonial migration as an essential domain for understanding American empire. See Sam Erman, "Citizens of Empire: Puerto Rico, Status, and Constitutional Change," *California Law Review* 102, no. 5 (October 2014): 1181; Sam Erman, "Meanings of Citizenship in the U.S. Empire: Puerto Rico, Isabel González, and the Supreme Court, 1898 to 1905," *Journal of American Ethnic History* 27, no. 4 (Summer 2008): 5–33; Christina Duffy Ponsa, "When Statehood Was Autonomy," in Neuman and Brown-Nagin, *Reconsidering the Insular Cases*, 1–28; Christina Duffy Ponsa, "'They Say I Am Not an American': The Non-Citizen National and the Law of American Empire," *Virginia Journal of International Law* 48, no. 4 (2008): 659; and Christina Duffy Ponsa, "Empire and the Transformation of Citizenship," in McCoy and Scarano, *Colonial Crucible*, 332–41.

14. Kramer, "Power and Connection," 1349.

15. Important pioneering works in forging the connection between migration, empire, and foreign relations include Meredith Oyen, *The Diplomacy of Migration: Transnational Lives and*

the Making of U.S.-Chinese Relations in the Cold War (Ithaca, NY: Cornell University Press, 2015); Madeline Y. Hsu, *The Good Immigrants: How the Yellow Peril Became the Model Minority* (Princeton, NJ: Princeton University Press, 2015); Donna Gabaccia, *Foreign Relations: American Immigration in Global Perspective* (Princeton, NJ: Princeton University Press, 2012); Kornel Chang, *Pacific Connections: The Making of the U.S.-Canadian Borderlands* (Berkeley: University of California Press, 2012); Robert C. McGreevey, "Empire and Migration: Coastwise Shipping, National Status, and the Legal Origins of Puerto Rican Migration to the United States," *Journal of the Gilded Age and Progressive Era* 11, no. 4 (October 2012): 553–73; Moon-Ho Jung, "Seditious Subjects: Race, State Violence, and the U.S. Empire," *Journal of Asian American Studies* 14, no. 2 (June 2011): 221–47; Eiichoro Azuma, *Between Two Empires: Race, History, and Transnationalism in Japanese America* (New York: Oxford University Press, 2005); Dorothy Fujita-Rony, *American Workers, Colonial Power: Philippine Seattle and the Transpacific West, 1919–1941* (Berkeley: University of California Press, 2003); and Catherine Ceniza Choy, *Empire of Care: Nursing and Migration in Filipino American History* (Durham, NC: Duke University Press, 2003).

16. See Paul Kramer, *The Blood of Government: Race, Empire, the United States, and the Philippines* (Chapel Hill: University of North Carolina Press, 2006); Fujita-Rony, *American Workers, Colonial Power.*

17. Adam Ewing, *The Age of Garvey: How a Jamaican Activist Created a Mass Movement and Changed Global Black Politics* (Princeton, NJ: Princeton University Press, 2014), 68; Jason M. Colby, *The Business of Empire: United Fruit, Race, and U.S. Expansion in Central America* (Ithaca, NY: Cornell University Press, 2011), 199–200.

18. See esp. Tabili, *"We Ask for British Justice."* For comparative work on American and British empires, see Julian Go, *Patterns of Empire: The British and American Empires, 1688 to the Present* (Cambridge: Cambridge University Press, 2011); and Phillip Darby, *Three Faces of Imperialism: British and American Approaches to Asia and Africa, 1870–1970* (New Haven, CT: Yale University Press, 1987).

19. For a useful discussion of agency and its variant forms, including both individual and collective acts of resistance as well as collaboration, see Walter Johnson, "On Agency," *Journal of Social History* 37, no. 1 (2003): 113–24. On the importance of attention to agency in imperial contexts, Paul Kramer has written, "Pulling back from the illusory association of empire with absolute power will allow historians to approach empires as complex circuits of agency in which bottom-up and mid-range claims-making was no less typical (if always less welcome) than top-down command." "Power and Connection," 1383. For a recent study of challenges to U.S. colonialism in Puerto Rico, see Solsiree del Moral, "Negotiating Colonialism: 'Race,' Class, and Education in Early-Twentieth-Century Puerto Rico," in McCoy and Scarano, *Colonial Crucible,* 135–144.

20. For pathbreaking work on the links between U.S. imperialism and Caribbean migration, see Jesse Hoffnung-Garskof, *A Tale of Two Cities: Santo Domingo and New York after 1950* (Princeton, NJ: Princeton University Press, 2008). Hoffnung-Garskof argues that U.S. concern over public opinion in Santo Domingo led to a loosening of visa requirements for migrants to the United States in the 1960s, and that U.S. invasions, occupations, and imperial policies in nations as diverse as Germany, Japan, Vietnam, and Cuba, among others, shaped a variety of migration streams to the United States in the twentieth century.

21. Paul Kramer articulates this binary and offers an illuminating discussion of transnational versus imperial approaches to immigration history in his essay "Power and Connection," 1382. Landmark works of transnational immigration history include Madeline Hsu, *Dreaming of Gold, Dreaming of Home: Transnationalism and Migration between the United States and South China,*

1882–1943 (Stanford, CA: Stanford University Press, 2000); and Adam McKeown, *Chinese Migrant Networks and Cultural Change: Peru, Chicago, Hawaii, 1900–1936* (Chicago: University of Chicago Press, 2001). For examples of an imperial approach to immigration history, see Paul A. Kramer, "Empire against Exclusion in Early 20th Century Trans-Pacific History," *Nanzan Review of American Studies* 33 (2011): 13–32; and Paul Kramer, "Imperial Openings: Civilization, Exemption, and the Geopolitics of Mobility in the History of Chinese Exclusion, 1868–1910," *Journal of the Gilded Age and Progressive Era* 14, no. 3 (2015): 317–47.

1. America's Caribbean Frontier

1. "Gov. Allen Inaugurated: Assumes Control of the Civil Government," *New York Times*, May 2, 1900.

2. Translations from the original Spanish are my own. On the U.S. invasion and the period of military occupation, see Fernando Picó, *Historia general de Puerto Rico* (Río Piedras, PR: Ediciones huracán, 2000), 223–33.

3. General Miles, "Proclama: Cuartel general del ejercito de los Estados Unidos, a los inhabitantes de Puerto Rico" (Ponce, Puerto Rico, July 29, 1898), quoted in Guillermo A. Baralt, *Buena Vista: Life and Work on a Puerto Rican Hacienda, 1833–1904* (Chapel Hill: University of North Carolina Press, 1999), 115; Bailey W. and Justine Whitfield Diffie, *Puerto Rico: A Broken Pledge* (New York: Vanguard Press, 1931), 3.

4. Circular of Geo. W. Davis, Brigadier-General, Commanding, Headquarters Department of Porto Rico, San Juan, PR, August 15, 1899. Annual reports of the War Department for the fiscal year ended June 30, 1900, Part 13, Report of the Military Governor of Porto Rico on Civil Affairs, Serial Set vol. no. 4088, Session vol. no. 14, 56th Cong., 2d Sess., H. Doc. 2 pt. 6, 27. See also James Wilson, "To the Portoriquenos," August 31, 1898, James Wilson Papers, Library of Congress.

5. Pedro Cabán, in his extensive study of U.S. colonial policy in Puerto Rico, provides a foundation for understanding the early period of U.S. rule. Pedro A. Cabán, *Constructing a Colonial People: Puerto Rico and the United States, 1898–1932* (Boulder, CO: Westview Press, 1999). For recent work that explores continuities between the Spanish and American periods, see Lanny Thompson, *Imperial Archipelago* (Honolulu: University of Hawa'ii Press, 2010); and Francisco A. Scarano, "Censuses in the Transition to Modern Colonialism: Spain and the United States in Puerto Rico," in McCoy and Scarano, *Colonial Crucible*, 210–19.

6. For a useful critique of U.S.-centric accounts of colonialism and the Spanish-Cuban-American War, see Louis A. Pérez Jr., *The War of 1898: The United States and Cuba in History and Historiography* (Chapel Hill: University of North Carolina Press, 1998).

7. Astrid Cubano Iguina, *Rituals of Violence in Nineteenth-Century Puerto Rico: Individual Conflict, Gender, and the Law* (Gainesville: University Press of Florida, 2006), 137–38.

8. Schmidt-Nowara argues that "most contemporary revisions of European imperialism, such as Frederick Cooper and Ann Stoler's *Tension of Empire*, ignore Spain's nineteenth-century colonial experience and the breakup of empire in the Caribbean and Pacific." Christopher Schmidt-Nowara, "'After Spain': A Dialogue with Joseph M. Fradera on Spanish Colonial Historiography," in Burton, *After the Imperial Turn*, 162–64. See also Christopher Schmidt-Nowara, *Interpreting Spanish Colonialism: Empires, Nations, and Legends* (Albuquerque: University of New Mexico Press, 2005), 5.

9. Mariano Negrón Portillo, *Las turbas republicanas* (Río Piedras, PR: Ediciones huracán, 1990), 25–26.

10. "En Expectativa," *La Democracia*, January 2, 1897.

11. *La Democracia*, January 2, 1897; "Las reformas," *La Democracia*, January 4, 1897; "Incógnita," *La Democracia*, January 5, 1897; "La comision y las reformas," *La Democracia*, January 15, 1897.

12. Iguina, *Rituals of Violence*, 139.

13. *La Democracia*, November 26, 1897.

14. *La Democracia*, November 26, 1897; "1897–1898," *La Democracia*, December 31, 1897.

15. "Detalles sobre el nuevo regimen," *La Democracia*, November 31, 1897; "La autonomia es un hecho," *La Democracia*, November 10, 1897. Astrid Cubano has shown a dramatic increase in eligible voters from 4 percent of the Puerto Rican population in 1873 to 16 percent in 1897 as a direct result of the Autonomy Charter. See Astrid Cubano Iguina, "Political Culture and Male Mass-Party Formation in Late-Nineteenth-Century Puerto Rico," *Hispanic American Historical Review* 78, no. 4 (November 1998): 656.

16. Juan R. Torruella, "The Insular Cases: A Declaration of Their Bankruptcy and My Harvard Pronouncement," in Neuman and Brown-Nagin, *Reconsidering the Insular Cases*, 64.

17. *La Democracia*, January 26, 1897.

18. The liberal Autonomist Party was also known as the Liberal Party after 1896. "Del regocijo y entusiasmo populates," *La Democracia*, November 26, 1897; "Poor maestro decor," *Ensayo Obrero*, December 19, 1897; Iguina, *Rituals of Violence*, 138–39; editorial, *Ensayo Obrero*, December 19, 1897.

19. "Recension del overo," *Ensayo Obrero*, September 30, 1897.

20. Eileen J. Suárez Findlay, *Imposing Decency: The Politics of Sexuality and Race in Puerto Rico, 1870–1920* (Durham, NC: Duke University Press, 1999), 58.

21. Jesse Hoffnung-Garskof, "To Abolish the Law of Castes: Merit, Manhood and the Problem of Colour in the Puerto Rican Liberal Movement, 1873–1892," *Social History* 36, no. 3 (August 2011): 314.

22. "La mano de hierro," *Ensayo Obrero*, February 6, 1898.

23. Julian Go, *American Empire and the Politics of Meaning: Elite Political Cultures in the Philippines and Puerto Rico during U.S. Colonialism* (Durham, NC: Duke University Press, 2008), 75; Christina Duffy Ponsa, "When Statehood Was Autonomy," in Neuman and Brown-Nagin, *Reconsidering the Insular Cases*, 16.

24. "Por nuestro decoro," *Ensayo Obrero*, December 19, 1897; "La Tía Javiera," *Ensayo Obrero*, January 30, 1898; "Alerta," *Ensayo Obrero*, January 30, 1898; Iguina, *Rituals of Violence*, 137–40.

25. "Mirando al porvenir," *Ensayo Obrero*, February 6, 1898.

26. Gonzalo F. Córdova, *Resident Commissioner Santiago Iglesias and His Times* (Río Piedras: Editorial de la Universidad de Puerto Rico, 1993), 55.

27. The Autonomist Party was founded in 1887 in Ponce and was originally inspired by a similar movement in Cuba. In seeking greater control over local affairs while remaining under Spanish rule, autonomists sought the power to make laws governing immigration and tariffs. See Harold J. Lidin, *History of the Puerto Rican Independence Movement* (Hato Rey, PR: Master typesetting of Puerto Rico, 1981), 1:113–36; and Marta Sánchez Olmeda, *Los movimientos independistas en puerto rico y su permeabilidad en la clase obrera* (Río Piedras, PR: Editorial Edil, 1991), 13.

28. Miles Galvin, *The Organized Labor Movement in Puerto Rico* (Rutherford, NJ: Fairleigh Dickinson University Press, 1979), 37.

29. Córdova, *Resident Commissioner*, 55–57.

30. "La alocución del General Henry," *La Democracia*, December 13, 1898.

31. Ponsa, "When Statehood Was Autonomy," 6.

32. On the politics of Puerto Rican elites in the period of U.S. occupation, see Go, *American Empire*, 77–82.

33. Eileen J. Findlay, "Love in the Tropics: Marriage, Divorce, and the Construction of Benevolent Colonialism in Puerto Rico, 1898–1910," in *Close Encounters of Empire: Writing the Cultural History of U.S.–Latin American Relations*, ed. Gilbert Joseph, Catherine C. LeGrand, and Ricardo D. Salvatore (Durham, NC: Duke University Press, 1998), 138; Iguina, "Political Culture," 660.

34. "Pro patria," *La Federación Obrera*, February 4, 1899; "Manifiesto," *Porvenir Social*, May 16, 1899.

35. "Información desempleo," *Porvenir Social*, December 3, 1898.

36. Findlay, *Imposing Decency*, 138; Ayala and Bernabe, *Puerto Rico in the American Century*, 17.

37. "Proyecto del reglamiento," *Porvenir Social*, December 30, 1898; "La Liga Obrera," *Porvenir Social*, December 30, 1898.

38. "Eco de Lares," *Porvenir Social*, May 18, 1899.

39. "Al Sr Secretario," *Porvenir Social*, May 25, 1899; "En huelga & afectuosa," *Porvenir Social*, May 13, 1899.

40. Findlay, *Imposing Decency*, 135.

41. Ibid., 139.

42. "De los Estados Unidos," *Porvenir Social*, April 8, 1899; "Partido Obrero," *Porvenir Social*, May 25, 1899.

43. General Davis, Governor of Puerto Rico, Statement made during the Hearings before the Committee on Pacific Islands and Puerto Rico of the U.S. Senate on Senate Bill 2264, "To Provide a Government for the Island of Puerto Rico, and for other purposes," (Washington, DC: Government Printing Office, 1900), 26, box Y6005, RG 287, National Archives Building, Washington, DC (hereafter cited as NAB).

44. Baralt, *Buena Vista*, 85.

45. Fernando López Tuero, *Isla de Puerto-Rico: Estudios de economía rural* (Puerto Rico: Imprenta del Boletin Mercantil, 1893), 27, quoted in Laird W. Bergad, *Coffee and the Growth of Agrarian Capitalism in Nineteenth-Century Puerto Rico* (Princeton, NJ: Princeton University Press), 171.

46. Bergad, *Coffee and the Growth of Agrarian Capitalism*, 170–73.

47. On the Puerto Rican state under U.S. rule, see Cabán, *Constructing a Colonial People*, and Ayala and Bernabe, *Puerto Rico in the American Century*, 14–32.

48. *Puerto Rico: A Guide to the Island of Boriquen* (New York: University Society, 1940), 89.

49. Davis, Statement made in the Hearings, 35.

50. On the coffee crisis, see Fernando Picó, *Al filo del poder: Subalternos y dominantes en Puerto Rico, 1739–1910* (Río Piedras: Editorial de la Universidad de Puerto Rico, 1993), 159–60. See also Baralt, *Buena Vista*, 113–30; and Bailey W. Diffie and Justine Whitfield Diffie, *Porto Rico: A Broken Pledge* (New York: Vanguard Press, 1931), 140. While these accounts stress the effects of the 1899 hurricane and declining world coffee prices on the island's coffee sector, I show how specific U.S. policies—from currency reform and coastwise shipping to free trade—aggravated this crisis.

51. *Huss v. New York and Puerto Rican Steamship Co.*, 182 U.S., 392 (1901).

52. "Cuban Ports Open to All: Only American Trading Ships, However, Can Clear for Puerto Rico," *New York Times*, August 16, 1898.

53. "A Mediaeval Colonial Policy," *New York Times*, November 19, 1898; "England and Our Colonial Policy," *New York Times*, November 20, 1898; "The American Shipbuilders," *New York Times*, November 26, 1898; "Pin Pricks," *New York Times*, January 8, 1899.

54. "Puerto Rican Shipping Law: Foreign Bottoms May Engage Temporarily in Trade with This Country," *New York Times*, May 4, 1899.

55. "The Puerto Rican Tariff," letter from Azel Ames, T. Larrinaga, R. Valdes, Lucas Amadeo, L. Sánchez Morales, and J. R. Latimer to the Editor, *New York Times*, February 21, 1900; Michael Willrich, *Pox: An American History* (New York: Penguin, 2011), 129, 147.

56. Petition of T. Larrinaga and Twelve Others to the U.S. Congress, February 20, 1900, box 196, folder Sen 56A-J27, RG 46, NAB. See, for example: "The laws which now compel us to use American ships only, as there are few in our harbors, give them the advantage of a monopoly at advanced freight rates; while other crafts, which bring to Puerto Rico commodities (that should come only from the U.S.), who would gladly accept lower rates, were we privileged to utilize them, return without cargoes." The coastwise laws were later reinforced by the Merchant Marine Act of 1920 (also known as the "Jones Act"). The Jones Act of 1920 is not to be confused with the Jones Act of 1917, which granted citizenship. See Nelson A. Denis, "The Jones Act: The Law Strangling Puerto Rico," *New York Times*, September 25, 2017.

57. On the San Ciriaco hurricane, see Raquel Rosario Rivera, "Una vision fotográfica y estadística de los estragos causados por el Huracán San Ciriaco en la isla de Puerto Rico," in *La llegada del Cíclope: Percepciones de San Ciriaco a cien años de su visita*, ed. Raquel Rosario Rivera (San Juan, PR: Fundación Puertorriqueña de las Humanidades, 2000), 9–17.

58. Davis, Statement made in the Hearings (1900), 34.

59. Ibid., 36.

60. Ibid., 35.

61. Congress eventually agreed to a much smaller grant than what Governor Davis requested. Congress granted $200,000 and President McKinley authorized the distribution of emergency food supplies. Cabán, *Constructing a Colonial People*; Davis, Statement made in the Hearings (1900), 66.

62. For the effects of San Ciriaco on migration, see Irene Fernández Aponte, "La dislocación poblacional y éxodo migratorio como resultado de San Ciriaco," in *La llegada del Cíclope: Percepciones de San Ciriaco a cien años de su visita* (San Juan, PR: Fundación Puertorriqueña de las Humanidades, 2000), 113–21.

63. Annual reports of the War Department for the fiscal year ended June 30, 1900, 22.

64. See Section 8 of the U.S. Constitution.

65. Annual reports of the War Department for the fiscal year ended June 30, 1900, 26.

66. Ibid., 38.

67. Ibid., 44.

68. Ibid.

69. Ángel G. Quintero Rivera, *Patricios y plebeyos: Burgueses, hacendados, artesanos y obreros: Las relaciones de clase en el Puerto Rico de cambio de siglo* (San Juan, PR: Ediciones Huracán, 1988), 83.

70. Annual reports of the War Department for the fiscal year ended June 30, 1900, 45; Quintero Rivera, *Patricios y plebeyos*, 83.

71. Annual reports of the War Department for the fiscal year ended June 30, 1900, 40.

72. Ibid., 59.

73. Ibid.

74. Eileen P. Scully, *Bargaining with the State from Afar: American Citizenship in Treaty Port China, 1844–1942* (New York: Columbia University Press, 2001), 5.

75. Annual reports of the War Department for the fiscal year ended June 30, 1900, 64.

76. As Pedro Cabán has written, the U.S. District Court in San Juan that was founded in 1900 through the Foraker Act served to keep U.S. citizens "beyond the reach of the local magistrates." Cabán, *Constructing a Colonial People*, 63. Eileen Scully has shown that the United States established a district court in China in 1906 in an effort to exert greater control over Americans there after a series of lenient decisions by the U.S. Consul threatened U.S.-China relations. Scully has argued

that the district court in China was a form of imperial power but, unlike in Puerto Rico and the Philippines, the power of this court was limited by the establishment of British courts in China. Scully, *Bargaining with the State from Afar*, 7–13.

77. Annual reports of the War Department for the fiscal year ended June 30, 1900, 58.

78. Fernando Picó, "La revolución puertorriqueña de 1898: La necesidad de un nuevo paradigma para entender el 98 puertorriqueño," *Historia y Sociedad* 10 (1998): 7–22.

79. "Los discursos de Mr. Davis," *La Democracia*, May 3, 1900.

80. "El régimen civil," *La Democracia*, May 2, 1900.

81. Ibid.

82. Annual reports of the War Department for the fiscal year ended June 30, 1900, 27.

83. Thompson, *Imperial Archipelago*, 195.

84. Senate Committee on Pacific Islands and Porto Rico, *Temporary Civil Government for Porto Rico*, 56th Cong., 1st Sess. (February 5, 1900), S. Rep. 249: 13.

85. Lanny Thompson has argued that U.S. statutes did not extend automatically to the Philippines. Thompson, *Imperial Archipelago*, 205.

86. L. S. Rowe, *The United States and Porto Rico: With Special Reference to the Problems Arising out of Our Contact with the Spanish-American Civilization* (New York: Longmans, Green, 1904), 152. On Rowe's role in Puerto Rico and the use of political science in imperial administration, see Courtney Johnson, "Understanding the American Empire: Colonialism, Latin Americanism, and Professional Social Science, 1898–1920," in McCoy and Scarno, *Colonial Crucible*, 181.

87. Rowe, *United States and Porto Rico*, 152.

88. An Act to Provide a Government for the Territory of Hawaii (31 Stat., 141, sec. 98), April 30, 1900.

89. William Taft, Secretary of War, to Hon. C. H. Grosvenor of the U.S. House of Representatives, April 5, 1904, Serial Set vol. no. 4676, Session vol. no. 50, 58th Cong., 2nd Sess., H. Doc. 660.

90. Memorandum of Charles E. Magoon, Law Officer, Bureau of Insular Affairs, to the Secretary of War, April 5, 1904, Serial Set vol. no. 4676, Session vol. no. 50, 58th Congress, 2nd Sess., H. Doc. 660.

91. *Huss v. New York and Puerto Rican Steamship Co.* 182 U.S. (1901).

92. Emily Rosenberg, *Financial Missionaries to the World: The Politics and Culture of Dollar Diplomacy, 1900–1930* (Cambridge, MA: Harvard University Press, 1999), 10.

93. Ibid., 11.

94. Ibid., 12.

95. Edwin Walter Kemmerer, *Modern Currency Reforms: A History and Discussion of Recent Currency Reforms in India, Porto Rico, Philippine Islands, Straits Settlements and Mexico* (New York: MacMillan, 1916), 199.

96. Ibid., 183.

97. Senator Morgan, *Congressional Record*, March 30, 1900 (Washington, DC: Government Printing Office, 1900), 3478.

98. Padilla Rivera Lidorio to the Governor of Puerto Rico, May 26, 1900, box 57, folder 10214, AGPR.

99. Governor Davis, *Annual Report for 1900*, 173, quoted in Kemmerer, *Modern Currency Reforms*, 212.

100. Governor Allen, *Annual Report*, May 1, 1901, quoted in Kemmerer, *Modern Currency Reforms*, 212.

101. Kemmerer, *Modern Currency Reforms*, 218.

102. Ibid., 219.

103. *Financial Missionaries to the World*, Rosenberg's survey of dollar diplomacy, includes a useful look at currency reform in Puerto Rico. Focused on situating U.S. financial reform in American cultural and political contexts, she pays less attention to the impact of these reforms on foreign peoples. Although Rosenberg argues that the arrival of the gold standard was only a temporary setback for Puerto Rican workers since wages eventually increased, evidence suggests that the effect on consumer prices increased the cost of living by more than 10 percent. See Rosenberg, *Financial Missionaries*, 14.

104. Davis, *Annual Report for 1900*, 173.

105. Kemmerer, *Modern Currency Reforms*, 220.

106. Ibid.

107. Statement of De Ford and Company, quoted in Kemmerer, *Modern Currency Reforms*, 224.

108. Kemmerer, *Modern Currency Reforms*, 180.

109. R. Oxio to the Governor of Puerto Rico, June 12, 1900, box 57, folder 10214, AGPR.

110. Isidor González, President of the Labor Union of Carolina to the Governor of Puerto Rico, May 7, 1900, box 57, folder 10214, AGPR; Governor of Puerto Rico to Isidor Gonzalez, May 17, 1900, box 57, folder 10214, AGPR.

111. "First Annual Report of Charles Allen, Governor of Porto Rico, 1900–1901," in Center for Puerto Rican Studies, History Task Force, *Sources for the Study of Puerto Rican Migration, 1879–1930* (New York: Research Foundation of the City University of New York, 1982), 14–15; quoted in Carmen Teresa Whalen and Victor Vázques-Hernández, eds., *Puerto Rican Diaspora: Historical Perspectives* (Philadelphia: Temple University Press, 2005), 7.

112. Petition of T. Larrinaga and Twelve Others to the U.S. Congress, February 20, 1900.

113. The Foraker Act, as it was passed in April of 1900, allowed for a temporary tariff on trade with the stipulation that by March 1, 1902, the Legislative Assembly of Puerto Rico and the U.S. president would decide permanently on either a continued tariff or free trade. "El bill Foraker," *La Democracia*, April 12, 1900.

114. Davis, *Annual Report for 1900*, 39.

115. Ibid., 200.

116. Ibid.

117. Ibid., 160.

118. Carmen Raffuci de Garcia suggests that supporters of the tariff were motivated in part by the desire of protectionists to set a precedent for U.S. governance of the Philippines. Carmen Raffuci de Garcia, *El gobierno civil y la Ley Foraker: Antecedentes históricos* (Río Piedras, PR: Editorial Universitaria, Universidad de Puerto Rico, 1981), 65.

119. Davis, *Annual Report for 1900*, 142.

120. Ibid., 142.

121. Thompson, *Imperial Archipelago*, 205.

122. April Merleaux, *Sugar and Civilization: American Empire and the Cultural Politics of Sweetness* (Chapel Hill: University of North Carolina Press, 2015), 32–37.

123. Free trade between Puerto Rico and the United States was not signed into law until July 25, 1901. "Free Trade Granted to the Porto Ricans," *New York Times*, July 26, 1901.

124. Section 3 of the Foraker Act reads: "Whenever the legislative assembly of Porto Rico shall have enacted and put into operation a system of local taxation to meet the necessities of the Government of Porto Rico, by this act established, and shall by resolution duly passed so notify the President, he shall make proclamation hereof, and thereupon all tariff duties on merchandise and articles going into Porto Rico from the United States or coming into the United States from Porto Rico, shall cease and from and after such date all such merchandise and articles shall be

entered at the several ports of entry free of duty." See also "The Porto Rican Tariff: Rumored in Washington That the President Will Remove the Duties in Three Months," *New York Times*, April 18, 1901.

125. "Free Trade with Porto Rico," *New York Times*, July 24, 1901.

126. On how the *Downes* decision reflected interests of the U.S. legislative and executive branches of government, see Sam Erman, "Citizens of Empire: Puerto Rico, Status, and Constitutional Change," *California Law Review* 102, no. 5 (October 2014): 73.

127. "Waited for Free Trade: The Swan, Laden with Porto Rican Sugar, Now in Port," *New York Times*, July 26, 1901.

128. "Porto Rico Declares for Free Trade: Joint Resolution of Assembly Approved by Governor Allen," *New York Times*, July 5, 1901; "Free Trade Granted to the Porto Ricans," *New York Times*, July 26, 1901. Puerto Rico was the only U.S. territory to be granted free trade. See Rogers M. Smith, "The Insular Cases, Differentiated Citizenship, and Territorial Statuses in the Twenty-First Century," in Neuman and Brown-Nagin, *Reconsidering the Insular Cases*, 110; and Bartholomew H. Sparrow, *The Insular Cases and the Emergence of American Empire* (Lawrence: University of Kansas Press, 2006), 226.

129. Hawai'ian sugar was the only other sugar exempt from the tariff. "Porto Rico as a Truck Farm," *New York Times*, August 1, 1901.

130. Ibid.

131. Negrón-Portillo, *Las turbas republicanas*, 45.

132. Go, *American Empire and the Politics of Meaning*, 150–51.

133. Third Annual Report of the Governor of Porto Rico, Covering the Period from July 1, 1902 to June 30, 1903 (Washington, DC: Government Printing Office, 1903), 77.

134. Christopher Schmidt-Nowara, "From Columbus to Ponce de León: Puerto Rican Commemorations between Empires, 1893–1908," in McCoy and Scarano, *Colonial Crucible*, 234.

135. The Insular Courts included forty-six municipal courts, one for each municipality, that heard civil cases, often involving property disputes. There were also forty-eight justice courts, one in each municipality and two in both Ponce and San Juan, where justices of the peace decided on all criminal cases with fines under $250 and sentences less than six months in prison. The most serious civil and criminal cases were heard by one of the five judicial district courts. Under the terms of the Foraker Act, only criminal cases involving a felony conviction could be appealed before the Supreme Court of the island. Third Annual Report of the Governor of Porto Rico, Covering the Period from July 1, 1902 to June 30, 1903, 28–29. On the similarly hybrid nature of the U.S. legal system in the Panama Canal Zone beginning with U.S. occupation in 1904, see Julie Greene, *The Canal Builders: Making America's Empire at the Panama Canal* (New York: Penguin Press, 2009), 272–75.

136. The Bill of Rights was originally conceived as a way of checking the power of the federal government and thereby placating Anti-Federalist fears of an all-powerful central government. But beginning in the 1920s, the Bill of Rights was gradually applied to check the power of states and local governments as well. See Akhil Reed Amar, *The Bill of Rights: Creation and Reconstruction* (New Haven, CT: Yale University Press, 1998), 290.

137. J. W. Burgess, "The Relation of the Constitution of the United States to Newly Acquired Territory," *Political Science Quarterly* 15, no. 3 (September 1900): 390.

138. Ibid., 391.

139. *Downes v. Bidwell*, no. 507, Supreme Court of the United States, 182 U.S. 244. Decided May 27, 1901.

140. Concurring Opinion of Justice White, *Downes v. Bidwell*, 182 U.S. at 341–42.

141. On the doctrine of incorporation, see Christina Duffy Ponsa and Burke Marshall, "Between the Foreign and the Domestic: The Doctrine of Territorial Incorporation, Invented and Reinvented," in Burnett and Marshall, *Foreign in a Domestic Sense*, 1–36.

142. By the terms of the Territorial Clause of the Constitution, Congress ruled with plenary, or near absolute, power over all American territorial acquisitions. Before 1898 such plenary power had always been temporary, however. In a pattern first established by the Northwest Ordinance of 1787, Congress ceded this power once territories became states. The Spanish-Cuban-American War of 1898 marked a break from this practice since the United States acquired Puerto Rico and the Philippines without the expectation of granting them statehood. Thus Congress held plenary power in Puerto Rico indefinitely.

143. Ponsa and Marshall, "Between the Foreign and the Domestic," 12–13.

144. Opinion of Justice Brown, *Downes v. Bidwell*, 182 U.S.

145. Charles Allen, Governor of Porto Rico, *First Annual Report, Governing the Period from May 1, 1900 to May 1, 1901* (Washington, DC: Government Printing Office, 1901), 65.

146. Ibid., 57.

147. Juan R. Torruella, circuit judge, United States Court of Appeals for the First Circuit, has argued that the Supreme Court's decisions in the Insular Cases reflected racial concerns of contemporaneous politics more than "the pursuit of legal doctrine." Juan R. Torruella, "The *Insular Cases*: The Establishment of a Regime of Political Apartheid," *University of Pennsylvania Journal of International Law* 29, no. 2 (Winter 2007): 283–347.

148. Opinion of Justice Brown, *Downes v. Bidwell*, 182 U.S.

149. Simeon E. Baldwin, "The Constitutional Questions Incident to the Acquisition and Government by the United States of Island Territory," *Harvard Law Review* 12 (1899): 415, quoted in Juan R. Torruella, "The Insular Cases: A Declaration of Their Bankruptcy," in Neuman and Brown-Nagin, *Reconsidering the Insular Cases*, 63.

150. Abbot Lawrence Lowell, "The Status of Our New Possessions: A Third View," *Harvard Law Review* 13, no. 3 (1899): 155–76; James Bradley Thayer, "Our New Possessions," *Harvard Law Review* 12, no. 7 (1899): 464–85.

151. Benjamin Allen Coates, *Legalist Empire: International Law and American Foreign Relations in the Early Twentieth Century* (New York: Oxford University Press, 2016), 46–57.

152. Chief Justice Fuller, with support of Justices Harlan, Brewer, and Peckham, wrote the dissenting opinion in the *Downes* case. *Downes v. Bidwell*, 182 U.S. at 347–75 (Fuller, C.J., dissenting). See Pedro A. Malavet, "The Constitution Follows the Flag . . . but Doesn't Quite Catch Up with It": The Story of *Downes v. Bidwell*," in *Race Law Stories*, ed. Rachel F. Moran and Devon W. Carbado (New York: Foundation Press, 2008), 133.

153. *Downes v. Bidwell*, 182 U.S. at 375–91 (Harlan, J., dissenting). See Malavet, "Constitution Follows the Flag," 111–46.

154. Rowe, *United States and Porto Rico*, 94.

155. *Reynolds v. United States*, 98 U.S., 145 (1878); *Callan v. Wilson* 127 U.S., 540 (1887).

156. Rowe, *United States and Porto Rico*, 92–94, 96.

157. Ibid., 96–97.

158. *Our New Possessions: Cuba, Puerto Rico, Hawaii, Philippines* (New York: American Book, 1899), 9; Trumbull White, *Our New Possessions* (Rock Island, IL: L. E. West, 1898), 309.

159. Robert Beisner, *Twelve against Empire: The Anti-Imperialists, 1898–1900* (New York: McGraw Hill, 1968), 17.

160. Quoted in Beisner, *Twelve against Empire*, 81.

161. "PR-EU," *La Democracia*, April 12, 1900.

162. Samuel Gompers, "Imperialism, Its Dangers and Wrongs," *American Federationist* 5, no. 9, November 1898.

163. Richard E. Welch Jr., *Response to Imperialism: The United States and the Philippine-American War, 1899–1902* (Chapel Hill: University of North Carolina Press, 1979), 85.

164. Speech of Mr. Wilson in the U.S. House of Representatives, February 22, 1900, Congressional Record, 56th Cong., 1st Sess. (Washington, DC: Government Printing Office, 1900), Pt. 3:2103.

165. F. Tennyson Neely, *Neely's Panorama of Our New Possessions* (New York: F. Tennyson Neely, 1898), 89.

166. Speech of Senator Albert Beveridge Jr., quoted in Ngai, *Impossible Subjects*, 101; and Thomas Gossett, *Race: The History of an Idea* (New York: Oxford University Press, 1997), 337–38.

167. Welch, *Response to Imperialism*, 87.

2. The Rise of National Status

1. Minutes of a Meeting of the Board of Special Inquiry, Barge Office, Port of New York, April 3, 1900, box 103, folder Sen 56A-F25, RG 46, NAB.

2. "A Puerto Rican Detained: Citizenship Questioned at Barge Office," *New York Times*, April 4, 1900.

3. Minutes of a Meeting of the Board of Special Inquiry, April 3, 1900.

4. Ibid.

5. Minutes of a Meeting of the Board of Special Inquiry, April 3, 1900; "A Puerto Rican Detained: Citizenship Questioned at Barge Office," *New York Times*, April 4, 1900.

6. Secretary Gage to Commissioner of Immigration, Barge Office, New York, April 4, 1900, box 103, folder Sen 56A-F25, RG 46, NAB; "Puerto Rican Allowed to Land," *New York Times*, April 5, 1900.

7. On the architecture of U.S. imperial law, see Sam Erman, "Citizens of Empire"; Erman, "Meanings of Citizenship in the U.S. Empire: Puerto Rico, Isabel González, and the Supreme Court, 1898 to 1905," *Journal of American Ethnic History* 27, no. 4 (Summer 2008): 5–33; Ponsa, "When Statehood Was Autonomy"; Christina Duffy Ponsa, "The Edges of Empire and the Limits of Sovereignty: American Guano Islands," *American Quarterly* 57, no. 3 (September 2005): 779–803; Christina Duffy Ponsa, "Empire and the Transformation of Citizenship," in McCoy and Scarano, *Colonial Crucible*, 332–41; Ponsa and Adriel I. Cepeda Derieux, "Los casos insulares: Doctrina desanexionista," *Revista Jurídica de la Universidad de Puerto Rico* 78, no. 3 (2009): 661. On the legal history of noncitizens under U.S. territorial control, see Guadalupe T. Luna, "On the Complexities of Race: The Treaty of Guadalupe Hidalgo and *Dred Scott v. Sanford*," *University of Miami Law Review* 53, no. 4 (1999): 691; and Pedro A. Malavet, "The Inconvenience of a 'Constitution [That] Follows the Flag . . . but Doesn't Quite Catch Up with It': From *Downes V. Bidwell* to *Boumediene v. Bush*," *Mississippi Law Journal* 80 (2010): 181.

8. In highlighting the role of colonial migrants in contesting imperial law, I build on the work of Mae Ngai and Linda Kerber on the history of migration and citizenship: Ngai, *Impossible Subjects*; and Linda Kerber, "Toward a History of Statelessness in America," *American Quarterly* 57, no. 3 (2005): 727–49. I also build on the legal scholarship of Sam Erman and Christian Duffy Ponsa on the 1904 case of *Gonzales v. Williams*: Erman, "Meanings of Citizenship"; and Ponsa, "'They Say I Am Not an American': The Non-Citizen and the Law of American Empire," *Virginia Journal of International Law* 48, no. 4 (2008): 659–718.

9. Annual Reports of the War Department for the fiscal year ending June 30, 1900, 95.

10. Ibid., 96, 116.

11. Ibid., 99.

12. On the discourse of "fitness for citizenship," see Matthew Frye Jacobson, *Barbarian Virtues: The United States Encounters Foreign Peoples at Home and Abroad, 1876–1917* (New York: Hill and Wang, 2000), 239–41.

13. Gary Gerstle, *American Crucible: Race and Nation in the Twentieth Century* (Princeton, NJ: Princeton University Press, 2001), 4.

14. General Davis, Governor of Puerto Rico, Statement made during the Hearings before the Committee on Pacific Islands and Puerto Rico of the U.S. Senate on Senate Bill 2264, "To Provide a Government for the Island of Puerto Rico, and for other purposes" (Washington, DC: Government Printing Office, 1900), 64, box Y6005, RG 287, NAB.

15. Henry Curtis, Statement made in the Hearings before the Committee on Pacific Islands and Puerto Rico of the U.S. Senate on Senate Bill 2264, "To Provide a Government for the Island of Puerto Rico, and for other purposes" (Washington, DC: Government Printing Office, 1900), 102, box Y6005, RG 287, NAB.

16. See Walter L. Williams, "United States Indian Policy and the Debate over Philippine Annexation: Implications for the Origins of American Imperialism," *Journal of American History* 66, no. 4 (March 1980): 810–31.

17. Annual Reports of the War Department for the Fiscal Year Ending June 30, 1900, 116.

18. Allen, "First Annual Report," in Whalen and Vázques-Hernández, *Puerto Rican Diaspora*, 98.

19. Ibid., 99.

20. Whitelaw Reid, *Problems of Expansion* (New York: Century, 1900), 13–14, 205–9.

21. Gary Okihiro, "Colonial Vision, Racial Visibility: Racializations in Puerto Rico and the Philippines during the Initial Period of U.S. Colonization," in *Racial Transformations: Latinos and Asians Remaking the United States*, ed. Nicholas de Genova (Durham, NC: Duke University Press, 2006), 36. See also Findlay, *Imposing Decency*, 119.

22. Annual Reports of the War Department for the fiscal year ended June 30, 1900, 94; Report on the Census of Porto Rico, 1899 (Washington, DC: Government Printing Office, 1900).

23. Annual Reports of the War Department for the fiscal year ending June 30, 1900, 35.

24. Ibid., 45.

25. Ponsa, '"They Say I Am Not an American,"' 684.

26. Annual Reports of the War Department for the fiscal year ending June 30, 1900, 107.

27. Ponsa, '"They Say I Am Not an American,"' 686–90.

28. *Temporary Civil Government for Porto Rico*, 56th Cong., 1st sess. (February 5, 1900), S. Rep. 249, in Ayala and Bernabe, *Puerto Rico in the American Century*, 21.

29. "Puerto Rico y el Hawaii: Dos criterios del gobierno. Siempre preteridos," *La Democracia*, June 1, 1900; reprinted in Reece B. Bothwell González, comp., *Puerto Rico: Cien años de lucha política* (Río Piedras, PR: Editorial Universitaria, 1979), 4:142.

30. Lucas Amadeo, Statement made in the Hearings before the Committee on Pacific Islands and Puerto Rico of the U.S. Senate on Senate Bill 2264, "To Provide a Government for the Island of Puerto Rico, and for other purposes" (Washington: Government Printing Office, 1900), 128, box Y6005, RG 287, NAB.

31. Ibid., 128.

32. Iguina, *Rituals of Violence*, 111–18.

33. Annual Reports of the War Department for the fiscal year ending June 30, 1900, 110.

34. Abbott Lawrence Lowell, "The Colonial Expansion of the United States," *Atlantic Monthly*, vol. 83, February 1899.

35. Ibid., 152.

36. Ibid.

37. Ibid.

38. Lowell, "Status of Our New Possessions," 155; Rogers M. Smith, "The Bitter Roots of Puerto Rican Citizenship," in Burnett and Marshall, *Foreign in a Domestic Sense*, 376. See also Christina Duffy Ponsa, "United States: American Expansion and Territorial Deannexation," *University of Chicago Law Review* 72, no. 3 (Summer 2005): 797–879. Ponsa observes that the memory of the Civil War weighed heavily in the Supreme Court's decisions in the Insular Cases, which interpreted the meaning of the Foraker Act and affirmed the unincorporated status of Puerto Rico.

39. On the origins of the national passport, see Radhika Viyas Mongia, "Race, Nationality, Mobility: A History of the Passport," in Burton, *After the Imperial Turn*, 196–216.

40. Pasaportes 1886–1889, Records of the Spanish Government of Puerto Rico, Political and Civil Affairs, box 161, RG 186, AGPR.

41. Virginia E. Sánchez Korrol, *From Colonia to Community: The History of Puerto Ricans in New York City, 1917–1948* (Westport, CT: Greenwood Press, 1983), 3–14.

42. *Chronicle*, University of Michigan, October 27, 1877.

43. Mariano Negrón-Portillo, "Puerto Rico: Surviving Colonialism and Nationalism," in *Puerto Rican Jam: Rethinking Colonialism and Nationalism*, ed. Frances Negron-Muntaner and Ramón Grosfoguel (Minneapolis: University of Minnesota Press, 2008), 55n9.

44. Ibid., 54.

45. Scholarship on Puerto Rican migration to the United States has largely focused on the post–World War II period. See esp. Carmen Teresa Whalen, *From Puerto Rico to Philadelphia: Puerto Rican Workers and Postwar Economies* (Philadelphia: Temple University Press, 2001); Julio Morales, *Puerto Rican Poverty and Migration: We Just Had to Try Elsewhere* (New York: Praeger, 1986); and Ramón Grosfoguel, *Colonial Subjects: Puerto Ricans in a Global Perspective* (Berkeley: University of California Press, 2003). *Labor Migration under Capitalism* offers a useful starting point for studying Puerto Rican migration. Centro de Estudios Puertorriqueños, City University of New York, *Labor Migration under Capitalism: The Puerto Rican Experience* (New York: Monthly Review Press, 1979), 93–164.

46. On early labor migrations from the island, see Igualdad Iglesias de Pagan, *El obrerismo en Puerto Rico, época de Santiago Iglesias, 1896–1905* (Palacia de Castilla: Editorial Juan Ponce de León, 1973).

47. Puerto Rican scholars Carmelo Rosario Natal, Raquel Rosario Rivera, and Iris López have begun to examine the early twentieth-century experience of migrants to Hawai'i. I build on this work by situating this experience in the larger context of U.S. empire, where employers, colonial officials, and migrants all grappled with the place of colonial subjects in the American republic. See Carmelo Rosario Natal, *Éxodo Puertorriqueño: Las emigraciones al Caribe y Hawaii, 1900–1910*, 4th ed. (Río Piedras, PR: Editoria Edil, 2001); Raquel Rosario Rivera, "Pasaporte a la angustia: Sufrimientos de los emigrados y familiares con destino a Hawaii," *Horizonte: Revista de la Pontificia Universidad Católica de Puerto Rico* 44, no. 87 (October 2002), 211–43; and Iris López, "Borinkis and Chop Suey: Puerto Rican Identity in Hawai'i, 1900 to 2000," in *The Puerto Rican Diaspora: Historical Perspectives*, ed. Carmen Teresa Whalen and Víctor Vázquez-Hernández (Philadelphia: Temple University Press, 2005), 43–49. See also JoAnna Poblete, *Islanders in the Empire: Filipino and Puerto Rican Laborers in Hawai'i* (Urbana: University of Illinois Press, 2014). For the earliest scholarly treatment of this subject, see Clarence Senior, *Puerto Rican Emigration* (Río Piedras: University of Puerto Rico, 1947).

48. Spreckels Sugar Company was one of the major Hawai'i-based sugar companies in the early twentieth century, shipping raw sugar to California for refining. Spreckels and other Hawai'ian sugar companies did not recruit Filipino contract laborers until 1906.

49. "Puertorriqueños que van a Hawaii," *La Correspondencia*, December 17, 1900.

50. "Por que no debe irse al Hawaii," *La Correspondencia*, August 9, 1900, 3.

51. Gunther Peck, *Reinventing Free Labor: Padrones and Immigrant Workers in the North American West, 1880–1930* (Cambridge: Cambridge University Press, 2000), 101–3.

52. Hawai'i was not made a state until 1959, when President Eisenhower signed into law the Admission Act. On June 27, 1959, Hawai'ians voted in a plebiscite 17 to 1 in favor of accepting statehood.

53. Padrones and contract laborers did enter the U.S. Southwest illegally in the early twentieth century. See Peck, *Reinventing Free Labor*.

54. The Hawai'ian Sugar Planters Association was founded in 1895 with the aim of consolidating the power of sugar planters throughout the islands. Chas. Hortzell, Secretary of Porto Rico, to Secretary of the Interior, Washington, DC, April 9, 1902, box 108, folder Sen 57A-F21, RG 46, NAB.

55. Victoriana Sánchez to Governor of Puerto Rico, October 1, 1901, box 17, folder 1421, AGPR.

56. Bernardino Milán of Sábana Grande to Governor of Puerto Rico, September 3, 1901, box 17, folder 1421, AGPR.

57. Assistant Secretary of Porto Rico to Miguel Serrano of Ponce, June 14, 1901, box 17, folder 1421, AGPR.

58. Rodulfo Medina and Manuel Serrano, of Yauco, Puerto Rico, to Governor of Puerto Rico, March 9, 1901, box 17, folder 1421, AGPR.

59. Mayor of Aguadilla to the Governor of Puerto Rico, August 20, 1901, box 17, folder 1421, AGPR.

60. Mayor of Ponce to Governor of Puerto Rico, March 4, 1901, box 17, folder 1421, AGPR.

61. Santiago Iglesias Pantín, *La Miseria*, April 18, 1901, reprinted in Igualdad Iglesias de Pagán, *El obrerismo en Puerto Rico*, 1–398.

62. Ibid.

63. Consul of France, San Juan, Puerto Rico to Governor of Puerto Rico, March 4, 1903, box 17, folder 1421 III, AGPR.

64. Mayor of Ponce to Governor of Puerto Rico, March 4, 1901, box 17, folder 1421, AGPR.

65. Pascual Jordan of Cabo Rojo to Governor of Puerto Rico, January 11, 1902, box 17, folder 1421, AGPR.

66. Here, I build on the work of historian Rosa Carrasquillo, who has shown that the rural poor in Puerto Rico made claims to "marginal citizenship" under Spanish rule by evading oppressive work contracts. Puerto Rican petitions for citizenship and labor rights under U.S. rule, I argue, had their roots in this earlier political culture. See Rosa E. Carrasquillo, *Our Landless Patria: Marginal Citizenship and Race in Caguas, Puerto Rico, 1880–1910* (Lincoln: University of Nebraska Press, 2006).

67. Petition Submitted by Puerto Ricans in the Hawaiian Plantation of Paulilo to the Governor of Puerto Rico, July 14, 1902, box 108, folder Sen 57A-F21, RG 46, NAB.

68. Ibid.

69. Frank Foster, "Sidelights on the Shorter Workday Demand," *American Federationist* 7, no. 11, November 1900, quoted in Lawrence Glickman, "Inventing the 'American Standard of Living': Gender, Race, and Working-Class Identity, 1880–1925," *Labor History* 24, nos. 2–3 (March 1, 1993): 228.

70. Chas. Hortzell to Secretary of the Interior, Washington, DC, April 9, 1902, box 108, folder Sen 57A-F21, RG 46, NAB.

71. Thos. Ryan to Governor of Hawaii, July 26, 1902, box 108, folder Sen 57A-F21, RG 46, NAB; Sanford Dole, Governor of Hawaii, to Secretary of the Interior, October 24, 1902, box 108, folder Sen 57A-F21, RG 46, NAB.

72. Hawes Report on the Paulilo Plantation, October 16, 1902, box 108, folder Sen 57A-F21, RG 46, NAB (hereafter cited as Hawes Report); Sanford Dole to A. G. Hawes, Jr. Relating to Investigations of Porto Rican Complaints at Paulilo, October 13, 1902, box 108, folder Sen 57A-F21, RG 46, NAB.

73. See, for example, the testimony of Dolores Rivera and Marcial Torres, Hawes Report, 1902.

74. Hawes Report, 1902.

75. Ibid.

76. Ibid.

77. For additional claims of low pay relative to other Hawai'ian sugar plantations, see the testimony of Nicolas Ortiz and Lareto Santiago, Hawes Report, 1902.

78. Hawes Report, 1902.

79. Ibid.

80. Hawes Report, 1902. Hawes completed his report in Honolulu on October 20, 1902, after spending less than two days on the sugar plantations.

81. Hawaiian Sugar Planters Association, Honolulu, Hawaii, to Governor of Puerto Rico, August 8, 1902, box 17, folder 1421, AGPR.

82. Ibid.

83. Ibid.

84. Quinta Medina to the Governor of Puerto Rico, September 8, 1902, box 17, folder 1421, AGPR.

85. Cirilo Betancourt and Twelve Other Members of the Free Federation of Workingmen to Governor of Puerto Rico, n.d., box 17, folder 1421, AGPR.

86. La Logia Modestia of Ponce, Puerto Rico, to Governor of Puerto Rico, April 1, 1902, box 17, folder 1421, AGPR.

87. William O. Smith, Secretary of the Hawaiian Sugar Planters' Association to Hon. H. E. Cooper, Governor of Hawaii, May 22, 1902, box 17, folder 1421, AGPR. The Smith Report begins with an investigation of the Koloa Plantation.

88. The trope of outside agitators has long been used by critics of migrant laborers' unionization efforts. See James Grossman, *Land of Hope: Chicago, Black Southerners and the Great Migration* (Chicago: University of Chicago Press, 1991).

89. Ibid.

90. Ibid.

91. Report of A. M. Brown, Esq., High Sheriff, Hilo, Hawaii Island, June 27, 1902, box 17, folder 1421, AGPR.

92. Lucia Cruz of Ponce to Governor of Puerto Rico, December 30, 1901, box 17, folder 1421, AGPR.

93. Miguel Serrano of Ponce to Governor of Puerto Rico, May 22, 1901, box 17, folder 1421, AGPR.

94. Ibid.

95. "Well Treated Over There," *San Juan News*, May 8, 1902.

96. J. C. Bills, Second Annual Report of the Bureau of Labor to Legislature of Porto Rico (San Juan, PR: Bureau of Supplies, Printing and Transportation, February 10, 1914), 99.

97. Ibid.

98. Federico Degetau to Treasury Secretary, September 16, 1903, box 123, folder 51637/1b, RG 85, NAB.

99. Federico Degetau to Treasury Secretary, September 16, 1903. For more on Degetau's legal perspective, see Ponsa, "'They Say I Am Not an American,'" 686–90; and Erman, "Citizens of Empire," 1181–1242.

100. Minutes of Board of Special Inquiry, Ellis Island, August 4, 1902, box 3299, folder 18848, RG 267, NAB.

101. Ibid.

102. Minutes of Board of Special Inquiry, Ellis Island, August 5, 1902, box 3299, folder 18848, RG 267, NAB. Domingo Collazo's wife was an aunt of Isabel González.

103. Ibid.

104. Minutes of Board of Special Inquiry, Ellis Island, August 7, 1902, box 3299, folder 18848, RG 267, NAB.

105. Petition of Domingo Collazo to the U.S. Circuit Court for the Southern District of New York, August 18, 1902, box 3299, folder 18848, RG 267, NAB.

106. Legal Brief of William B. Anderson, Counsel for William Williams, U.S. Commissioner of Immigration at the Port of New York, September 17, 1902, U.S. Circuit Court for the Southern District of New York, box 45, folder 51637/1, RG 85, NAB.

107. U.S. Circuit Court Decision in the Matter of Isabel González, October 7, 1902, box 3299, folder 18848, RG 267, NAB.

108. Quoted in the Order of the Supreme Court to the Circuit Court for the Southern District of New York, January 4, 1904, box 3299, folder 18848, RG 267, NAB.

109. Letter to the Commissioner of Immigration, Ellis Island, October 9, 1902, box 45, folder 51637/1, RG 85, NAB.

110. "In the matter of the Petition of Isabel González for a Writ of Habeas Corpus" to the U.S. Supreme Court, February 4, 1903, box 3299, folder 18848, RG 267, NAB. See also Assignment of Errors, In the Matter of the Petition of Isabel González for a Writ of Habeas Corpus, January 15, 1903, box 3299, folder 18848, RG 267, NAB.

111. Motion to Advance Hearing in the Supreme Court, March 11, 1903, submitted by the Courdert Brothers, attorneys for Isabel González, box 3299, folder 18848, RG 267, NAB.

112. U.S. Attorney General to Mr. Cortelyou, Washington, DC, 1903, box 123, folder 51637/1b, RG 85, NAB.

113. Amicus Brief of Federico Degetau, 1903, box 3299, folder 18848, RG 267, NAB. See also Degetau's protest against the detention of other Puerto Ricans on Ellis Island, including Mary Coy: Protest of Puerto Rican Resident Commissioner, Federico Degetau, September 16, 1903, box 123, folder 51637/1b, RG 85, NAB.

114. "Porto Ricans Not Aliens," *New York Times*, January 5, 1904.

115. On national status, see Dorothy Fujita-Rony, *American Workers, Colonial Power: Philippine Seattle and the Transpacific West, 1919–1941* (Berkeley: University of California Press, 2003); and Ngai, *Impossible Subjects*, 100.

116. Sam Erman has shown how González recognized the limits of her legal victory. Erman, "Meanings of Citizenship."

117. *Nation* 78, no. 2010, January 7, 1904.

118. George B. Cortelyou, Secretary of the Bureau of Immigration, to William Dillingham, April 19, 1904, box 123, folder 51637/1b, RG 85, NAB.

119. Ibid.

120. The González name was misspelled in the official Supreme Court ruling *Gonzales v. Williams* (1904). As much as possible, in this book I have presented the spelling of Spanish names

as I found them in the original archival documents. U.S. colonial documents often misspelled Spanish names and omitted accents.

121. Eugenia Arbona, "Puerto Ricans in St. Louis Requesting Aid," January 11, 1905, box 258, folder 2437, AGPR.

122. New York and Porto Rico Steamship Company, "Letter to the Governor of Porto Rico," January 30, 1905, box 258, folder 2437, AGPR; Arbona, "Puerto Ricans in St. Louis Requesting Aid," 1905.

123. Arbona, "Puerto Ricans in St. Louis Requesting Aid," 1905.

124. Glickman, "Inventing the 'American Standard of Living,'" 231–34.

125. On reading migrant narratives against the grain, see Eileen Findlay, "Portable Roots: Latin New Yorker Community Building and the Meanings of Women's Return Migration in San Juan, Puerto Rico, 1960–2000," *Caribbean Studies* 37, no. 2 (July–December 2009): 3–43. Findlay argues that narratives are "meaning-making activities, a place in which story-tellers spin particular interpretations of past events, in light of their present" (8).

126. N. C. Dauron, "Letter in Support of Puerto Ricans in St. Louis," January 19, 1905, box 258, folder 2437, AGPR.

127. N. C. Dauron, "Letter in Support of Puerto Ricans in St. Louis," 1905. See also the letters of support of Mrs. P. J. Toomey, Miss Mary F. Mulcahy, Miss Mary Ames of Queen's Daughters, a Catholic charity in St. Louis; and Queen's Daughters, "Letter in Support of Puerto Ricans in St. Louis," January 30, 1905; all in box 258, folder 2437, AGPR.

128. María Casalduo, "My Sister Abandoned in St. Louis," January 21, 1905, box 258, folder 2437, AGPR.

129. María Casalduo, "My Sister Abandoned in St. Louis," 1905.

130. Arturo Córdova, "Letter in Support of Puerto Ricans in St. Louis," January 20, 1905, box 258, folder 2437, AGPR.

131. Matos Bernier, "Commission Appointed to Investigate Puerto Ricans in Saint Louis," January 21, 1905, box 258, folder 2437, AGPR.

132. St. Louis Cordage Co., "Letter to the Governor of Puerto Rico," February 2, 1905, box 258, folder 2437, AGPR.

133. Ibid.

134. Ibid.

135. Degetau to Governor Hunt, May 27, 1904, and February 10, 1905, box 17, folder 1276, AGPR.

136. See Supreme Court Justice Bradley's dissent in the Slaughterhouse Cases, 83 U.S. 36, 21 L. Ed. 394 (1873).

137. On the post–Civil War labor market, see Jacqueline Jones, *American Work: Four Centuries of Black and White Labor* (New York: W. W. Norton, 1998); Katharine Bjork, "Incorporating an Empire: From Deregulating Labor to Regulating Leisure in Cuba, Puerto Rico, and the Philippines, 1898–1909" (PhD diss., University of Chicago, 1998), 24–68; and Sven Beckert, "From Tuskegee to Togo: The Problem of Freedom in the Empire of Cotton," *Journal of American History* 92, no. 2 (2005): 498–526.

3. Labor Networks

1. Papers of Santiago Iglesias, quoted in Clarence Senior, *Santiago Iglesias: Labor Crusader* (Hato Rey, PR: Inter American University Press, 1972), 23.

2. Santiago Iglesias helped found early labor unions on the island after his arrival in San Juan in 1896. Córdova, *Resident Commissioner Santiago Iglesias*, 47. Puerto Ricans founded the first

labor federation on the island just after the U.S. takeover in 1898, but because of conflicts among different labor leaders, the FLT did not emerge as the most powerful labor union until 1905. Findlay, *Imposing Decency*, 138.

3. Gompers coined the phrase "pure and simple" in 1893 to distinguish the AFL from Socialists. Julie Greene, *Pure and Simple Politics: The American Federation of Labor and Political Activism, 1881–1917* (Cambridge: Cambridge University Press, 1998), 2.

4. On the AFL's disregard for Mexican immigrant workers in the Southwest in the period before 1916, see Peck, *Reinventing Free Labor*, 209. Peck notes that "when Samuel Gompers made a trip to Mexico City in 1916 and concluded that Mexican workers should be brought into his organization, El Paso union officials stubbornly refused to make any such efforts."

5. Several important studies of Puerto Rican labor history have situated the AFL's support of workers on the island within Puerto Rican history. In privileging the island context, these studies have treated the period of AFL involvement in isolation from developing strains of nativist ideology within U.S. mainland labor organizations. According to this view, the AFL's campaign in Puerto Rico was a simple act of inclusion. For an example of work that focuses on the island context in isolation from the mainland, see Carlos Sanabria, "The Puerto Rican Organized Workers' Movement and the AFL, 1901–1934" (PhD diss., City University of New York, 2000), 192. Similarly, Arturo Morales Carrión has argued that Gompers came to support the AFL's campaign on the island out of "warm feelings for the inhabitants." Arturo Morales Carrión, *Puerto Rico: A Political and Cultural History* (New York: W. W. Norton, 1983), 178. Joseph Bedford has also argued that "Gompers seemed genuinely moved by what he had seen of labor conditions in Puerto Rico." Joseph Bedford, "Samuel Gompers and the Caribbean: The AFL, Cuba, and Puerto Rico, 1898–1906," *Labor's Heritage* 6, no. 4 (1995): 17, George Meany Memorial Archives, National Labor College, Silver Spring, MD. Historian Ángel G. Quintero Rivera has taken exception to this line of argument, hypothesizing that because U.S. colonial law allowed Puerto Ricans unrestricted entrance to the mainland, the AFL was interested in organizing on the island as a way of mitigating the flow of laborers to the mainland. See Gervasio L. García and A. G. Quintero Rivera, *Desafío y solidaridad: Breve historia del movimiento obrero puertorriqueño* (Río Piedras, PR: Ediciones Huracán, 1982), 37. Rivera also posits this as a hypothesis in a personal interview with historian Miles Galvin, "Personal interview, Angel G. Quintero Rivera, January 25, 1972," quoted in Galvin, *Organized Labor Movement*, 56. I build on this work by showing how the AFL's mainland concerns about immigration also shaped its involvement in Puerto Rico.

6. Daniel E. Bender and Jana K. Lipman, *Making the Empire Work: Labor and United States Imperialism* (New York: New York University Press, 2015), 14–15.

7. New scholarship has called for drawing together the study of labor, migration, and empire. Daniel Bender and Jana Lipman have argued that "U.S. immigration history needs to wrestle with histories of U.S. empire, and in the process, help integrate the histories of empire, labor, migration, indigeneity, and foreign relations." See Bender and Lipman, *Making the Empire Work*, 18; Leon Fink, ed., *Workers across the Americas: The Transnational Turn in Labor History* (New York: Oxford University Press, 2011); and Julie Greene, "Builders of Empire: Rewriting the Labor and Working-Class History of Anglo-American Global Power," *Labor: Studies in Working-Class History of the Americas* 13, nos. 3–4 (2016): 1–10. Earlier historians, including some nationalists and independistas, showed little interest in such linkages and excoriated Iglesias for leading the rank and file of the labor movement away from the nationalist project. See Olmeda, *Los movimientos independistas*, 30.

8. While Jorge Cruz and other Puerto Ricans migrated to the United States as contract laborers in the years immediately following the U.S. takeover of the island, migration picked up dramatically after the granting of U.S. citizenship in 1917. New York became the primary

destination for migrants. By 1920, 7,719 Puerto Ricans lived in New York, 1,667 of whom were classified by the U.S. census as black. The 1920s saw a dramatic rise in Puerto Rican migration, with some 38,000 migrating to New York. U.S. Bureau of the Census, *Fourteenth Census of the United States*, vol. 2, Population, 1920, 630, 635, 640; U.S. Bureau of the Census, *Fifteenth Census of the United States*, vol. 2, Population, 1930, 157; Sánchez Korrol, *From Colonia to Community*. In the years after World War II, migration to New York averaged 40,000 each year. As anthropologist Philippe Bourgois has written, the Puerto Rican migration became one of the largest waves of immigration in modern U.S. history. Philippe Bourgois, *In Search of Respect: Selling Crack in El Barrio* (Cambridge: Cambridge University Press, 2003), 51.

9. See Paul Kramer, "Imperial Openings: Civilization, Exemption, and the Geopolitics of Mobility in the History of Chinese Exclusion, 1868–1910," *Journal of the Gilded Age and Progressive Era* 14, no. 3 (2015): 317–47. Kramer argues that "imperial histories of migration give mobility not just to migrants, but to states and the forces of capital" in "Empire against Exclusion in Early 20th Century Trans-Pacific History," *Nanzan Review of American Studies* 33 (2011): 15.

10. Findlay, *Imposing Decency*, 139.

11. Dionicio Nodín Valdés, *Organized Agriculture and the Labor Movement before the UFW: Puerto Rico, Hawai'i, California* (Austin: University of Texas Press, 2011), 43.

12. Senior, *Santiago Iglesias*, 22.

13. On the currency crisis, see chapter 1. Puerto Rican pesos were exchanged for U.S. dollars at a rate of 1 peso (Puerto Rican) to $.60 (U.S.) as a result of the 1900 Foraker Act. Kemmerer, *Modern Currency Reforms*, 199; Padilla Rivera Lidorio to the Governor of Puerto Rico, May 26, 1900, box 57, folder 10214, AGPR.

14. Santiago Iglesias Pantín, *Luchas emancipadoras: Crónicas de Puerto Rico* (San Juan, PR: n.p., 1958), 174. On the history of the Insular Police under U.S. rule, see Kevin Santiago-Valles, "American Penal Forms and Colonial Spanish Custodial-Regulatory Practices in Fin de Siècle Puerto Rico," in McCoy and Scarano, *Colonial Crucible*, 94.

15. Samuel Gompers, *Seventy Years of Life and Labor: An Autobiography* (New York: E. P. Dutton, 1925), 2:70.

16. Córdova, *Resident Commissioner*, 54.

17. See Iglesias Pantín, *Luchas emancipadoras*, 249: "Iglesias y otros trabajadores fueron sentenciados a sufrir prisión por términos distintos bajo el fundamento de que habían conspirado para aumentar los salarios y mejorar las condiciones de vida."

18. David Montgomery, "Workers' Movements in the United States Confront Imperialism: The Progressive Era Experience," *Journal of the Gilded Age and Progressive Era* 7, no. 1 (January 2008): 22.

19. Iglesias was arrested along with seven other workers for organizing a strike against being paid in Spanish silver, the currency that had been depreciated in the 1900 change in currency, known as the *canje*. Iglesias was sentenced under Spanish law to a prison term of four years, three months, and one day for the crime of "conspiracy to raise the price of labor." See "The Conspiracy to Raise the Price of Labor," *American Federationist* 9, no. 1 (January 1902); and Córdova, *Resident Commissioner*, 97.

20. The Clayton Antitrust Act of 1914 exempted unions from the 1890 Sherman Antitrust Act.

21. Samuel Gompers to Governor Hunt, Puerto Rico, December, 1901, published in *American Federationist* 9, no. 2 (February 1902).

22. Editorial, *New York Evening Post*, quoted in Samuel Gompers to Governor Hunt, Puerto Rico, December 1901, *American Federationist* 9, no. 2 (February1902).

23. See "Progress in Porto Rico," Proceedings of the AFL Annual Conventions, 1902, 15. At its annual convention in 1901, the AFL declared that American workers' "sense of justice had been outraged by the arrest of the representative of the AFL and his fellow workers . . . for endeavoring

to increase wages and secure better conditions." See AFL Annual Convention Records, 1901, 230, George Meany Memorial AFL-CIO Archive, Special Collections and University Archives, University of Maryland Libraries (hereafter cited as AFL-CIO Archive).

24. AFL Annual Convention Records, 1902, 15, AFL-CIO Archive.

25. "Progress in Porto Rico," Proceedings of the AFL Annual Conventions, 1902, 15, AFL-CIO Archive.

26. Bernard Mandel, *Samuel Gompers: A Biography* (Yellow Springs, OH: Antioch Press, 1963), 9.

27. Ibid., 14.

28. Ibid., 17–19.

29. Gompers, *Seventy Years of Life and Labor*, 70.

30. Samuel Gompers, "Imperialism, Its Dangers and Wrongs," *American Federationist* 5, no. 9 (November 1898).

31. "Puerto Rican Detained," *Nation* 70, April 12, 1900.

32. Ibid.

33. Mandel, *Samuel Gompers*, 332.

34. Hearing on Immigration Bill, House Committee on Immigration and Naturalization, U.S. House of Representatives (Washington, DC: Government Printing Office, 1910), box 1041, folder 53072/2A, RG 85, NAB.

35. Ibid.

36. Ibid.

37. Quoted in John Higham, *Strangers in the Land: Patterns of American Nativism, 1865–1925* (New York: Atheneum, 1978), 71–72.

38. Edward F. McSweeney, Assistant U.S. Commissioner of Immigration, at the Port of New York, "Problems of Immigration," *American Federationist* 9, no. 1 (January 1902).

39. "Why He Came to Porto Rico," *American Federationist* 11, no. 2 (February 22, 1904); Jacobson, *Barbarian Virtues*, 85.

40. John Commons, *Races and Immigrants in America* (New York: MacMillan, 1907), 151.

41. Samuel Gompers, "An Address before a Meeting of the Washington, D.C., Central Labor Union," March 24, 1904, reprinted in *The Samuel Gompers Papers* 6, ed. Peter Albert (Urbana: University of Illinois Press, 1997), 245–258.

42. Ngai, *Impossible Subjects*, 116.

43. Thompson, *Imperial Archipelago*, 30.

44. Ibid., 37.

45. Puerto Rican labor organizers first contacted the AFL in 1900 when they requested assistance in securing freedom of assembly. The AFL subsequently passed resolutions calling for an investigation of the island in 1901, 1902, and 1903. See American Federation of Labor, *American Federation of Labor: History, Encyclopedia, Reference Book; Guide to AFL Convention Records* (Washington, DC: n.p., 1919).

46. Gompers left New York on February 14, 1904. Samuel Gompers, "President Gompers in Porto Rico," February 15, 1904, Written aboard the S.S. *Coamo*, published in the *American Federationist* 11, no. 4 (April 1904).

47. Ibid.

48. "Why He Came to Porto Rico," *American Federationist* 11, no. 2 (February 22, 1904).

49. Samuel Gompers, "In Porto Rico," *American Federationist* 11, no. 5 (May 1904).

50. Ibid.

51. Ibid.

52. On Gompers and the wider politics of the AFL in this period, see Greene, *Pure and Simple Politics*.

53. Gompers, "In Porto Rico," *American Federationist* 11, no. 5 (May 1904).

54. Ibid.

55. Samuel Gompers, "President Gompers in Porto Rico, February 21, 1904," *American Federationist* 11, no. 4 (April 1904).

56. Gompers, "Address before a Meeting of the Washington, D.C., Central Labor Union," March 24, 1904.

57. Gompers, "President Gompers in Porto Rico, February 21, 1904."

58. Samuel Gompers, "Address before Federacion Regional, February 22, 1904," published in *American Federationist* 11, no. 4 (April 1904).

59. Gompers, "Address before a Meeting of the Washington, D.C., Central Labor Union," March 24, 1904.

60. Gompers, "Address before Federacion Regional," February 22, 1904.

61. African Americans who migrated north in the years before World War I often worked in agriculture rather than industry. See Cindy Hahamovitch, *The Fruits of Their Labor: Atlantic Coast Farmworkers and the Making of Migrant Poverty, 1870–1945* (Chapel Hill: University of North Carolina Press, 1997), 35.

62. "Trade Union Attitude toward Colored Workers," *American Federationist* 8, no. 4 (April 1901).

63. Samuel Gompers, "The Negro in the AF of L," editorial, *American Federationist* 18, no. 1 (January 1911).

64. Bender and Lipman, *Making the Empire Work*, 18. See also Marilyn Lake and Henry Reynolds, *Drawing the Global Colour Line: White Men's Countries and the International Challenge of Racial Equality* (Cambridge: Cambridge University Press, 2008).

65. Samuel Gompers, "Extract from Address on Porto Rico Delivered at the Masonic Temple," April 13, c. 1904, *American Federationist*, n.d.

66. Statement of Santiago Iglesias, *AFL Convention Records*, 1904, 21–170.

67. Ibid.

68. Ibid.

69. Ayala and Bernabe, *Puerto Rico in the American Century*, 35–39.

70. Statement of Mr. William Willoughby, Treasurer of Porto Rico, quoted in Samuel Gompers, "Extract from Address on Porto Rico Delivered at the Masonic Temple," April 13, c. 1904.

71. Statement of Samuel Gompers, quoted in Samuel Gompers "Extract from Address on Porto Rico Delivered at the Masonic Temple," April 13, c. 1904.

72. President Taft to Samuel Gompers, October 12, 1905, quoted in Samuel Gompers, "Porto Rican Labor Situation," *American Federationist* 12, no. 12 (December 1905).

73. Gompers, "Porto Rican Labor Situation," *American Federationist* 12, no. 12 (December 1905).

74. Ibid. On subsequent efforts to employ Puerto Ricans in the Panama Canal Zone, see Greene, *Canal Builders*, 67.

75. Greene, *Canal Builders*, 88–92.

76. Gompers, "Porto Rican Labor Situation," *American Federationist* 12, no. 12 (December 1905).

77. Santiago Iglesias, "Strike of Agricultural Laborers in Porto Rico," *American Federationist* 12, no. 16 (June 1905): 380–81.

78. Ibid.

79. Ayala and Bernabe, *Puerto Rico in the American Century*, 63.

80. This strike came on the heels of a successful strike earlier that year. In January 1905, more than 5,000 sugarcane workers along the northern coast walked out in protest of their low wages. By February 13, the sugar plantation owners agreed to increase the wage range from

30 to 62 centavos for a twelve- to fourteen-hour workday to 50 to 75 centavos a day. "San Juan, Porto Rico, April 24, 1905," *Washington Star*, May 7, 1905, excerpted in *Samuel Gompers Papers* 6, 423–429.

81. Ibid.

82. Ibid.

83. Ibid.

84. Santiago Iglesias, "Strike of Agricultural Laborers in Porto Rico," *American Federationist* 12, no. 16 (June 1905); "El Meeting de Ayer," *El Águila*, April 17, 1905.

85. "An Excerpt from an Article in the *Washington Star*," May 7, 1905, in *Samuel Gompers Papers* 6, 423–29.

86. Ibid.

87. Greene, *Canal Builders*, 92.

88. "San Juan, Porto Rico, April 24, 1905," *Washington Star*, May 7, 1905.

89. Santiago Iglesias reported on May 29, 1905, that no cane fires had been set by striking sugar workers. Governor Winthrop contested this claim, stating that various fires had indeed been set. See "San Juan, Porto Rico, April 24, 1905," *Washington Star*, May 7, 1905.

90. Ibid.

91. "An Excerpt from an Article in the *Washington Star*," May 7, 1905, in *Samuel Gompers Papers* 6, 423–29.

92. "General Strike," *El Águila*, November 23, 1905.

93. Santiago Iglesias, "About the Strike," *El Águila*, November 28, 1905.

94. For important new work showing the agency of agricultural workers, particularly those in the tobacco sector, see Teresita A. Levy, *Puerto Ricans in the Empire: Tobacco Growers and U.S. Colonialism* (New Brunswick, NJ: Rutgers University Press, 2015), 64–71.

95. "Sobre el Café," *El Águila*, April 27, 1905.

96. "What Brazil Gets: Deal against Uncle Sam," *El Águila*, October 24, 1905.

97. "Mr. Larrinaga Waxes Enthusiastic," *El Águila*, October 25, 1905.

98. Proceedings of the AFL Conventions, AFL Convention of 1904, 183, AFL-CIO Archive.

99. "Boycott en Puerto Rico," *El Águila*, March 26, 1906.

100. "Workingmen Don't Want to Strike but May Have to," *El Águila*, September 10, 1905; Samuel Gompers to Santiago Iglesias, August 4, 1905, in *Samuel Gompers Papers* 6, 470–71.

101. Samuel Gompers to Santiago Iglesias, August 4, 1905, in *Samuel Gompers Papers* 6, 470–71.

102. "Strike Is On," *El Águila*, September 22, 1905.

103. "The Failure: Labor Strike Amounts to Nothing and Is Peaceful," *El Águila*, September 23, 1905.

104. Petition of the Women's Protective Local of San Juan to the U.S. House of Representatives, February 24, 1912, box 626, folder HR 62A-H13.1, RG 233, NAB.

105. San Juan Typographical Union of San Juan, February 23, 1912; Free Federation of Workingmen of Porto Rico, February 25, 1912; Painters, Decorators and Paperhangers of San Juan, February 23, 1912; Bricklayers Local of San Juan, February 23, 1912; Journeyman Barber's Local Union of San Juan, February 23, 1912; Carpenters and Joiners Local of San Juan, February 24, 1912; Cigarmakers of Caguas, February 29, 1912; United Brotherhood of Carpenters and Joiners of Arecibo, February 29, 1912; Hod carriers of Arecibo, February 29, 1912; International Longshoremen's Association of Arecibo, February 29, 1912; United Brotherhood of Carpenters and Joiners Union of Juncos, March 2, 1912; Boot and Shoe Workers Union of Arecibo, February 29, 1912; Agricolas Local Union of Juncos, February 28, 1912; Bricklayers Local of Arecibo, February 29, 1912; Tobacco Strippers' Local of Juncos, February 27, 1912; Bakers Local Union of San German, March 11, 1912; Carpenters and Joiners of Puerta de Tierra, February 25, 1912; Bakers and Confectionary Workers of Juncos, February 27, 1912; Cigarmakers Local of Juncos,

February 25, 1912; Central Labor Union of Arecibo, February 29, 1912; Central Labor Union of San Juan, February 25, 1912; all in box 626, folder HR 62A-H13.1, RG 233, NAB.

106. Santiago Iglesias to President Taft, May 11, 1910, box 626, folder HR 62A-H13.1, RG 233, NAB.

107. Though the Puerto Rican Assembly passed a bill in March of 1912 to create its own Bureau of Labor in an attempt to preempt efforts in Washington, workers viewed it as illegitimate. The working-class newspaper *Unión Obrera*, for example, decried the bureau, stating the need for a bureau that would "treat laborers like people, and not caciques, who believe laborers to be inferior beings." Echoing the protest of the *Unión Obrera*, Iglesias asked Congress to use the power of federal law to create a genuine bureau of labor, one not subject to the interests of the Unionist Party then in control of the island government. The Unionist Party, which was controlled by large landowners who favored low corporate taxes and antagonized the working class, dominated island politics from 1904 (when the party changed its name from Federal to Unionist) until after the passage of the Jones Act in 1917. Luis Muñoz Rivera, in fact, had lobbied Congress against passing the Olmstead Bill, which would have established a department of labor, on the grounds that the bureau should be established by the island government rather than Washington. All in Statement of Santiago Iglesias, Hearings before the Committee on Insular Affairs, U.S. Senate, May 2–4, 1912, box Y4–1710, RG 287, NAB. See Valdés, *Organized Agriculture*, 48; Erman, "Citizens of Empire," 53.

108. Santiago Iglesias to President Taft, November 27, 1909, box 626, folder HR 62A-H13.1, RG 233, NAB.

109. Ibid.

110. Ibid.

111. In addition to the Philippines, some thirty-nine states had established bureaus of labor by 1912, beginning with the bureau run by Carroll Wright in Massachusetts. Statement of Secretary of War Henry Stimson, Hearings before the Committee on Insular Affairs, U.S. Senate, May 2–4, 1912, box Y4–1710, RG 287, NAB.

112. Established within the U.S. War Department in 1898, the Division of Customs and Insular Affairs became the Bureau of Insular Affairs in 1902. The BIA was charged with administering customs and civil affairs in Puerto Rico and the Philippines. Frank McIntyre served as BIA assistant chief in 1907–8 and 1910–12; he served as BIA chief during 1912–18 and 1920–29.

113. Statement of Frank McIntyre, Assistant to the Chief of the Bureau of Insular Affairs, Hearings before the Committee on Insular Affairs, U.S. Senate, May 2–4, 1912, box Y4–1710, RG 287, NAB.

114. Statement of Samuel Gompers, Hearings before the Committee on Insular Affairs, U.S. Senate, May 2–4, 1912, box Y4–1710, RG 287, NAB.

115. Hahamovitch, *Fruits of Their Labor*, 70.

116. Secretary Morrison of the American Federation of Labor to the U.S. Senate, March 18, 1912, quoted in Santiago Iglesias Pantín, *A People without a Country: Appeal for U.S. Citizenship for the People of Porto Rico* (Washington DC: American Federation of Labor, 1912), 18.

117. Ibid.

118. Gompers, "Address before Federacion Regional," February 22, 1904.

119. Gompers, "Address before a Meeting of the Washington, DC, Central Labor Union," March 24, 1904.

120. Samuel Gompers. "President Gompers Speaks to Workingmen," San Juan, PR, February 25, 1904, *American Federationist* 11, no. 4 (April 1904).

121. "Porto Rico Pleads for Justice," *American Federationist* 12, no. 10 (October 1905).

122. Ibid.

123. On the development of anti-American sentiment in Puerto Rico in this period, see Julian Go, "Anti-Imperialism in the U.S. Territories after 1898," in *Empire's Twin: U.S. Anti-Imperialism from the Founding Era to the Age of Terrorism*, ed. Ian Tyrrell and Jay Sexton (Ithaca, NY: Cornell University Press, 2015), 79–96.

124. Statement of Samuel Gompers, Senate Hearings on H.R. 20048, "A Bill to Make Porto Ricans Citizens of the United States," Hearings before the Committee on Pacific Islands and Porto Rico, U.S. Senate, May 7, 1912.

125. *Report of President Gompers to the American Federation of Labor Annual Convention*, Atlanta, 1911, quoted in Iglesias Pantín, *People without a Country*, 13.

126. Statement of Santiago Iglesias, President of the Free Federation of Workingmen of Porto Rico, in Iglesias Pantín, *People without a Country*, 30.

127. Petition of the Central Federated Union of Greater New York and Vicinity to the U.S. Congress, March 18, 1912, box 626, folder HR 62A-H13.1, RG 233, NAB. Citizenship backers also included assorted groups with an interest in the welfare of America's new colonial subjects such as the University of Michigan Alumni Association of Puerto Rico, the Porto Rican Alliance of New York City, and the Lake Mohonk Conference. In one example, the University of Michigan Alumni Association of Puerto Rico, at its annual banquet in San Juan in 1911, adopted a resolution stating that the "granting of American citizenship is nothing more than an act of justice to a worthy people, more than one million in number." Resolution of the University of Michigan Alumni Association of Puerto Rico, December 30, 1911, box 626, folder HR 62A-H13.1, RG 233, NAB.

128. On the election of Woodrow Wilson and its effects on the movement for Philippine Independence, see Paul Kramer, *The Blood of Government: Race, Empire, the United States, and the Philippines* (Chapel Hill: University of North Carolina Press, 2006), 350.

129. Ibid., 344.

130. Samuel Gompers, "Immigration—Up to Congress," *American Federationist* 18, no. 1 (January 1911).

131. A. A. Graham, "The Un-Americanization of America," *American Federationist* 17, no. 4 (April 1910); "Lid off the Melting Pot," *American Federationist* 19, no. 3 (March 1912); Gompers, "Immigration—Up to Congress," *American Federationist* 18, no. 1 (January 1911).

132. Petition of the Men's Protective Local of Cabo-Rojo, Porto Rico, affiliated with the American Federation of Labor, to the U.S. House of Representatives, February 14, 1912, box 626, folder HR 62A-H13.1, RG 233, NAB. Similar petitions were sent to the House from a variety of AFL affiliates on the island, including the United Brotherhood of Carpenters and Joiners, No. 1582 of Arecibo, February 29, 1912; Central Labor Union of Arecibo, February 29, 1912; Hod Carriers and Building Laborers Union No. 260 of Arecibo, February 29, 1912; Cigar Makers Int. Union of America, No. 467 of Arecibo, February 29, 1912; International Longshoremen's Association of Arecibo, February 29, 1912; Painters, Decorators, Paperhangers Local Union No. 550 of San Juan, February 23, 1912; San Juan Typographical Union, February 23, 1912; Federación Libre de las Trabajadores, February 23, 1912; Journeymen Barbers Local Union No. 602 of San Juan, February 23, 1912; Bricklayer's Local Union No. 10982 of San Juan, February 23, 1912; Women's Protective Local Union No. 11752 of San Juan, February 24, 1912; Central Labor Union of San Juan, February 25, 1912; Carpenters and Joiners Local Union No. 1450 of San Juan, February 24, 1912; Journeymen Tailors Union of America, February 26, 1912; joint advisory board of the Cigarmakers' Local Union of Puerto Rico, February 25, 1912; Carpenters and Joiners Local Union of Puerto de Tierra, San Juan, February 25, 1912; Cigarmakers Local Union of San Juan, February 24, 1912; Central Labor Union of Caguas, Puerto Rico, February 20, 1912; Men's Protective Local

Union of Cabo Rojo, March 4, 1912; Bricklayers Union of Arecibo, February 29, 1912; all in box 626, folder HR 62A-H13.1, RG 233, NAB.

133. Christopher Capozzola, "The Secret Soldiers' Union: Labor and Soldier Politics in the Philippine Scout Mutiny of 1924," in Bender and Lipman, *Making the Empire Work*, 85.

4. Citizenship and Statelessness

1. U.S. army training of Puerto Ricans in these battalions first began in 1899. "Uncle Sam's Man-Factory in Porto Rico," *Harper's Weekly*, February 1, 1902. On the U.S. project of educating colonial subjects for citizenship, see Julian Go, "Chains of Empire, Projects of State: Political Education and U.S. Colonial Rule in Puerto Rico and the Philippines," *Comparative Studies in Society and History* 42, no. 2 (April 2000): 333–62. Go argues that though U.S. officials aimed to establish a system of tutelage for both Puerto Ricans and Filipinos, like most colonial projects this initiative was never realized in full and "unfolded in ways that transgressed its initial premises."

2. "Uncle Sam's Man-Factory in Porto Rico."

3. Illinois Republican James Mann proposed an amendment to the Jones Act in 1917 that would have granted Puerto Rico woman suffrage in advance of the Nineteenth Amendment. The Mann Amendment failed to pass, however, and it was not until 1929, more than a decade after the Nineteenth Amendment passed in Washington, that the Puerto Rican legislature extended woman suffrage to the island. See Allison L. Sneider, *Suffragists in an Imperial Age: U.S. Expansion and the Woman Question, 1870–1929* (New York: Oxford University Press, 2008), 134.

4. Puerto Rican labor leaders employed this term to describe their political and economic position within the U.S. empire. See Iglesias Pantín, *People without a Country*, 1–31.

5. Scholars have long argued that the United States granted citizenship in 1917 in order to draft Puerto Ricans into World War I. Yet new work has allowed for other possible causes. I suggest the granting of citizenship had roots in both the U.S. colonial project and Puerto Rican–led movements on the island.

6. For a useful critique of American exceptionalism, see Alexander Keyssar, *The Right to Vote: The Contested History of Democracy in the United States* (New York: Basic Books, 2000), xvi–xxi. In describing the approach of midcentury "consensus" historians, Keyssar writes: "The expansion of democratic political rights in the United States was not deemed to require explanation; it was the nation's natural destiny" (xix). Keyssar argues instead that the history of citizenship in the United States is marked by contestation and contingency. Keyssar's study does not include Puerto Rico.

7. Kerber, "Toward a History of Statelessness."

8. Christina Duffy Ponsa has explored the limits of citizenship in the context of U.S. empire. She argues that U.S. empire needs to be understood in terms of the tension between the extension and withholding of national power. See Ponsa, "Edges of Empire."

9. See Manuel Maldonado-Denis, *Puerto Rico: A Socio-Historic Interpretation* (New York: Random House, 1972), 108. The legal scholar José A. Cabranes has noted that Pedro Albizu Campos, a leader of the independence movement, claimed in 1930 that the need for conscripting soldiers in World War I prompted the Jones Act. Cabranes attempted to refute this claim in 1979, arguing that aliens were still subject to the military draft. José A. Cabranes, *Citizenship and the American Empire: Notes on the Legislative History of the United States Citizenship of Puerto Ricans* (New Haven, CT: Yale University Press, 1979), 13–16. This debate has continued with recent scholarship exploring the complex roots of the Jones Act more fully. Harry Franqui-Rivera has argued that the notion that the Jones Act was passed to conscript soldiers has become a Puerto Rican nationalist

myth and that, in fact, the "need for soldiers was unrelated to the granting of citizenship in 1917." Harry Franqui-Rivera, "National Mythologies: U.S. Citizenship for the People of Puerto Rico and Military Service," *Memorias: Revista Digital de Historia y Arqueología desde el Caribe*, no. 21 (September–December 2013): 5–21. In contrast, Bartholomew Sparrow and Jennifer Lamm have claimed that "making Puerto Ricans U.S. citizens would make the draft that much easier to implement." Bartholomew Sparrow and Jennifer Lamm, "Puerto Ricans and U.S. Citizenship in 1917: Imperatives of Security," *CENTRO: Journal of the Center for Puerto Rican Studies* 29, no. 1 (Spring 2017): 303. For the broader context of the Jones Act, see Edgardo Meléndez, "Comments on the Jones Act and the Grant of U.S. Citizenship to Puerto Ricans," *CENTRO: Journal of the Center for Puerto Rican Studies* 29, no. 1 (Spring 2017): 316–27.

10. When Germany expressed interest in buying the Danish West Indies during World War I, U.S. officials, seeking to maintain the Caribbean as an exclusive sphere of U.S. influence, moved quickly to purchase the islands for the United States. Given the U.S. practice in Puerto Rico and the Philippines of withholding citizenship, the government of Denmark delayed the deal out of concern for the citizenship status of the islands' residents. For officials in Washington, granting citizenship in Puerto Rico became a prerequisite to purchasing the Danish West Indies (the U.S. Virgin Islands) in 1917. See Carrión, *Puerto Rico*; and Charles Callan Tansill, *The Purchase of the Danish West Indies* (Baltimore: Johns Hopkins Press, 1932). On the larger U.S. interest in national security, see Sparrow and Lamm, "Puerto Ricans and U.S. Citizenship in 1917," 284–315.

11. José Cabranes argues that citizenship was granted as a kind of reward for calmly accepting U.S. rule. In his words: "The basic colonial relationship was rarely directly challenged. United States citizenship thus inevitably was considered a means of acknowledging the special place of Puerto Rico among the new colonial territories and of expressing the virtually universal expectation of a permanent relationship." José A. Cabranes, *Citizenship*, 52–53. Still others have argued that the U.S. government supported citizenship as a means of discouraging the growth of the independence movement. See María del Pilar Argüelles, *Morality and Power: The U.S. Colonial Experience in Puerto Rico from 1898 to 1948* (Lanham, MD: University Press of America, 1996), 40.

12. To argue that workers' agency is an important consideration in this debate is not to suggest, of course, that all Puerto Ricans supported calls for U.S. citizenship. Opinion on the island was divided, especially after 1905. The Unionist Party, dominated by Autonomist elites like Muñoz Rivera, controlled the Puerto Rican House of Delegates from 1904 to 1924. Unionists pressed for increased self-rule and supported the continuation of Puerto Rican citizenship until Congress allowed for a plebiscite to permanently decide the question of citizenship. At the same time, the FLT labor movement and the island's Republican Party supported U.S. citizenship. Calls for independence increased as the U.S. Congress repeatedly ignored the Unionist Party's demands for a plebiscite. Independence activists decried AFL and FLT support of U.S. citizenship as an impediment to forming a sovereign Puerto Rican nation-state. Though activists had called for independence since the early twentieth century, the independence movement remained a small, minority movement in the period before 1930. See Wilfredo Mattos Cintrón, "The Struggle for Independence: The Long March to the Twenty-First Century," in *Colonial Dilemma: Critical Perspectives on Contemporary Puerto Rico*, edited by Edwin Meléndez and Edgardo Meléndez (Boston, MA: South End Press, 1993), 201; Ché Paralitici, *Sentencia Impuesta: 100 Años de Encarcelamientos por la Independencia de Puerto Rico* (San Juan, PR: Ediciones Puerto Rico Histórico, 2004); Findlay, *Imposing Decency*, 142; Fernando Picó, *History of Puerto Rico: A Panorama of Its People* (Princeton, NJ: Markus Wiener, 2006), 250; and Kal Wagenheim, *Puerto Rico: A Profile* (New York: Praeger, 1975), 67.

13. Goldwin Smith, *The United States: An Outline of Political History, 1492–1871* (New York: MacMillan, 1893).

14. *Giles v. Harris*, 189 U.S. 475 (1903).

15. Quoted in "Recent Views of the Fifteenth Amendment," *Harper's Weekly*, May 23, 1903.

16. *New York Sun*, quoted in "Recent Views of the Fifteenth Amendment," *Harper's Weekly*, May 23, 1903.

17. A. R. Colquhoun, *North American Review*, 1903, quoted in "Recent Views of the Fifteenth Amendment," *Harper's Weekly*, May 23, 1903.

18. Ibid.

19. Ibid.

20. Ibid.

21. On such arguments in the case of the Philippines, see Ngai, *Impossible Subjects*, 99.

22. Henry Brannon, *A Treatise on the Rights and Privileges Guaranteed by the Fourteenth Amendment to the Constitution of the United States* (Cincinnati, OH: W. H. Anderson, 1901), 33.

23. The Civil Rights Act of July 14, 1870, granted African Americans the right to naturalize.

24. Brannon, *Treatise on the Rights and Privileges*, 30.

25. Aide-de-Camp, Headquarters, Department of Porto Rico, San Juan, to Dr. Variano Asenjo, Lares, Porto Rico, June 15, 1899, box 179, folder 3728, AGPR. See Nationality Act of July 14, 1870 (16 Stat. 25). See also Ngai, *Impossible Subjects*, 38.

26. Copy of Revised Statutes of the U.S. 1899. "There is no Court now in existence on the Island which has authority to naturalize Aliens. Section 2165, Revised Statutes confers this power upon certain courts," box 179, folder 3728, AGPR.

27. Dr. Valeriano Asenjo to Governor Davis, July 1899, box 179, folder 3728, AGPR.

28. Brannon, *Treatise on the Rights and Privileges*, 30.

29. Ian Haney López, *White by Law: The Legal Construction of Race* (New York: New York University Press, 1996), 35–40.

30. In *Gonzales v. Williams*, 192 U.S. 1 (1904), the U.S. Supreme Court defined Puerto Ricans as nationals loyal to the United States but exempt from immigration restrictions. See also "Porto Ricans Not Aliens," *New York Times*, January 5, 1904.

31. Charles Tyler, "Our Record in Porto Rico," *Harper's Weekly*, October 28, 1905. Congress began to allow for naturalization of Puerto Ricans through the 1906 Bureau of Immigration and Naturalization Act.

32. Ibid.

33. Congress began to allow naturalization in 1906 through the Bureau of Immigration and Naturalization Act, but it was not until the 1915 federal court ruling *In re Giralde* that Puerto Ricans in the United States could be considered white and thereby naturalize in U.S. courts more easily. Charles Venator-Santiago, "Mapping the Contours of the History of the Extension of U.S. Citizenship to Puerto Rico, 1898–Present," *CENTRO: Journal of the Center for Puerto Rican Studies* 29, no. 1 (Spring 2017): 46.

34. Valdés, *Organized Agriculture*, 49.

35. George Bird Arias, "A Plea for Porto Ricans," Lake Mohonk Conference, October 23, 1907, box 90, folder SEN 62A-F17, RG 46, NAB; also found in *Proceedings of the Twenty-Fifth Annual Lake Mohonk Conference of Friends of the Indian and Other Dependent Peoples* (New York: Lake Mohonk Conference, 1907).

36. Hon. Manuel Rossy to Santiago Iglesias Pantín, October 30, 1911, quoted in Iglesias Pantín, *People without a Country*, 11.

37. Petition of the Municipalities of Puerto Rico to the U.S. Congress, quoted in "Porto Rico Pleads for Justice," *American Federationist* 12, no. 10 (October 1905).

38. Memorial of the House of Delegates of Porto Rico to the Congress of the United States of America, San Juan, January 6, 1906, box 415, folder HR 59A-H10.1, RG 233, NAB.

39. Ibid.

40. Report of Governor Winthrop, San Juan, Puerto Rico, January 15, 1906, quoted in Iglesias Pantín, *People without a Country*, 14.

41. Ibid.

42. Several others in Washington also supported citizenship. President Theodore Roosevelt sent a special message to Congress in 1905 requesting that citizenship be granted: "I can not see how any harm can possibly result from it, and it seems to me a matter of right and justice to the people of Porto Rico." Assorted U.S. senators and congressmen from both the Republican and Democratic Parties joined Roosevelt in supporting the measure. Representative Williams of Mississippi argued on the House floor: "We ought no longer to keep the people of Puerto Rico in the status where they are now, where they are adjudged to be neither foreigners nor citizens—neither fish, flesh, nor fowl." Representative Cooper of Wisconsin concurred, and quoted from the Republican Party platform: "We believe that the Native inhabitants of Porto Rico should be at once collectively made citizens of the United States." Special Message of President Theodore Roosevelt to Congress, December 11, 1905; Speech of Representative Williams of Mississippi to the U.S. House of Representatives, May 8, 1908; Speech of Representative Cooper of Wisconsin to the U.S. House of Representatives, January 6, 1909; all quoted in Iglesias Pantín, *People without a Country*, 1–31.

43. Statement of Henry Stimson, Senate Hearings on H.R. 20048, A Bill to Make Porto Ricans Citizens of the United States, Hearings before the Committee on Pacific Islands and Porto Rico, U. S. Senate, May 7, 1912, 4.

44. Ibid., 8.

45. Ibid., 4.

46. Ibid.

47. Ibid., 8.

48. Ibid.

49. Secretary of Porto Rico Post, July 7, 1905, quoted in Iglesias Pantín, *People without a Country*, 13.

50. Frederic Dean, "Question of Self Rule Sets Puerto Rico Seething," *New York Times*, February 18, 1912.

51. Ibid.

52. During the 1912 Senate Hearings many of the same questions of fitness for citizenship recurred. Secretary of War Henry Stimson, for example, stated his belief that racial differences between Latins and Anglo-Saxons were insurmountable, so much so that making Puerto Rico an American state would be inadvisable. When asked to clarify his objection to ultimately granting the island statehood, Stimson explained, "The racial difference is a very great difference." Statement of Henry Stimson, 4.

53. Dean, "Question of Self Rule," *New York Times*, February 18, 1912; Elihu Root to Mr. Rivera, Porto Rican Delegate to the U.S., March 10, 1912, quoted in Iglesias Pantín, *People without a Country*, 1–31; "Root against Vote for Porto Ricans," *New York Times*, February 15, 1912.

54. President Taft to Santiago Iglesias, quoted in "Porto Ricans Must Wait," *New York Times*, April 17, 1912. On Santiago Iglesias, see Iglesias Pantín, *Luchas emancipadoras*; Senior, *Santiago Iglesias*.

55. Erman, "Citizens of Empire," 63.

56. Independence Party of Puerto Rico to Luis Muñoz Rivera, Resident Commissioner of Porto Rico in the U.S. House of Representatives, April 15, 1912, box 90, folder SEN 62S-F17, RG 46, NAB; Statement of Luis Muñoz Rivera, Resident Commissioner of Puerto Rico in the U.S. House of Representatives, Senate Hearings on H.R. 20048, A Bill to Make Porto Ricans Citizens of the United States, Hearings before the Committee on Pacific Islands and Porto Rico, U.S. Senate, May 7, 1912; both in Law Library, Library of Congress.

57. "Make War on Birds: People of Porto Rico Eat Everything That Flies, and Even the Unhatched Eggs," *Los Angeles Times*, May 5, 1912, 15.

58. Ibid.

59. William Willoughby held a PhD from Johns Hopkins University and eventually served as president of the American Political Science Association. White social scientists like Willoughby lent their support to U.S. colonial projects by granting ideologies of racial hierarchy the prestige of science. Robert Vitalis, *White World Order, Black Power Politics: The Birth of American International Relations* (Ithaca, NY: Cornell University Press, 2015), 43–47.

60. Report of Mr. Larrinaga, the Resident Commissioner of Puerto Rico, before the Committee of Pacific Islands, U.S. Senate, 1912, box 90, folder SEN 62A-F17, RG 46, NAB.

61. Because the office of resident commissioner was not attached to any formal administrative office in the U.S. House of Representatives, the records and personal papers of Larrinaga and other resident commissioners are nowhere to be found in the U.S. National Archives.

62. Samuel Gompers, president of the AFL, made a second trip to Puerto Rico in 1914, in part to investigate these conditions. During his visit, the cigar makers and tobacco workers were in the midst of a seventeen-week strike. Gompers supported the strike, even when the governor asked strikers to relent and return to work. In response, Gompers and the AFL asked Congress to undertake an extensive investigation of working conditions on the island. AFL Convention Records, 1914, 53–364. Report of Mr. Larrinaga, Resident Commissioner of Puerto Rico, before the Committee of Pacific Islands, U.S. Senate, 1912, box 90, folder SEN 62A-F17, RG 46, NAB.

63. On rising anti-imperialist sentiment in Central America during the war and after, see Jason M. Colby, "Progressive Empire: Race and Tropicality in United Fruit's Central America," in Bender and Lipman, *Making the Empire Work*, 300–301.

64. Statement of Samuel Gompers, Hearings before the Committee on Pacific Islands and Porto Rico, United States Senate, 64th Cong., 1st Sess. on S. 1217, A Bill to Provide a Civil Government for Porto Rico, and for other purposes, January 28, 1916 (Washington, DC: Government Printing Office, 1916), box Y6005, RG 287, NAB.

65. On the FLT's worker education program known as "Cruzada del Ideal" that began in 1909 to address the 90 percent illiteracy rate among agricultural workers, see Valdés, *Organized Agriculture*, 43–45. On the agency of agricultural workers in other sectors of the island economy, see Levy, *Puerto Ricans in the Empire*, 64.

66. Similarly, increased wartime demand for copper used in munitions helped fuel the 1917 strike of copper miners in Bisbee, Arizona. See Katherine Benton-Cohen, *Borderline Americans: Racial Division and Labor War in the Arizona Borderlands* (Cambridge, MA: Harvard University Press, 2009), 198. On the 1915 sugar strike, see García and Rivera, *Desafío y Solidaridad*.

67. Statement of P. Rivera Martinez, Hearings before the Commission on Industrial Relations, U.S. Senate, Labor Conditions in Porto Rico, 1915, 64th Cong., 1st Sess., Senate Documents, vol. 29, no. 6939, Washington DC, May 26, 1915, 11037.

68. Santiago Iglesias to President Wilson, June 4, 1915, AFL Convention Documents in AFL Records of the Gompers Era, reels 25–33, 1909–1925, Library of Congress.

69. Statement of Juncos Residents, Hearings before the Commission on Industrial Relations, U.S. Senate, Labor Conditions in Porto Rico, 1915, 11044.

70. Santiago Iglesias, "Strike of Porto Rican Agricultural Workers," *American Federationist* 22, no. 4 (April 1915).

71. Affidavit No. 861, Exhibit H, Statement of Mr. Lucas E. Castro, Hearings before the Commission on Industrial Relations, U.S. Senate, Labor Conditions in Porto Rico, 1915, 11044.

72. Statement of Santiago Iglesias, Hearings before the Commission on Industrial Relations, U.S. Senate, Labor Conditions in Porto Rico, 1915, 11044.

73. Affidavits Nos. 867–870 of Luis Sanchez Ocana, Juan Roman, Jose Maria Pereira, and Juan Rivera witnessed before the notary public of Juncos, Porto Rico, Mr. Pedro Santanna, Jr., Hearings before the Commission on Industrial Relations, U.S. Senate, Labor Conditions in Porto Rico, 1915, 64th Cong., 1st Sess., Senate Documents, vol. 29, no. 6939, 11044. See also Affidavit No. 863 of Mr. Modesto Martinez, a doctor in Juncos, who reported that he saw police clubbing innocent workers. Hearings before the Commission on Industrial Relations, U.S. Senate, Labor Conditions in Porto Rico, 1915, 11183.

74. Affidavit No. 1016 of Mr. Rafael Lopez Landron, Attorney for the accused workers in the February Strike in Vieques, Hearings before the Commission on Industrial Relations, U.S. Senate, Labor Conditions in Porto Rico, 1915, 11044.

75. Statement of Mr. Travieso, Hearings before the Commission on Industrial Relations, U.S. Senate, Labor Conditions in Porto Rico, 1915, 11125.

76. Affidavit No. 1016 of Mr. Rafael Lopez Landron, Attorney for the accused workers in the February Strike in Vieques, Hearings before the Commission on Industrial Relations, U.S. Senate, Labor Conditions in Porto Rico, 1915, 11044.

77. Iglesias "Strike of Porto Rican Agricultural Workers."

78. Statement of Santiago Iglesias, Hearings before the Commission on Industrial Relations, U.S. Senate, Labor Conditions in Porto Rico, 1915, 11049.

79. Statement of Santiago Iglesias, Hearings before the Commission on Industrial Relations, U.S. Senate, Labor Conditions in Porto Rico, 1915, 11047.

80. Affidavit No. 1016 of Mr. Rafael Lopez Landron, Attorney for the accused workers in the February Strike in Vieques, Hearings before the Commission on Industrial Relations, U.S. Senate, Labor Conditions in Porto Rico, 1915, 11044.

81. Affidavit of Nicomedes Rivera, Emillio Fariza, Jose M. Roman, and Pablo Ramirez, Hearings before the Commission on Industrial Relations, U.S. Senate, Labor Conditions in Porto Rico, 1915, 11066.

82. Affidavit of Sofia Rivera, February Strike in Vieques, Hearings before the Commission on Industrial Relations, U.S. Senate, Labor Conditions in Porto Rico, 1915, 11067.

83. Telegram of M. F. Rojas, Chairman Strike Committee, Arecibo, to Justicia, Free Federation, San Juan, February 16, 1915, Hearings before the Commission on Industrial Relations, U.S. Senate, Labor Conditions in Porto Rico, 1915, 11066.

84. Statement of Santiago Iglesias, February Strike in Vieques, Hearings before the Commission on Industrial Relations, U.S. Senate, Labor Conditions in Porto Rico, 1915, 11066.

85. Telegram of Santiago Iglesias to Governor Yager, February 20, 1915, quoted in Hearings before the Commission on Industrial Relations, U.S. Senate, Labor Conditions in Porto Rico, 1915, 11065.

86. During part of the Sugar Strike of 1915, the governor of Puerto Rico declared martial law in the rural zones. E. Landron, Mayor of Arecibo, to the Governor of Porto Rico, February 21, 1915, quoted in Hearings before the Commission on Industrial Relations, U.S. Senate, Labor Conditions in Porto Rico, 1915, 11065.

87. Iglesias, "Strike of Porto Rican Agricultural Workers."

88. Statement of Santiago Iglesias, Hearings before the Commission on Industrial Relations, U.S. Senate, Labor Conditions in Porto Rico, 1915, 11065.

89. For similar patterns of protest among British subjects in Jamaica, see Diana Paton, *No Bond but the Law: Punishment, Race and Gender in Jamaican State Formation, 1780–1870* (Durham, NC: Duke University Press, 2004), 122–99.

90. Santiago Iglesias to President Wilson, June 4, 1915.

91. Ibid.

92. Affidavit signed by 233 witnesses and read by Chairman Walsh, Hearings before the Commission on Industrial Relations, U.S. Senate, Labor Conditions in Porto Rico, 1915, 11059.

93. Statement of Santiago Iglesias, Hearings before the Commission on Industrial Relations, U.S. Senate, Labor Conditions in Porto Rico, 1915, 11081.

94. Affidavit of Alberto Fernandez before Leopoldo Tormes Garcia, the Notary Public of the city of Ponce, Porto Rico, March 1915, Hearings before the Commission on Industrial Relations, U.S. Senate, Labor Conditions in Porto Rico, 1915, 11063. Fernandez's account is supported by fifteen other affidavits entered into the 1915 Senate Hearings.

95. Hemenegildo Robledo to the Governor of Porto Rico, excerpted in Hearings before the Commission on Industrial Relations, U.S. Senate, Labor Conditions in Porto Rico, 1915, 11062; Statement of Santiago Iglesias, Hearings before the Commission on Industrial Relations, U.S. Senate, Labor Conditions in Porto Rico, 1915, 11062.

96. Santiago Iglesias to President Wilson, June 4, 1915.

97. Statement of Santiago Iglesias, Hearings before the Commission on Industrial Relations, U.S. Senate, Labor Conditions in Porto Rico, 1915, 64th Cong., 1st Sess., Senate Documents, vol. 29, no. 6939, 11061.

98. Iglesias, "Strike of Porto Rican Agricultural Workers."

99. On the Ponce Riot of 1905, see Statement of Santiago Iglesias, Hearings before the Commission on Industrial Relations, U.S. Senate, Labor Conditions in Porto Rico, 1915, 11059.

100. Santiago Iglesias and the AFL disputed Travieso's claim that it was the laborers in Vieques who fired first. See statement of Travieso, Hearings before the Commission on Industrial Relations, U.S. Senate, Labor Conditions in Porto Rico, 1915, 11126.

101. Statement of Travieso, Hearings before the Commission on Industrial Relations, U.S. Senate, Labor Conditions in Porto Rico, 1915, 11127.

102. Statement of Travieso, Hearings before the Commission on Industrial Relations, U.S. Senate, Labor Conditions in Porto Rico, 1915, 11133.

103. Governor Yager to the Insular Police of Puerto Rico, February 25, 1915, quoted in Hearings before the Commission on Industrial Relations, U.S. Senate, Labor Conditions in Porto Rico, 1915, 11133.

104. Governor Yager regularly opposed prolabor legislation backed by the FLT. On Yager's opposition to organized labor on the island, see Caban, *Constructing a Colonial People*, 242; and Valdés, *Organized Agriculture*, 46.

105. Cable to General McIntyre, February 26, 1915.

106. Ibid.

107. Santiago Iglesias to President Wilson, June 4, 1915.

108. Samuel Gompers to President Woodrow Wilson, July 29, 1915.

109. Santiago Iglesias to President Wilson, June 4, 1915.

110. Nelson Lichtenstein, Susan Strasser, and Roy Rosenzweig, *Who Built America? Working People and the Nation's Economy, Politics, Culture, and Society* (New York: Worth, 2000), 2:245.

111. Ibid., 246.

112. Statement of Manuel Rodriguez Serra, Hearings before the Committee on Pacific Islands and Porto Rico, U.S. Senate, 64th Cong., 1st Sess. on S. 1217, A Bill to Provide a Civil Government for Porto Rico, and for other purposes, January 28, 1916 (Washington, DC: Government Printing Office, 1916), box Y6005, RG 287, NAB.

113. Ibid.

114. Ibid.

115. Petition of the Porto Rico Bar Association to the U.S. Congress, January 24, 1916, Hearings before the Committee on Pacific Islands and Porto Rico, U.S. Senate.

116. Statement of Cay Coll Cuchi, Hearings before the Committee on Pacific Islands and Porto Rico, U.S. Senate.

117. Statement of Samuel Gompers, Hearings before the Committee on Pacific Islands and Porto Rico, U.S. Senate.

118. Ibid.

119. Statement of John Lennon, Hearings before the Committee on Pacific Islands and Porto Rico, U.S. Senate.

120. Statement of Samuel Gompers, Hearings before the Committee on Pacific Islands and Porto Rico, U.S. Senate.

121. Statement of Coy Coll Cuchi, Hearings before the Committee on Pacific Islands and Porto Rico, U.S. Senate.

122. Cabranes, *Citizenship and the American Empire*, 53.

123. President Wilson's Third Annual Message to Congress, December 17, 1915, quoted in Carrión, *Puerto Rico*, 193. Wilson's primary interest in the Jones Bill may not have been U.S. citizenship per se, but rather extending to Puerto Rico a greater measure of autonomy as a way to cultivate pro-American sentiment. See Sparrow and Lamm, "Puerto Ricans and U.S. Citizenship in 1917," 298.

124. In urging Congress to declare war on Germany in 1917, President Wilson argued, "The world must be made safe for democracy." President Woodrow Wilson's War Message, Congressional Record, 65th Cong., 1st Sess., 102–4. On the connections between the U.S. woman suffrage movement, World War I, and Puerto Rico, see Sneider, *Suffragists*, 120; and Wagenheim, *Puerto Rico*, 69.

125. Statement of Hon. Willis Sweet of Porto Rico, Hearings before the Committee on Pacific Islands and Porto Rico, U.S. Senate.

126. Statements of Senator Vardaman and Samuel Gompers, Hearings before the Committee on Pacific Islands and Porto Rico, U.S. Senate.

127. Statement of Samuel Gompers, Hearings before the Committee on Pacific Islands and Porto Rico, U.S. Senate.

128. On the racialist argument regarding fitness for citizenship in Puerto Rico as well as in the Philippines, see Jacobson, *Barbarian Virtues*, 240.

129. Statement of Senator Vardaman, Hearings before the Committee on Pacific Islands and Porto Rico, U.S. Senate; Statement of Samuel Gompers, Hearings before the Committee on Pacific Islands and Porto Rico, U.S. Senate.

130. Ibid.

131. Valdés, *Organized Agriculture*, 48.

132. "Declares Porto Rico Wants Autonomy," *New York Times*, September 21, 1912.

133. Ayala and Bernabe, *Puerto Rico in the American Century*, 28.

134. Statement of Manuel Rodriguez Serra, Hearings before the Committee on Pacific Islands and Porto Rico, U.S. Senate.

135. Ibid.

136. Statement of Cay Coll Cuchi, member of the Puerto Rican House of Delegates, Hearings before the Committee on Pacific Islands and Porto Rico, U.S. Senate.

137. Wagenheim, *Puerto Rico*, 69. Historians of the Jones Act who have focused more on unionist opposition to U.S. citizenship than on FLT support for U.S. citizenship have understood the Jones Act as simply an act of external domination, arguing that "Puerto Ricans became Americans in spite of themselves." See Ronald Fernandez, *The Disenchanted Island: Puerto Rico and the United States in the Twentieth Century* (Westport, CT: Praeger, 1996), 73.

138. "Muñoz Rivera establece su posición con respecto a la estadidad, la independencia y la ciudadanía," *La Democracia*, April 13, 1914, reprinted in Reece B. Bothwell González, comp., *Puerto Rico: Cien años de lucha política* (Río Piedras, PR: Editorial Universitaria, 1979), 4:281.

139. "Manifiesto Dirigido a los Unionistas por Luis Muñoz Rivera, Desde Washington," *La Democracia*, 1913, reprinted in Bothwell González, *Puerto Rico*, 4:260.

140. Ibid.

141. Statement of Senator Broussard, Hearings before the Committee on Pacific Islands and Porto Rico, U.S. Senate.

142. Statement of Mr. Cay Coll Cuchi, Hearings before the Committee on Pacific Islands and Porto Rico, U.S. Senate.

143. Statement of Manuel Rodriguez Serra, Hearings before the Committee on Pacific Islands and Porto Rico, U.S. Senate.

144. Erman, "Citizens of Empire," 60.

145. U.S. Statutes at Large, 39:951–68.

146. Samuel Gompers to Frank Morrison, January 15, 1916, in *Samuel Gompers Papers* 9, ed. Peter Albert (Urbana: University of Illinois Press, 2003), 371–72. For a comparison of the Jones Acts in Puerto Rico and the Philippines, see Rick Baldoz and César Ayala, "The Bordering of America: Colonialism and Citizenship in the Philippines and Puerto Rico," *CENTRO: Journal of the Center for Puerto Rican Studies* 25, no. 1 (Spring 2013): 76–105.

147. Cabranes, *Citizenship*, 17.

148. According to an October 18, 1918, letter from Major General Frank McIntyre, chief of the Bureau of Insular Affairs, to Governor Arthur Yager of Puerto Rico, those who "declared their intention of not becoming citizens of the United States . . . are not exempted from military duty under the Selective Service Act." Reprinted in Bureau of Supplies, Printing, and Transportation, Report of the Adjutant General to the Governor of Puerto Rico on the Operation of the Military Registration and Selective Draft in Puerto Rico 93 (1924), quoted in Cabranes, *Citizenship*, 17.

149. Ibid. Noncitizens such as Native American nationals on the mainland were subject to the World War I draft. The Jones Act passed in March of 1917—one month before the United States entered World War I and two months before Congress passed the Selective Service Draft Act in May of 1917. The selective service statute of 1917 stipulated that the president was authorized to draft "all male citizens, or male persons not alien enemies who have declared their intention to become citizens." Act of May 18, 1917, chap. 15, 2, 40 Stat. 76, quoted in Cabranes, *Citizenship*, 16. See also John Whiteclay Chambers II, *To Raise an Army: The Draft Comes to Modern America* (London: Free Press, 1987), 231–32.

150. Paul A. Kramer, "Power and Connection: Imperial Histories of the United States in the World," *American Historical Review* 116, no. 5 (December 2011):1383.

5. "Working People Going North"

1. Arthur Yager, Governor of Puerto Rico, to Frank McIntyre, Chief of the Bureau of Insular Affairs, U.S. War Department, April 20, 1917, box 1107, folder 26697, RG 350, National Archives at College Park, MD (hereafter cited as NACP).

2. Manuel V. Dominich, Commissioner of the Interior of Porto Rico, to William B. Wilson, Secretary of Labor, Washington, DC, May 19, 1918, box 6, folder 20/60, RG 174, NACP.

3. On Filipino migrations, see Rick Baldoz, *The Third Asiatic Invasion: Empire and Migration in Filipino America, 1898–1946* (New York: New York University Press, 2011); Ngai, *Impossible Subjects*; and Fujita-Rony, *American Workers, Colonial Power*. On Mexican migrations, see Benton-Cohen, *Borderline Americans*; Peck, *Reinventing Free Labor*, Zaragosa Vargas, *Proletarians of the North: A History of Mexican Industrial Workers in Detroit and the Midwest, 1917–1933* (Berkeley: University

of California Press, 1993). On labor migrations more broadly in this period, see also Greene, "Labor of Empire"; Cindy Hahamovitch, "Creating Perfect Immigrants: Guest Workers of the World in Historical Perspective," *Labor History* 44, no. 1 (2003): 69–94; and George Sanchez, "Race, Nation, and Culture in Recent Immigration Studies," *Journal of American Ethnic History* 18, no. 4 (1999): 66–84.

4. Ngai, *Impossible Subjects*, 91–166.

5. "New England Publishers Protect Manufacturers," Memorandum to the Department of Labor, July 13, 1917, box 5, folder 20/31, RG 174, NACP.

6. Norfolk and Western Railway, to Wm. Redfield, Washington DC, October 26, 1917, box 5, folder 20/31, RG 174, NACP.

7. On the rhetoric of labor shortages in this period, see Hahamovitch, *Fruits of Their Labor*, 82.

8. Samuel Gompers to William B. Wilson, August 3, 1917, box 6, folder 20/60, RG 174, NACP.

9. Report on Farm Labor in California, Commissioner of Labor, State of California, June 1917, quoted in Memorandum as to the Supply of Labor of J. W. Sullivan to Herbert Hoover, August 21, 1917, box 5, folder 20/31, RG 174, NACP.

10. Memorandum as to the Supply of Labor of J. W. Sullivan to Herbert Hoover, August 21, 1917, box 5, folder 20/31, RG 174, NACP.

11. Hahamovitch, *Fruits of Their Labor*, 95–97.

12. The Department of Labor entertained the possibility of recruiting laborers from other countries as well but usually decided against extending the order of May 23, 1917, beyond the Mexican case. In one example, the secretary of labor William B. Wilson denied the request of growers in Florida to allow workers from the Bahamas to enter the country. In a handwritten note on the subject, Wilson wrote that there was a fundamental difference between admitting laborers from Mexico, Canada, and Puerto Rico, on the one hand, and countries like the Bahamas, on the other. "The principle is the same but the psychology is different. For that reason I don't deem it advisable to extend the order." William B. Wilson, Secretary of Labor, to W.J. Spillman, Chief, Office of Markets, Department of Agriculture, September 14, 1917, box 6, folder 20/60, RG 174, NACP. The Department of Labor also rejected the possibility of repealing Chinese Exclusion. John P. White, President of the United Mine Workers, to the Secretary of Labor, June 14, 1917.

13. Congress passed the Immigration Act of 1917 on February 5, overriding President Wilson's December 14, 1916, veto. The law banned illiterate immigrants over the age of sixteen.

14. Secretary of Labor to W.J. Spillman, Chief, Office of Markets, Department of Agriculture, September 14, 1917, box 6, folder 20/60, RG 174, NACP; Office of Farm Management, Department of Agriculture, to the Assistant Secretary of Labor, August 30, 1917, box 6, folder 20/60, RG 174, NACP.

15. Benton-Cohen, *Borderline Americans*, 97.

16. Alexandra Minna Stern, "Eugenics and Racial Classification in Modern Mexican America," in *Race and Classification: The Case of Mexican America*, ed. Ilona Katzew and Susan Deans-Smith (Stanford, CA: Stanford University Press, 2009), 166.

17. Ibid., 168.

18. Samuel Gompers to William B. Wilson, August 3, 1917, box 6, folder 20/60, RG 174, NACP.

19. Assistant to the Secretary of Labor to Miss R. Lee Guard, Secretary to Mr. Gompers, October 19, 1917, box 6, folder 20/60, RG 174, NACP; Samuel Gompers, President of the American Federation of Labor, to William B. Wilson, Secretary of Labor, September 26, 1917, box 6, folder 20/60, RG 174, NACP.

20. Samuel Gompers, President of the American Federation of Labor, to William B. Wilson, Secretary of Labor, September 26, 1917, box 6, folder 20/60, RG 174, NACP.

21. Memorandum of William B. Wilson to the Commissioner-General, June 12, 1917, box 6, folder 20/60, RG 174, NACP.

22. Memorandum as to the Supply of Labor, J. W. Sullivan to Herbert Hoover, August 21, 1917, box 5, folder 20/31, RG 174, NACP.

23. Cablegram from F. C. Roberts, San Juan, Puerto Rico, to Louis F. Post, Assistant Secretary of Labor, Washington DC, November 1, 1917, box 6, folder 20/60, RG 174, NACP.

24. Secretary William B. Wilson, U.S. Department of Labor, Washington, DC, to Manuel V. Dominich, San Juan, Puerto Rico, May 29, 1918, box 6, folder 20/60, RG 174, NACP.

25. Memorandum to Chief, Construction Service, Office of the Quartermaster General, Washington, DC, February 4, 1924, box 312, folder 1493–238, RG 350, NACP. Puerto Ricans also served in U.S. military occupations overseas. See Micah Wright, "Building an Occupation: Puerto Rican Laborers in the Dominican Republic, 1916–1924," *Labor: Studies in Working-Class History of the Americas* 13, nos. 3–4 (2016): 83–103.

26. Report of the Constructing Quartermaster, Camp Jackson, South Carolina, from February 22, 1918, to April 1, 1919, 16, Camp Jackson Completion Reports 1917–1919, box 136, RG 92, NACP.

27. Ibid.

28. Report of the Constructing Quartermaster, Camp Jackson, 17.

29. At Camp Bragg outside Fayetteville, North Carolina, similar conditions prevailed. The U.S. Employment Service of the Department of Labor recruited 1,800 Puerto Ricans to work at Bragg. As in Camp Jackson, Puerto Ricans at Bragg were housed in segregated units, separated within the camp from both white and black barracks. When forty-two died from the influenza epidemic at Bragg, the majority were Puerto Ricans. Camp Bragg officials reported that the Puerto Ricans "were of little or no use" and were returned to the island "due to their inefficiency." Completion Report, Field Artillery Cantonment, Camp Bragg, Office of the Constructing Quartermaster, Fayetteville, North Carolina, July 1919, Camp Bragg Completion Reports 1917–1919, box 37, RG 92, NACP.

30. Report of the Constructing Quartermaster, Camp Jackson, 18.

31. Wm. Lay Patterson, Assistant to Chief of Bureau, to Chief, Bureau of Navigation, Navy Department, Washington, DC, June 6, 1923, box 312, folder 1493–238, RG 350, NACP.

32. Ibid.

33. Gaspar Castillo, Bayamon, Puerto Rico to the Governor of Puerto Rico, San Juan, April 15, 1923, box 312, folder 1493–238, RG 350, NACP.

34. Wm. Lay Patterson, Assistant to Chief of Bureau, to Gaspar Castillo, Bayamon, Puerto Rico, June 22, 1923, box 312, folder 1493–238, RG 350, NACP.

35. J. M. Carson, Brigadier General, Q. M. Corps to Major General Frank McIntyre, Chief of Bureau of Insular Affairs, May 11, 1921, box 312, folder 1493–238, RG 350, NACP.

36. Dr. Charles Paz to the Secretary of War, March 23, 1922, box 312, folder 1493–238, RG 350, NACP.

37. Chas. C. Walcutt, Jr. to Dr. C. Barletta Paz, 615 Canal Street, New Orleans, LA, March 31, 1922, box 312, folder 1493–238, RG 350, NACP.

38. Concha Garcia to the Governor of Porto Rico, San Juan, August 14, 1922, box 312, folder 1493–238, RG 350, NACP.

39. Felix Pagan Merly to Chief of the Bureau of Insular Affairs, May 9, 1922, box 312, folder 1493–238, RG 350, NACP.

40. Chas. C. Walcutt, Jr. to Felix Pagan Merly, May 23, 1922, box 312, folder 1493–238, RG 350, NACP.

41. Craig Robertson, *The Passport in America: The History of a Document* (New York: Oxford University Press, 2010), 160–61.

42. Richard Campbell, Commissioner of Naturalization, U.S. Department of Labor, to Chief, Bureau of Insular Affairs, War Department, April 30, 1919, box 180, folder 1390, Archivo General de Puerto Rico, San Juan (hereafter cited as AGPR).

43. British colonial subjects entering England in this period faced similar challenges as employers took full advantage of workers' ambiguous legal status. On the example of black alien seamen working in British merchant shipping, see Laura Tabili, *"We Ask for British Justice": Workers and Racial Difference in Late Imperial Britain* (Ithaca, NY: Cornell University Press, 1994), 121.

44. Chas. C. Walcutt, Jr., Acting Chief of the Bureau of Insular Affairs, to Arthur Yager, Governor of Porto Rico, June 11, 1919, box 180, folder 1390, AGPR.

45. Ibid.

46. Arthur Yager, Governor of Puerto Rico, to Chas. Walcutt, Jr., Chief, Bureau of Insular Affairs, War Department, Washington, DC, June 25, 1919, box 180, folder 1390, AGPR.

47. William Phillip, Assistant Secretary of State, to the Secretary of War, October 6, 1919, box 180, folder 1390, AGPR.

48. Ibid. President Theodore Roosevelt granted the U.S. State Department the authority to issue passports to residents of U.S. insular possessions in 1902. See Erman, "Citizens of Empire," 39.

49. Telegram from Arthur Yager, Governor of Puerto Rico, to the Secretary of War, Washington, DC, April 30, 1917, box 180, folder 1390, AGPR.

50. On the history of conscription in the context of early twentieth-century American liberalism, see Eliot A. Cohen, *Citizens and Soldiers: The Dilemmas of Military Service* (Ithaca, NY: Cornell University Press, 1985), 134–51. Memorandum of the Secretary of War on Application of pending Army Bill to Porto Rico, May 1, 1917, box 180, folder 1390, AGPR.

51. Nancy Gentile Ford, "'Mindful of the Traditions of His Race': Dual Identity and Foreign-Born Soldiers in the First World War," *Journal of American Ethnic History* 16, no. 2 (1997): 35.

52. Benjamin Heber Johnson, *Revolution in Texas: How a Forgotten Rebellion and Its Bloody Suppression Turned Mexicans into Americans* (New Haven, CT: Yale University Press, 2003), 151; Christopher Capozzola, *Uncle Sam Wants You: World War I and the Making of the Modern American Citizen* (New York: Oxford University Press, 2008), 23–54.

53. Though some like García protested the draft, others supported the war effort as a struggle for liberty. On Puerto Rican resistance to and support for the draft, see Ché Paralitici, *No quiero mi cuerpo pa' tambor: El servicio militar obligatorio en Puerto Rico* (San Juan, PR: Ediciones Puerto Rico Histórico, 1998).

54. *Garcia v. Townshend*, 251 U.S. 567 (1920), U.S. Supreme Court Records and Briefs, 7.

55. Ibid.

56. Ibid., 9.

57. Ibid., 29.

58. Ibid., 39.

59. Ibid., 29, 14.

60. "Porto Ricans Are American Citizens," broadside issued by the Bureau of Insular Affairs, War Department, October 12, 1920, box 180, folder 1390, AGPR.

61. There was precedent for U.S. immigration officials to issue government documents known as "border-crossing cards" (not passports) to Mexicans following enactment of the Immigration Act of 1917. See St. John, *Line in the Sand*, 180.

62. For a useful discussion of internal colonialism and labor reserves in American imperial contexts, see Bender and Lipman, *Making the Empire Work*, 8–9.

63. Thomas H. Gill, President, T. H. Gill Company, Greenville, North Carolina, to Frank McIntyre, Chief, Bureau of Insular Affairs, October 7, 1920, box 312, folder 1493–238, RG 350, NACP.

64. Horace Towner, Governor of Puerto Rico, to General Frank McIntryre, July 10, 1923, box 456, folder 2876, RG 350, NACP. On the Great Migration and the role of northern labor agents in recruiting blacks from the South, see Jacqueline Jones, *A Dreadful Deceit: The Myth of Race from the Colonial Era to Obama's America* (New York: Basic Books, 2013), 232.

65. Horace Towner, Governor of Puerto Rico, to Joseph Ransdell, Senator from Louisiana, June 8, 1923, box 312, folder 1493–238, RG 350, NACP.

66. Senator Ransdell to John W. Weeks, Secretary of War, June 23, 1923, box 312, folder 1493–238, RG 350, NACP.

67. R. H. Jordan, Major, Q. M. O., to Frank McIntyre, Bureau of Insular Affairs, June 14, 1923, box 312, folder 1493–238, RG 350, NACP.

68. "Report on the Emigration of Porto Rican Laborers to Arizona," by the Assistant Commissioner of Agriculture, October 11, 1926, box 312, folder 1493–238, RG 350, NACP.

69. Report on the Puerto Rican Situation in Arizona, by E.J. Walker, Arizona Cotton Growers' Association, General Manager, submitted to Frank McIntyre, Chief, Bureau of Insular Affairs, February 9, 1927, box 312, folder 1493, RG 350, NACP.

70. On the Johnson-Reed Act and immigrant exclusion, see Ngai, *Impossible Subjects*, 21–55.

71. Quoted in Frank McIntyre, Chief of the Bureau of Insular Affairs, to Governor Horace Towner, San Juan, February 17, 1927, box 312, folder 1493, RG 350, NACP.

72. Report on the Puerto Rican Situation in Arizona, by E.J. Walker, Arizona Cotton Growers' Association, General Manager, submitted to Frank McIntyre, Chief, Bureau of Insular Affairs, February 9, 1927, box 312, folder 1493, RG 350, NACP.

73. Benton-Cohen, *Borderline Americans*, 248.

74. Stern, "Eugenics and Racial Classification," 168.

75. Benton-Cohen, *Borderline Americans*, 203–38.

76. Memorandum of Santiago Iglesias, Secretary, American Federation of Labor, September 1926, box 312, folder 1493–238, RG 350, NACP.

77. Hahamovitch "Creating Perfect Immigrants," 80.

78. Zaragosa Vargas, *Proletarians of the North*, 83.

79. Peck, *Reinventing Free Labor*, 198–225.

80. Ibid., 171.

81. "Nation Watches Plan for Aiding Labor Shortage," *Arizona Republican*, Phoenix, August 1, 1926, box 312, folder 1493-A, RG 350, NACP.

82. *Porto Rico Progress*, September 8, 1926, box 312, folder 1493-A, RG 350, NACP. On the history of Chinese migrants in the agricultural regions of Louisiana and the Caribbean and the racial ideologies by which racial nativists defined them as "coolies" and cheap laborers, see Moon-Ho Jung, *Coolies and Cane: Race, Labor and Sugar in the Age of Emancipation* (Baltimore, MD: Johns Hopkins University Press, 2006).

83. On the partnership between business and the state in this period, see Emily Rosenberg, *Spreading the American Dream: American Economic and Cultural Expansion, 1890–1945* (New York: Hill and Wang, 1982), 138–61. See also Sven Beckert, *Monied Metropolis: New York City and the Consolidation of the American Bourgeoisie, 1850–1896* (Cambridge: Cambridge University Press, 2001); and Frank McIntyre, Chief of the Bureau of Insular Affairs, to Horace Towner, Governor of Puerto Rico, February 23, 1926, box 312, folder 1493–238, RG 350, NACP.

84. Frank McIntyre, Chief of the Bureau of Insular Affairs, to Conrado Andino, Ponce, Puerto Rico, December 29, 1925, box 312, folder 1493–238, RG 350, NACP.

85. Report on the Puerto Rican Situation in Arizona, by E.J. Walker, Arizona Cotton Growers' Association, General Manager, submitted to Frank McIntyre, Chief, Bureau of Insular Affairs, February 9, 1927, box 312, folder 1493, RG 350, NACP.

86. As part of the commissioner's effort to monitor contract laborers going to the United States, a survey of potential employers was developed. Questions included, "Does the state government morally or materially guarantee through writing a strict compliance with the stipulated conditions?" "If the laborer is married or leaves his family in Porto Rico, which will be the condition of such a family and how will it receive the aid of the laborer who supports it?" Chas. C. Walcutt, Jr., Assistant to the Chief of the Bureau of Insular Affairs, Washington, DC, to Franco Viques, Philadelphia, PA, May 3, 1923, box 312, folder 1493–238, RG 350, NACP.

87. "Report on the Emigration of Porto Rican Laborers to Arizona," by the Assistant Commissioner of Agriculture, October 11, 1926, box 312, folder 1493–238, RG 350, NACP.

88. Report on the Puerto Rican Situation in Arizona, by E.J. Walker, Arizona Cotton Growers' Association, General Manager, submitted to Frank McIntyre, Chief, Bureau of Insular Affairs, February 9, 1927, box 312, folder 1493, RG 350, NACP.

89. Juan Flores, foreword to *A Puerto Rican in New York and Other Sketches*, by Jesús Colón, 2nd ed. (New York: International, 1982), ix; Bernardo Vega, *Memoirs of Bernardo Vega: A Contribution to the History of the Puerto Rican Community in New York*, ed. César Andreu Iglesias, trans. Juan Flores (New York: Monthly Review Press, 1984), 19–26, 92–100.

90. Santiago Iglesias to Frank McIntyre, October 2, 1926, box 312, folder 1493–238, RG 350, NACP.

91. Frank McIntyre to Santiago Iglesias, October 9, 1926, box 312, folder 1493–238, RG 350, NACP.

92. Cable from Governor Towner of Puerto Rico, San Juan, to Dr. James Bague, Cotton Growers Association, Phoenix, AZ, September 27, 1926, box 312, folder 1493–238, RG 350, NACP.

93. Telegram from the Phoenix Central Trades Council to William Green, American Federation of Labor, September 1926, box 312, folder 1493–238, RG 350, NACP.

94. Collected telegrams to William Green, American Federation of Labor, September 1926, box 312, folder 1493–238, RG 350, NACP.

95. Telegram from the Central Labor Council of Phoenix to William Green, President, American Federation of Labor, September 1926, box 312, folder 1493–238, RG 350, NACP.

96. William Green succeeded Samuel Gompers as AFL president in 1924. Telegram from the Central Labor Council of Phoenix to William Green, President, American Federation of Labor, September 1926, box 312, folder 1493–238, RG 350, NACP.

97. Memorandum of Santiago Iglesias, Secretary, American Federation of Labor, September 1926, box 312, folder 1493–238, RG 350, NACP.

98. Ibid.

99. The Congress of the Pan-American Federation of Labor grew out of the International Labor Conference of Pan American Countries held in Laredo, TX, in November 1918. AFL calls for restricting labor migration from member nations to the United States had earlier caused a rift in the congress. In June of 1919, the AFL approved a resolution calling for a ban on immigration from Europe and Mexico for four years. Latin American representatives to the Pan-American Federation took offense and threatened to dissolve the congress. Gompers later made amends by claiming the measure was necessary to protect the jobs and standard of living of American soldiers returning from the World War. See "Gompers Explains Immigrant Problem," *New York Times*, July 10, 1919.

100. "American Labor Federation Satisfied Effective Restrictions to Be Placed on Immigration of Porto Rican Labor," *Arizona Gazette*, October 12, 1926, box 312, folder 1493, RG 350, NACP.

101. Ibid.

102. E.J. Walker, Arizona Cotton Growers Association, to Mr. Frank McIntyre, Chief of Bureau of Insular Affairs, War Department, Washington, DC, August 30, 1928, box 312, folder 1493, RG 350, NACP.

103. Ibid.

104. Report on the Puerto Rican Situation in Arizona, by E.J. Walker, Arizona Cotton Growers' Association, General Manager, submitted to Frank McIntyre, Chief, Bureau of Insular Affairs, February 9, 1927, box 312, folder 1493, RG 350, NACP.

105. Ibid.

106. Manolo Hernandez, Florence, AZ, to Don Salomon Hernandez, Comerio, PR, January 11, 1927, box 312, folder 1493, RG 350, NACP.

107. Bacilo Rivera, Litchfield Camp 51, Arizona, USA, n.d., box 312, folder 1493, RG 350, NACP.

108. E.J. Walker to Frank McIntyre, November 4, 1926, box 312, folder 1493, RG 350, NACP.

109. Santiago Iglesias, Spanish Language Secretary of the American Federation of Labor, to General Frank McIntyre, Chief of Bureau of Insular Affairs, February 2, 1927, box 312, folder 1493, RG 350, NACP.

110. Quoted in "Arizona Cotton Growers Lose in Labor Experiment," *Porto Rico Progress*, November 10, 1926, box 312, folder 1493-A, RG 350, NACP.

111. "Immigrants Who Are Not Immigrants," *Galveston News*, June 29, 1929, box 312, folder 1493-A, RG 350, NACP.

112. Telegram of Governor Towner to Frank McIntyre, War Department, November 28, 1927, box 312, folder 1493, RG 350, NACP.

113. "Gore Plans to Colonize Puerto Ricans in Florida," *New York Herald Tribune*, June 29, 1933, box 312, folder 1493-A, RG 350, NACP.

114. "Gore Asks Florida O.K. on Sugar Plan," Associated Press, December 28, 1933, box 312, folder 1493-A, RG 350, NACP.

115. "Statement of Prudencio Rivera Martinez on the Suggestion for an Emigration of Puerto Rican Families," *El Mundo*, San Juan, PR, May 23, 1933, box 312, folder 1493-A, RG 350, NACP. Social critics argued that conditions in the U.S. cotton belt resembled colonialism abroad. In 1921 William Pickens of the NAACP dubbed the region the "American Congo." See Jones, *Dreadful Deceit*, 233.

116. 1920 Census figures quoted in E. M. Lewis, "A General Staff Study: Importation of Porto Ricans as an Asset to the Military Manpower of Hawai'i," Headquarters Hawaiian Department, U.S. War Department, August 7, 1925, box 312, folder 1493-A, RG 350, NACP.

117. On the use of segmented labor in the banana zones of United Fruit Company in Costa Rica and Guatemala, see Jason M. Colby, *The Business of Empire: United Fruit, Race, and U.S. Expansion in Central America* (Ithaca, NY: Cornell University Press, 2011).

118. As the American-born generation (Nisei) came of age, political observers took note. The University of Hawai'i sociologist Romanzo Adams predicted in 1936 that by the mid-1940s two-thirds of the Asian population in Hawai'i would be able to vote. Dean Itsuji Saranillio, "Colliding Histories: Hawai'i Statehood at the Intersection of Asians 'Ineligible to Citizenship' and Hawaiians 'Unfit for Self-Government,'" *Journal of Asian American Studies* 13, no. 3 (October 2010): 295.

119. "Lenroot Sees Menace by Japanese in Hawai'i," *Washington Post*, April 12, 1923.

120. E.M. Lewis, "A General Staff Study: Importation of Porto Ricans as an Asset of the Military Manpower of Hawai'i," Headquarters Hawaiian Department, U.S. War Department, August 7, 1925, box 456, folder 2876, RG 350, NACP.

121. Memorandum of Frank McIntyre to the Secretary of War, U.S. War Department, April 12, 1923, box 456, folder 2876, RG 350, NACP.

122. E.M. Lewis, "A General Staff Study: Importation of Porto Ricans as an Asset of the Military Manpower of Hawai'i," Headquarters Hawaiian Department, U.S. War Department, August 7, 1925, box 456, folder 2876, RG 350, NACP.

123. Ibid.

124. Memorandum to the Bureau of Insular Affairs, "Immigration of Porto Rican Laborers to Hawai'i," August 30, 1921, box 456, folder 2876, RG 350, NACP.

125. Petition of Pedro Guzman et al., to the Porto Rican House of Delegates, March 5, 1919, box 456, folder 2876, RG 350, NACP.

126. Ibid.

127. F. L. Amadeo, Secretary of House of Representatives, Puerto Rico, to Félix Córdova Dávila, Resident Commissioner, Washington, DC, April 30, 1919.

128. Petition of Pedro Guzman et al., to the Porto Rican House of Delegates, March 5, 1919, box 456, folder 2876, RG 350, NACP.

129. Ibid.

130. Poblete, *Islanders in the Empire*, 79–80; Susan K. Serrano, "Dual Consciousness about Law and Justice: Puerto Ricans' Battle for U.S. Citizenship in Hawai'i," *CENTRO: Journal of the Center for Puerto Rican Studies* 29, no. 1 (Spring 2017): 164–201.

131. E. M. Lewis, "A General Staff Study: Importation of Porto Ricans as an Asset of the Military Manpower of Hawai'i," Headquarters Hawaiian Department, U.S. War Department, August 7, 1925, box 456, folder 2876, RG 350, NACP.

132. Ibid.

133. "El Hawaii está Considerando la Importación de Trabajadores Puertorriqueños para sus Plantaciones," *La Democracia*, December 19, 1930.

134. Quoted in Kramer, *Blood of Government*, 414.

135. "Hawai'i Seeks Laborers: Sugar Planters May Bring in Men from Porto Rico," *New York Times*, December 6, 1930.

136. "Hawai'i Seeks Labor Supply," July 27, 1931, Newspaper clipping file, Bureau of Insular Affairs, box 456, folder 2876, RG 350, NACP.

137. "Hawaiian Labor Problem," n.d., 1931, Newspaper clipping file, Bureau of Insular Affairs, box 456, folder 2876, RG 350, NACP.

138. "Hoover's Visit Spurs Porto Rican Migration," April 24, 1931, Associated Press, Newspaper clipping file, Bureau of Insular Affairs, box 456, folder 2876, RG 350, NACP.

139. See Kramer, *Blood of Government*, 414.

140. Even after the Welch Bill failed, anti-Filipino forces in Washington continued to seek a legislative means of exclusion. Paul Kramer has argued that the anti-Filipino forces behind the proposed 1930 Welch Bill later helped pass the 1934 Tydings McDuffie Act, eventually granting independence in 1946. See Kramer, *Blood of Government*, 414, 423.

141. "Los Puertorriqueños no deben pensar por ahora embarcarse para Los Estados Unidos," Clippings File, August 31, 1931, box 312, folder 1493-A, RG 350, NACP.

142. By 1940 the Hawai'ian Sugar Planters Association had still not recruited the 100,000 workers from Puerto Rico that it had planned in 1930. The Puerto Rican population in Hawai'i numbered 6,671 in the 1930 census, and, through natural increase, rose to 8,296 in 1940. See Robert C. Schmitt, *Demographic Statistics of Hawaii: 1776–1965* (Honolulu: University of Hawai'i Press, 1968), and Robert C. Schmitt, *Historical Statistics of Hawaii* (Honolulu: University of Hawai'i Press, 1977), 25–27.

6. Colonial Migrants in New York

1. "Starving Family: Ptomaine Victims: Parents and Four Children, Discovered Ill in a Bare Room, Are Aided by Police," *New York Times*, January 15, 1921.

2. "Story of a Porto Rican Family," n.d., box 312, folder 1493-A, RG 350, NACP.

3. Frank Martinez, New York, to Félix Córdova Dávila, Washington, DC, January 19, 1921, box 312, folder 1493–238, RG 350, NACP.

4. R. A. Sierra to Hon. Félix Córdova Dávila, Resident Commissioner of Porto Rico, Washington, DC, January 15, 1921, box 456, folder 2876, RG 350, NACP.

5. Cable from Arthur Yager to the Bureau of Insular Affairs, January 26, 1921, box 456, folder 2876, RG 350, NACP.

6. One of numerous organizations in the *colonia*, the Asociación Portorriqueña was based at 244 West 114th Street in New York. G. O'Neill, President of the Asociación Portorriqueña to Newton Baker, Secretary of War, February 19, 1921, box 312, folder 1493–238, RG 350, NACP.

7. G. O'Neill, President of the Asociación Portorriqueña to Newton Baker, Secretary of War, February 19, 1921, box 312, folder 1493–238, RG 350, NACP.

8. "A la memoria de Gonzalo O'Neill," n.d., box 2, folder 1, Erasmo Vando Papers, Puerto Rican Diaspora Archives, Centro de Estudios Puertorriqueños, Hunter College, New York. See also Lorrin Thomas, *Puerto Rican Citizen: History and Political Identity in Twentieth-Century New York City* (Chicago: University of Chicago Press, 2010), 52–53.

9. Sánchez Korrol, *From Colonia to Community*, 196.

10. E. Victor Fiol Ramós, "La petitión dirigida para que las autoridades municipals de Nueva York atendeiesen a los puertorriqueños necesitados y que fué atendida," *La Democracia*, March 7, 1921.

11. Frank McIntyre to Arthur Yager, February 17, 1921, box 456, folder 2876, RG 350, NACP.

12. Félix Córdova Dávila, Resident Commissioner, Washington, DC, to Jose Cruzado, New York, December 31, 1920, box 312, folder 1493–238, RG 350, NACP.

13. Kramer, "Power and Connection," 1382.

14. *Puerto Rico Progress*, October 1, 1931.

15. Richard Enright, New York City Police Commissioner, to Frank McIntyre, Chief, Bureau of Insular Affairs, February 14, 1921, box 312, folder 1493–238, RG 350, NACP.

16. On the history of New York state-level immigration restrictions that originally targeted Irish paupers in the late nineteenth century, and the influence of such state laws on federal immigration policy in the twentieth century, see Hidetaka Hirota, "The Moment of Transition: State Officials, the Federal Government, and the Formation of American Immigration Policy," *Journal of American History* 99, no. 4 (March 2013): 1092–1108.

17. Francisco E. Balderrama and Raymond Rodríguez, *Decade of Betrayal: Mexican Repatriation in the 1930s* (Albuquerque: University of New Mexico Press, 2006), 120–21.

18. Congress first enacted the Bureau of Immigration and Naturalization Act (BINA) in 1906 to allow Puerto Ricans to naturalize, but the meaning of the law was later clarified in the 1915 ruling. Charles Venator-Santiago, "Mapping the Contours of the History of the Extension of U.S. Citizenship to Puerto Rico, 1898–Present," *CENTRO: Journal of the Center for Puerto Rican Studies* 29, no. 1 (Spring 2017): 46.

19. G. O'Neill to Félix Córdova Dávila, February 17, 1921, box 312, folder 1493–238, RG 350, NACP.

20. "From New York," letter of E. Victor Fiol Ramós, *La Democracia*, San Juan, PR, January 27, 1921.

21. Robert F. Foerster, "The Racial Problems Involved in Immigration from Latin America and the West Indies to the United States," report submitted to the Secretary of Labor, U.S. Department of Labor (Washington, DC: Government Printing Office, 1925).

22. Ibid., 35.

23. Ibid., 44.

24. Ibid., 48.

25. Melissa Nobles, *Shades of Citizenship: Race and the Census in Modern Politics* (Stanford, CA: Stanford University Press, 2000), 68.

26. Ibid., 73–74.

27. Ibid., 68–69, 73–74.

28. Thomas A. Guglielmo, *White on Arrival: Italians, Race, Color, and Power in Chicago, 1890–1945* (New York: Oxford University Press, 2004), 5–13.

29. Matthew Frye Jacobson, *Whiteness of a Different Color: European Immigrants and the Alchemy of Race* (Cambridge, MA: Harvard University Press, 1998), 222.

30. Ngai, *Impossible Subjects*, 254.

31. Foerster, "Racial Problems," 53, 59.

32. Ibid., 2, 61.

33. Clara E. Rodríguez, "Racial Themes in the Literature," in *Hispanic New York: A Sourcebook*, ed. Claudio Iván Remeseira (New York: Columbia University Press, 2010).

34. Lawrence R. Chenault, "The Puerto Rican Migrant in New York City" (PhD diss., Columbia University, 1938), 150. For a more recent treatment of this subject, see Nancy S. Landale and R. S. Oropesa, "White, Black, or Puerto Rican? Racial Self-Identification among Mainland and Island Puerto Ricans," *Social Forces* 81, no. 1 (September 2002): 236.

35. Rodriguez, "Racial Themes in the Literature," 120.

36. "Porto Rican Enters Protest," *New York Times*, July 15, 1923.

37. Ibid.

38. Ibid.

39. "Puerto Rico pide que se les considere iguales a los demas 'American citizens,'" *La Prensa*, March 21, 1924.

40. Petition of the Telegraph Operators of Ponce, Puerto Rico, to Frank McIntyre, Chief of the Bureau of Insular Affairs, Washington, DC, June 29, 1923, box 312, folder 1493-A, RG 350, NACP.

41. Fred Armstrong, "A Ray of Light," *La Democracia*, San Juan, June 27, 1923.

42. F. Vall Spinoza to Frank McIntyre, June 23, 1923, box 312, folder 1493-A, RG 350, NACP.

43. Fred Armstrong, "Insular Transport Service," *La Democracia*, n.d. (c. 1923), box 312, folder 1493-A, RG 350, NACP.

44. Fred Armstrong, "Immigration," *La Democracia*, April 10, 1923.

45. Colby, *Business of Empire*, 122–23.

46. "Siervos coloniales" in the original Spanish. "La situación actual en Puerto Rico es el resultado del vicioso sistem colonial," *El Tiempo*, October 1, 1926.

47. Ibid.

48. Ibid.

49. "Porto Rican Labor Imports Suspended," *Christian Science Monitor*, October 12, 1926.

50. "Informe rendido por el senador Iglesias sobre su estudio," *El Mundo*, May 5, 1932.

51. Governor Towner to General McIntyre, June 1, 1927, box 312, folder 1493, RG 350, NACP.

52. Jaime Bague, Acting Commissioner, Puerto Rican Bureau of Labor and Agriculture, to the Governor of Puerto Rico, May 27, 1927, box 312, folder 1493, RG 350, NACP.

53. "Los portorriqueños no son extranjeros," Tribuna Libre, *La Prensa*, August 6, 1926.

54. Thomas, *Puerto Rican Citizen*, 51.

55. "Los portorriqueños no son extranjeros."

56. "Cohesion Hispana en Harlem, *La Prensa*, August 10, 1926. See also "Liga Cívica Hispana en Nueva York," *La Prensa*, August 5, 1926; and "Quedó constituida el domingo la Liga Portorriqueña e Hispana en Harlem," August 10, 1926.

57. Thomas, *Puerto Rican Citizen*, 54–55.

58. Ibid.

59. Gabriel Haslip-Viera, "The Evolution of the Latino Community in New York City: Early Nineteenth Century to the Present," in *Latinos in New York: Communities in Transition*, ed. Gabriel Haslip-Viera and Sherrie L. Baver (Notre Dame, IN: University of Notre Dame Press, 1996), 8.

60. Ibid., 7–9.

61. Ibid.

62. *New York American*, c. February 5, 1931, quoted in "Rechazando un insulto," *La Democracia*, February 5, 1931.

63. "Rechazando un insulto," *La Democracia*, February 5, 1931.

64. "150,000 Porto Ricans Give New York Headache: Welfare Bodies Meet April 11 to Study Problems," *Baltimore Afro-American*, April 12, 1930.

65. Ibid.

66. "Repatriating Porto Ricans," *Porto Rico Progress*, January 8, 1931, 13, box 312, folder 1493-A, RG 350, NACP.

67. *Puerto Rico Progress*, October 1, 1931.

68. For what little has been written on the subject, see Thomas, *Puerto Rican Citizen*, 93.

69. George J. Sanchez, *Becoming Mexican American: Ethnicity, Culture, and Identity in Chicano Los Angeles, 1900–1945* (New York: Oxford University Press, 1995), 215–16.

70. Irma Watkins-Owens, *Blood Relations: Caribbean Immigrants and the Harlem Community, 1900–1930* (Bloomington: Indiana University Press, 1996), 169; Lara Putnam, *Radical Moves: Caribbean Migrants and the Politics of Race in the Jazz Age* (Chapel Hill: University of North Carolina Press, 2013).

71. Thomas, *Puerto Rican Citizen*, 93.

72. Mexicans in Rockdale, IL, to the Chicago Mexican Consulate, December 30, 1930, Archivo de la Secretaría de Relaciones Exteriores, Mexico City, IV-354-4, quoted in Balderrama, *Decade of Betrayal*, 115.

73. "Los Portorriqueños," *Grafico*, March 27, 1927, 2, quoted in Thomas, *Puerto Rican Citizen*, 55.

74. Balderrama, *Decade of Betrayal*, 102.

75. Ibid.

76. "The Anti-Filipino Riots," *Los Angeles Times*, January 28, 1930.

77. Ibid.

78. Ibid.

79. Sanchez, *Becoming Mexican American*, 215–16.

80. "Great Migration Back to Mexico Under Way," *Los Angeles Times*, April 12, 1931.

81. Ibid.

82. "Two Views on Immigration," *Washington Post*, March 30, 1927.

83. "Pair Accused of Immigrant Fraud," *Los Angeles Times*, April 12, 1931.

84. "Two Seized as Agents of Citizenship 'Racket': Police Charge Suspects Sold Forged Porto Rican Birth Certificates to Aliens," *New York Times*, April 12, 1931.

85. "New York Police Waging War on Alien Criminals: Ellis Island Packed with Those Who Will Be Sent Back from Whence They Came to Plague the United States," *Boston Globe*, March 6, 1931, 4.

86. Ibid.

87. Ibid.

88. Ibid.

89. "Puerto Ricans Here Are Put at 100,000: Migration to This Country That Began after the Spanish-American War Is Still Under Way," *New York Times*, June 19, 1932.

90. "150,000 Porto Ricans Give New York Headache: Welfare Bodies Meet April 11 to Study Problems," *Baltimore Afro-American*, April 12, 1930.

91. "Alien Student Ruling Affects 150 at Howard," *Baltimore Afro-American*, October 22, 1932.

92. *Balzac v. Porto Rico*, 258 U.S. 298 (1922), quoted in Bartholomew H. Sparrow, "The Centennial of *Ocampo v. United States*: Lessons from the Insular Cases," in Neuman and Brown-Nagin, *Reconsidering the Insular Cases*, 47.

93. Memorandum from F. LeJ. Parker, Acting Chief of the Bureau of Insular Affairs to the Secretary of War, August 17, 1933, box 312, folder 1493, RG 350, NACP.

94. Ngai, *Impossible Subjects*. See also Richard S. Kim, *The Quest for Statehood: Korean Immigrant Nationalism and U.S. Sovereignty, 1905–45* (New York: Oxford University Press, 2011).

95. Memorandum from F. LeJ. Parker, Acting Chief of the Bureau of Insular Affairs to the Secretary of War, August 17, 1933, box 312, folder 1493, RG 350, NACP.

96. Sánchez Korrol, *From Colonia to Community*, 178.

97. Unsigned letter to President Franklin Delano Roosevelt, August 11, 1933, box 312, folder 1493, RG 350, NACP.

98. F. LeJ. Parker to Theodore Roosevelt Jr., January 17, 1931, box 312, folder 1493, RG 350, NACP.

99. Thomas, *Puerto Rican Citizen*, 41.

100. Alexander Keyssar, "The Strange Career of Voter Suppression," *New York Times*, February 12, 2012.

101. Thomas, *Puerto Rican Citizen*, 185.

102. Ibid.; Joseph P. Fitzpatrick, *Puerto Rican Americans: The Meaning of Migration to the Mainland* (Englewood Cliffs, NJ: Prentice-Hall, 1971), 57–58.

103. Interview with Homero Rosado, Brooklyn College, Brooklyn, NY, November 1980, quoted in Sánchez Korrol, *From Colonia to Community*, 183.

104. Carlos R. Soltero, *Latinos and American Law: Landmark Supreme Court Cases* (Austin: University of Texas Press, 2006), 50–56.

105. Soltero, *Latinos and American Law*, 56.

106. "La organización del voto," *La Prensa*, October 9, 1924.

107. "Hay que inscribirse: Votar!," *La Prensa*, October 9, 1928; "La organización del voto," *La Prensa*, October 9, 1924; "El voto portorriqueño en Nueva York," *La Prensa*, October 15, 1923. See also "Los portorriqueños deben inscribirse esta semana," *La Prensa*, October 11, 1923.

108. Thomas, *Puerto Rican Citizen*, 51.

109. "El voto portorriqueño en Nueva York," *La Prensa*, October 15, 1923.

110. "La organización del voto," *La Prensa*, October 9, 1924.

111. "El voto portorriqueño en Nueva York," *La Prensa*, October 15, 1923.

112. Ibid.

113. "Los 40,000 votos portorriqueños de aquí son una gran fuerza política," *La Prensa*, March 8, 1927.

114. Interview with Ramón Colón, Puerto Rican Oral History Project, 1973–74, Long Island Historical Society, Brooklyn, NY, quoted in Sánchez Korrol, *From Colonia to Community*, 186.

115. Donna R. Gabaccia, *Foreign Relations: American Immigration in Global Perspective* (Princeton: Princeton University Press, 2012), 108. On the Irish case, see David Sim, *A Union Forever: The Irish Question and U.S. Foreign Relations in the Victorian Age* (Ithaca, NY: Cornell University Press, 2013).

116. Gabaccia, *Foreign Relations*, 118–19.

117. Thomas, *Puerto Rican Citizen*, 97.

Conclusion

1. "Sees Little Hope of Raising Bars to Immigrants," Jewish Telegraphic Agency, March 4, 1935.

2. "Puerto Rican Curb Urged: Reimer Warns Free Entry Here Is Adding to Slum Problem," *New York Times*, May 20, 1937.

3. Tabili, *"We Ask for British Justice,"* 183.

4. Laura Briggs has argued that the rise of "culture of poverty" theories in the mid-twentieth century signaled a shift from ideas of biological or racial determinism to ideas of cultural determinism. Laura Briggs, *Reproducing Empire: Race, Sex, Science, and U.S. Imperialism in Puerto Rico* (Berkeley: University of California Press, 2002), 165.

5. "Republicans Win Control at Albany," *New York Times*, November 9, 1938.

6. "Republicans Drop an Assemblyman," *New York Times*, June 30, 1938.

7. On the failure of Puerto Ricans to win sustained political recognition in the 1930s and 1940s, see Thomas, *Puerto Rican Citizen*, 102–32.

8. On post–World War II histories, see Whalen, *From Puerto Rico to Philadelphia*; Clara Rodríguez, *Puerto Ricans: Born in the U.S.A.* (Boulder, CO: Westview Press, 1991); Bourgois, *In Search of Respect*; Lilia Fernández, *Brown in the Windy City: Mexicans and Puerto Ricans in Postwar Chicago* (Chicago: University of Chicago Press, 2012); Eileen J. Suárez Findlay, *We Are Left without a Father Here: Masculinity, Domesticity, and Migration in Postwar Puerto Rico* (Durham, NC: Duke University Press, 2014); and Edgardo Meléndez, *Sponsored Migration: The State and Puerto Rican Postwar Migration to the United States* (Columbus: The Ohio State University Press, 2017). See also Juan Gonzalez, *Harvest of Empire: A History of Latinos in America* (New York: Viking, 2000).

9. In 2012, 4.9 million Puerto Ricans lived on the U.S. mainland and 3.5 million lived on the island. D'Vera Cohen, Eileen Patten, and Mark Hugo Lopez, "Puerto Rican Population Declines on Island, Grows on U.S. Mainland," August 11, 2014, *Pew Research Center: Hispanic Trends*, accessed March 17, 2017, http://www.pewhispanic.org/2014/08/11/puerto-rican-population-declines-on-island-grows-on-u-s-mainland/.

Bibliography

Archives and Other Repositories

Archivo General de Puerto Rico, San Juan (AGPR)
Baker Library, Harvard Business School, Boston
Centro de Estudios Puertorriqueños, Hunter College, New York
Collección Puertorriqueña, University of Puerto Rico, Río Piedras
George Meany Memorial AFL-CIO Archive, Special Collections and University Archives, University of Maryland Libraries, College Park
Library of Congress, Washington, DC
National Archives at Boston, Waltham, MA
National Archives at College Park, MD (NACP)
National Archives at New York, New York
National Archives Building, Washington, DC (NAB)
New York Public Library, New York
Special Collections and University Archives, University of Maryland Libraries, College Park
Widener Library, Harvard University, Cambridge, MA

Newspapers and Periodicals

El Águila (Ponce, Puerto Rico)
American Federationist (New York)
Arizona Republican (Phoenix)
Baltimore Afro-American
Chicago Defender
Christian Science Monitor (Boston)
La Correspondencia (San Juan)
La Democracia (Ponce)
Ensayo Obrero (San Juan)
La Federación Obrera (San Juan)
Galveston News (Houston)
Grafico (New York)
Los Angeles Times
El Mundo (San Juan)
New York Evening Post
New York Herald Tribune
New York Times
Porvenir Social (San Juan)
Porto Rico Progress (San Juan)
La Prensa (New York)
El Tiempo (San Juan)
Union Obrera (Mayaguez, Puerto Rico)
Washington Post (Washington, DC)
Washington Star (Washington, NJ)

Printed Primary Sources

Albert, Peter, ed. *The Samuel Gompers Papers*. Urbana: University of Illinois Press, 1997, 2003.

American Federation of Labor. *American Federation of Labor: History, Encyclopedia, Reference Book; Guide to AFL Convention Records*. Washington, DC: n.p., 1919.

Arias, George Bird. "A Plea for Porto Ricans." In *Proceedings of the Twenty-Fifth Annual Lake Mohonk Conference of Friends of the Indian and Other Dependent Peoples*. New York: Lake Mohonk Conference, 1907.

Baldwin, Simeon E. "The Constitutional Questions Incident to the Acquisition and Government by the United States of Island Territory." *Harvard Law Review* 12 (1899): 393–416.

Brannon, Henry. *A Treatise on the Rights and Privileges Guaranteed by the Fourteenth Amendment to the Constitution of the United States*. Cincinnati, OH: W. H. Anderson, 1901.

Burgess, J. W. "The Relation of the Constitution of the United States to Newly Acquired Territory." *Political Science Quarterly* 25, no. 3 (September 1900): 381–98.

Commons, John. *Races and Immigrants in America*. New York: MacMillan, 1907.

Gompers, Samuel. *Seventy Years of Life and Labor: An Autobiography*. Vol. 2. New York: E. P. Dutton, 1925.

Iglesias Pantín, Santiago. *Luchas emancipadoras: Crónicas de Puerto Rico*. San Juan, PR: n.p., 1958.

——. *A People without a Country: Appeal for U.S. Citizenship for the People of Porto Rico*. Washington, DC: American Federation of Labor, 1912.

Kemmerer, Edwin Walter. *Modern Currency Reforms: A History and Discussion of Recent Currency Reforms in India, Porto Rico, Philippine Islands, Straits Settlements and Mexico*. New York: MacMillan, 1916.

Lowell, Abbott Lawrence. "The Colonial Expansion of the United States." *Atlantic Monthly*, vol. 83, February 1899.

——. "The Status of Our New Possessions: A Third View." *Harvard Law Review* 13, no. 3 (1899): 155–76.

Neely, F. Tennyson. *Neely's Panorama of Our New Possessions*. New York: F. Tennyson Neely, 1898.

Our New Possessions: Cuba, Puerto Rico, Hawaii, Philippines. New York: American Book, 1899.

Puerto Rico: A Guide to the Island of Boriquén. Compiled and written by the Puerto Rico Reconstruction Administration in cooperation with the Writers' Program of the Work Projects Administration; sponsored by the Puerto Rico Department of Education. New York: University Society, 1940.

Reid, Whitelaw. *Problems of Expansion*. New York: Century, 1900.

Rowe, L. S. *The United States and Porto Rico: With Special Reference to the Problems Arising out of Our Contact with the Spanish-American Civilization*. New York: Longmans, Green, 1904.

Schmitt, Robert C. *Demographic Statistics of Hawaii, 1776–1965*. Honolulu: University of Hawai'i Press, 1968.

——. *Historical Statistics of Hawaii*. Honolulu: University of Hawai'i Press, 1977.

Smith, Goldwin. *The United States: An Outline of Political History, 1492–1871*. New York: MacMillan, 1893.

Tansill, Charles Callan. *The Purchase of the Danish West Indies*. Baltimore: Johns Hopkins Press, 1932.

Thayer, James Bradley. "Our New Possessions." *Harvard Law Review* 12, no. 7 (1899): 464–85.

Tuero, Fernando López. *Isla de Puerto-Rico: Estudios de economía rural*. Puerto Rico: Imprenta del Boletin Mercantil, 1893.

White, Trumbull. *Our New Possessions*. Rock Island, IL: L. E. West, 1898.

Secondary Sources

Amar, Akhil Reed. *The Bill of Rights: Creation and Reconstruction*. New Haven, CT: Yale University Press, 1998.

Aponte, Irene Fernández. "La dislocalización poblacional y el éxodo migratorio como resultado del huracán de San Ciriaco." In *La llegada del Cíclope: Percepciones de San Ciriaco a cien años de su visita*, edited by Raquel Rosario Rivera, 113–21. San Juan, PR: Fundación Puertorriqueña de las Humanidades, 2000.

Argüelles, María del Pilar. *Morality and Power: The U.S. Colonial Experience in Puerto Rico from 1898 to 1948*. Lanham, MD: University Press of America, 1996.

Ayala, César J., and Rafael Bernabe. *Puerto Rico in the American Century: A History since 1898*. Chapel Hill: University of North Carolina Press, 2007.

Azuma, Eiichiro. "Racial Struggle, Immigrant Nationalism, and Ethnic Identity: Japanese and Filipinos in the California Delta," *Pacific Historic Review* 67, no. 2 (1998): 163–99.

Balderrama, Francisco E., and Raymond Rodríguez. *Decade of Betrayal: Mexican Repatriation in the 1930s*. Rev. ed. Albuquerque: University of New Mexico Press, 2006. First published in 1995.

Baldoz, Rick. *The Third Asiatic Invasion: Empire and Migration in Filipino America, 1898–1946*. New York: New York University Press, 2011.

Baldoz, Rick, and César Ayala. "The Bordering of America: Colonialism and Citizenship in the Philippines and Puerto Rico." *CENTRO: Journal of the Center for Puerto Rican Studies* 25, no. 1 (Spring 2013): 76–105.

Baralt, Guillermo A. *Buena Vista: Life and Work on a Puerto Rican Hacienda, 1833–1904*. Chapel Hill: University of North Carolina Press, 1999.

Beckert, Sven. "From Tuskegee to Togo: The Problem of Freedom in the Empire of Cotton." *Journal of American History* 92, no. 2 (2005): 498–526.

——. *Monied Metropolis: New York City and the Consolidation of the American Bourgeoisie, 1850–1896*. Cambridge: Cambridge University Press, 2001.

Bedford, Joseph. "Samuel Gompers and the Caribbean: The AFL, Cuba, and Puerto Rico, 1898–1906." *Labor's Heritage* 6, no. 4 (1995): 4–25.

Beisner, Robert *Twelve against Empire: The Anti-Imperialists, 1898–1900*. New York: McGraw Hill, 1968.

Bender, Daniel E., and Jana K. Lipman. *Making the Empire Work: Labor and United States Imperialism*. New York: New York University Press, 2015.

Benton-Cohen, Katherine. *Borderline Americans: Racial Division and Labor War in the Arizona Borderlands*. Cambridge, MA: Harvard University Press, 2009.

Bergad, Laird W. *Coffee and the Growth of Agrarian Capitalism in Nineteenth-Century Puerto Rico*. Princeton, NJ: Princeton University Press, 1983.

Bjork, Katharine. "Incorporating an Empire: From Deregulating Labor to Regulating Leisure in Cuba, Puerto Rico, and the Philippines, 1898–1909." PhD diss., University of Chicago, 1998.

Bothwell González, Reece B., comp. *Puerto Rico: Cien años de lucha política*. Vol. 4. Río Piedras, PR: Editorial Universitaria, Universidad de Puerto Rico, 1979.

Bourgois, Philippe. *In Search of Respect: Selling Crack in El Barrio*. Cambridge: Cambridge University Press, 2003.

Briggs, Laura. *Reproducing Empire: Race, Sex, Science, and U.S. Imperialism in Puerto Rico*. Berkeley: University of California Press, 2002.

Burnett, Christina Duffy, and Burke Marshall, eds. *Foreign in a Domestic Sense: Puerto Rico, American Expansion, and the Constitution*. Durham, NC: Duke University Press, 2001.

Burton, Antionette, ed. *After the Imperial Turn: Thinking with and through the Nation*. Durham, NC: Duke University Press, 2003.

Cabán, Pedro A. *Constructing a Colonial People: Puerto Rico and the United States, 1898–1932*. Boulder, CO: Westview Press, 1999.

Cabranes, José A. *Citizenship and the American Empire: Notes on the Legislative History of the United States Citizenship of Puerto Ricans*. New Haven, CT: Yale University Press, 1979.

Capozzola, Christopher. "The Secret Soldiers' Union: Labor and Soldier Politics in the Philippine Scout Mutiny of 1924." In Bender and Lipman, *Making the Empire Work*, 85–103.

——. *Uncle Sam Wants You: World War I and the Making of the Modern American Citizen*. New York: Oxford University Press, 2008.

Carrasquillo, Rosa E. *Our Landless Patria: Marginal Citizenship and Race in Caguas, Puerto Rico, 1880–1910*. Lincoln: University of Nebraska Press, 2006.

Carrión, Arturo Morales. *Puerto Rico: A Political and Cultural History*. New York: W. W. Norton, 1983.

Centro de Estudios Puertorriqueños, City University of New York. *Labor Migration under Capitalism: The Puerto Rican Experience*. New York: Monthly Review Press, 1979.

Chambers, John Whiteclay, II. *To Raise an Army: The Draft Comes to Modern America*. London: Free Press, 1987.

Chenault, Lawrence R. "The Puerto Rican Migrant in New York City." PhD diss., Columbia University, 1938.

Cheng, Lucie, ed. *Immigration under Capitalism: Asian Workers in the United States before World War II*. Berkeley: University of California Press, 1984.

Cintrón, Wilfredo Mattos. "The Struggle for Independence: The Long March to the Twenty-First Century." In *Colonial Dilemma: Critical Perspectives on Contemporary Puerto Rico*, edited by Edwin Meléndez and Edgardo Meléndez, 201–14. Boston, MA: South End Press, 1993.

Coates, Benjamin Allen. *Legalist Empire: International Law and American Foreign Relations in the Early Twentieth Century*. New York: Oxford University Press, 2016.

Cohen, D'Vera, Eileen Patten, and Mark Hugo Lopez. "Puerto Rican Population Declines on Island, Grows on U.S. Mainland." *Pew Research Center: Hispanic Trends*, August 11, 2014. Accessed March 17, 2017. http://www.pewhispanic.org/2014/08/11/puerto-rican-population-declines-on-island-grows-on-u-s-mainland/.

Cohen, Eliot A. *Citizens and Soldiers: The Dilemmas of Military Service*. Ithaca, NY: Cornell University Press, 1985.

Colby, Jason M. *The Business of Empire: United Fruit, Race, and U.S. Expansion in Central America*. Ithaca, NY: Cornell University Press, 2011.

——. "Progressive Empire: Race and Tropicality in United Fruit's Central America." In Bender and Lipman, *Making the Empire Work*, 289–311.

Córdova, Gonzalo F. *Resident Commissioner Santiago Iglesias and His Times*. Río Piedras: Editorial de la Universidad de Puerto Rico, 1993.

Diffie, Bailey W., and Justine Whitfield Diffie. *Puerto Rico: A Broken Pledge*. New York: Vanguard Press, 1931.

Dudziak, Mary, and Leti Volpp, eds. Introduction to "Legal Borderlands: Law and the Construction of American Borders." Special issue, *American Quarterly* 57, no. 3 (September 2005): 593–610.

Erman, Sam. "Citizens of Empire: Puerto Rico, Status, and Constitutional Change." *California Law Review* 102, no. 5 (October 2014): 1181–1242.

——. "Meanings of Citizenship in the U.S. Empire: Puerto Rico, Isabel González, and the Supreme Court, 1898 to 1905." *Journal of American Ethnic History* 27, no. 4 (2008): 5–33.

Fernández, Lilia. *Brown in the Windy City: Mexicans and Puerto Ricans in Postwar Chicago*. Chicago: University of Chicago Press, 2012.

Fernandez, Ronald. *The Disenchanted Island: Puerto Rico and the United States in the Twentieth Century*. Westport, CT: Praeger, 1996.

Findlay, Eileen J. Suárez. "Love in the Tropics: Marriage, Divorce, and the Construction of Benevolent Colonialism in Puerto Rico, 1898–1910." In *Close Encounters of Empire: Writing the Cultural History of U.S.–Latin American Relations*, edited by Gilbert M. Joseph, Catherine C. LeGrand, and Ricardo D. Salvatore, 139–72. Durham, NC: Duke University Press, 1998.

——. *Imposing Decency: The Politics of Sexuality and Race in Puerto Rico, 1870–1920*. Durham, NC: Duke University Press, 1999.

——. "Portable Roots: Latin New Yorker Community Building and the Meanings of Women's Return Migration in San Juan, Puerto Rico, 1960–2000." *Caribbean Studies* 37, no. 2 (July–December 2009): 3–43.

——. *We Are Left without a Father Here: Masculinity, Domesticity, and Migration in Postwar Puerto Rico*. Durham, NC: Duke University Press, 2014.

Fink, Leon ed. *Workers across the Americas: The Transnational Turn in Labor History*. New York: Oxford University Press, 2011.

Fitzpatrick, Joseph P. *Puerto Rican Americans: The Meaning of Migration to the Mainland*. Englewood Cliffs, NJ: Prentice-Hall, 1971.

Flores, Juan. Foreword to *A Puerto Rican in New York and Other Sketches*, by Jesús Colón, ix–xvii. 2nd ed. New York: International, 1982. Originally published in 1961.

Ford, Nancy Gentile. "'Mindful of the Traditions of His Race': Dual Identity and Foreign-Born Soldiers in the First World War." *Journal of American Ethnic History* 16, no. 2 (1997): 35–57.

Franqui-Rivera, Harry. "National Mythologies: U.S. Citizenship for the People of Puerto Rico and Military Service." *Memorias: Revista Digital de Historia y Arqueología desde el Caribe*, no. 21 (September–December 2013): 5–21.

Fujita-Rony, Dorothy. *American Workers, Colonial Power: Philippine Seattle and the Transpacific West, 1919–1941*. Berkeley: University of California Press, 2003.

Gabaccia, Donna. *Foreign Relations: American Immigration in Global Perspective*. Princeton, NJ: Princeton University Press, 2012.

Galvin, Miles. *The Organized Labor Movement in Puerto Rico*. Rutherford, NJ: Fairleigh Dickinson University Press, 1979.

Garcia, Carmen Raffuci de. *El gobierno civil y la Ley Foraker: Antecedentes históricos*. Río Piedras, PR: Editorial Universitaria, Universidad de Puerto Rico, 1981.

García, Gervasio L., and A. G. Quintero Rivera. *Desafío y solidaridad: Breve historia del movimiento obrero puertorriqueño*. Río Piedras, PR: Ediciones Huracán, 1982.

Gerstle, Gary. *American Crucible: Race and Nation in the Twentieth Century*. Princeton, NJ: Princeton University Press, 2001.

Glickman, Lawrence. "Inventing the 'American Standard of Living': Gender, Race, and Working-Class Identity, 1880–1925." *Labor History* 24, nos. 2–3 (March 1, 1993): 221–35.

Go, Julian. *American Empire and the Politics of Meaning: Elite Political Cultures in the Philippines and Puerto Rico during U.S. Colonialism*. Durham, NC: Duke University Press, 2008.

——. "Anti-Imperialism in the U.S. Territories after 1898." In *Empire's Twin: U.S. Anti-Imperialism from the Founding Era to the Age of Terrorism*, edited by Ian Tyrrell and Jay Sexton, 79–96. Ithaca, NY: Cornell University Press, 2015.

——. "Chains of Empire, Projects of State: Political Education and U.S. Colonial Rule in Puerto Rico and the Philippines." *Comparative Studies in Society and History* 42, no. 2 (April 2000): 333–62.

Gonzalez, Juan. *Harvest of Empire: A History of Latinos in America*. New York: Viking, 2000.

Gossett, Thomas. *Race: The History of an Idea*. New York: Oxford University Press, 1997.

Greene, Julie. "Builders of Empire: Rewriting the Labor and Working-Class History of Anglo-American Global Power." *Labor: Studies in Working-Class History of the Americas* 13, nos. 3–4 (2016): 1–10.

——. *The Canal Builders: Making America's Empire at the Panama Canal*. New York: Penguin Press, 2009.

——. *Pure and Simple Politics: The American Federation of Labor and Political Activism, 1881–1917*. Cambridge: Cambridge University Press, 1998.

Grosfoguel, Ramón. *Colonial Subjects: Puerto Ricans in a Global Perspective*. Berkeley: University of California Press, 2003.

Grossman, James. *Land of Hope: Chicago, Black Southerners and the Great Migration*. Chicago: University of Chicago Press, 1991.

Guglielmo, Thomas A. *White on Arrival: Italians, Race, Color, and Power in Chicago, 1890–1945*. New York: Oxford University Press, 2004.

Hahamovitch, Cindy. "Creating Perfect Immigrants: Guest Workers of the World in Historical Perspective." *Labor History* 44, no. 1 (2003): 69–94.

——. *The Fruits of Their Labor: Atlantic Coast Farmworkers and the Making of Migrant Poverty, 1870–1945*. Chapel Hill: University of North Carolina Press, 1997.

Haslip-Viera, Gabriel. "The Evolution of the Latino Community in New York City: Early Nineteenth Century to the Present." In *Latinos in New York: Communities in Transition*, edited by Gabriel Haslip-Viera and Sherrie L. Baver, 3–29. Notre Dame, IN: University of Notre Dame Press, 1996.

Higham, John. *Strangers in the Land: Patterns of American Nativism, 1865–1925*. New York: Atheneum, 1978.

Hirota, Hidetaka. "The Moment of Transition: State Officials, the Federal Government, and the Formation of American Immigration Policy." *Journal of American History* 99, no. 4 (March 2013): 1092–1108.

Hoffnung-Garskof, Jesse. "To Abolish the Law of Castes: Merit, Manhood and the Problem of Colour in the Puerto Rican Liberal Movement, 1873–1892." *Social History* 36, no. 3 (August 2011): 312–42.

Iglesias de Pagan, Igualdad. *El obrerismo en Puerto Rico, época de Santiago Iglesias (1896–1905): Guía cronológica del Movimiento Obrero organizado y del Partido Socialista y Obrero de Puerto Rico*. Palencia de Castilla: Ediciones Juan Ponce de León, 1973.

Iguina, Astrid Cubano. "Political Culture and Male Mass-Party Formation in Late-Nineteenth-Century Puerto Rico." *Hispanic American Historical Review* 78, no. 4 (November 1998): 631–62.

——. *Rituals of Violence in Nineteenth-Century Puerto Rico: Individual Conflict, Gender, and the Law*. Gainesville: University Press of Florida, 2006.

Jacobson, Matthew Frye. *Barbarian Virtues: The United States Encounters Foreign Peoples at Home and Abroad, 1876–1917*. New York: Hill and Wang, 2000.

——. *Whiteness of a Different Color: European Immigrants and the Alchemy of Race*. Cambridge, MA: Harvard University Press, 1998.

Johnson, Benjamin Heber. *Revolution in Texas: How a Forgotten Rebellion and Its Bloody Suppression Turned Mexicans into Americans*. New Haven, CT: Yale University Press, 2003.

Johnson, Courtney. "Understanding the American Empire: Colonialism, Latin Americanism, and Professional Social Science, 1898–1920." In McCoy and Scarano, *Colonial Crucible*, 175–92.

Jones, Jacqueline. *American Work: Four Centuries of Black and White Labor*. New York: W. W. Norton, 1998.

——. *A Dreadful Deceit: The Myth of Race from the Colonial Era to Obama's America*. New York: Basic Books, 2013.

Jung, Moon-Ho. *Coolies and Cane: Race, Labor and Sugar in the Age of Emancipation*. Baltimore, MD: Johns Hopkins University Press, 2006.

Kerber, Linda K. "Toward a History of Statelessness in America." *American Quarterly* 57, no. 3 (2005): 727–49.

Keyssar, Alexander. *The Right to Vote: The Contested History of Democracy in the United States*. New York: Basic Books, 2000.

Kim, Richard S. *The Quest for Statehood: Korean Immigrant Nationalism and U.S. Sovereignty, 1905–45*. New York: Oxford University Press, 2011.

Kramer, Paul A. *The Blood of Government: Race, Empire, the United States, and the Philippines*. Chapel Hill: University of North Carolina Press, 2006.

——. "Empire against Exclusion in Early 20th Century Trans-Pacific History." *Nanzan Review of American Studies* 33 (2011): 13–32.

——. "Imperial Openings: Civilization, Exemption, and the Geopolitics of Mobility in the History of Chinese Exclusion, 1868–1910." *Journal of the Gilded Age and Progressive Era* 14, no. 3 (2015): 317–47.

——. "Power and Connection: Imperial Histories of the United States in the World." *American Historical Review* 116, no. 5 (December 2011): 1348–91.

Lake, Marilyn, and Henry Reynolds. *Drawing the Global Colour Line: White Men's Countries and the International Challenge of Racial Equality*. Cambridge: Cambridge University Press, 2008.

Landale, Nancy S., and R. S. Oropesa. "White, Black, or Puerto Rican? Racial Self-Identification among Mainland and Island Puerto Ricans." *Social Forces* 81, no. 1 (September 2002): 231–54.

Levy, Teresita A. *Puerto Ricans in the Empire: Tobacco Growers and U.S. Colonialism*. New Brunswick, NJ: Rutgers University Press, 2015.

Lichtenstein, Nelson, Susan Strasser, and Roy Rosenzweig. *Who Built America? Working People and the Nation's Economy, Politics, Culture, and Society*. Vol. 2, *1877 to the Present*. New York: Worth, 2000.

Lidin, Harold J. *History of the Puerto Rican Independence Movement*. Vol. 1. Hato Rey, PR: Master typesetting of Puerto Rico, 1981.

López, Ian Haney. *White by Law: The Legal Construction of Race*. New York: New York University Press, 1996.

López, Iris. "Borinkis and Chop Suey: Puerto Rican Identity in Hawai'i, 1900 to 2000." In *The Puerto Rican Diaspora: Historical Perspectives*, edited by Carmen Teresa Whalen and Víctor Vázquez-Hernández, 43–67. Philadelphia: Temple University Press, 2005.

Luna, Guadalupe T. "On the Complexities of Race: The Treaty of Guadalupe Hidalgo and *Dred Scott v. Sanford*." *University of Miami Law Review* 53, no. 4 (1999): 691–716.

Malavet, Pedro A. "The Constitution Follows the Flag . . . but Doesn't Quite Catch Up with It": The Story of Downes v. Bidwell." In *Race Law Stories*, ed. Rachel F. Moran and Devon W. Carbado (New York: Foundation Press, 2008), 111–46.

——. "The Inconvenience of a 'Constitution [That] Follows the Flag . . . but Doesn't Quite Catch Up with It': From *Downes v. Bidwell* to *Boumediene v. Bush*." *Mississippi Law Journal* 80 (2010): 181–257.

Maldonado-Denis, Manuel. *Puerto Rico: A Socio-Historic Interpretation*. New York: Random House, 1972.

Meléndez, Edgardo. "Comments on the Jones Act and the Grant of U.S. Citizenship to Puerto Ricans." *CENTRO: Journal of the Center for Puerto Rican Studies* 29, no. 1 (Spring 2017): 316–27.

——. *Sponsored Migration: The State and Puerto Rican Postwar Migration to the United States*. Columbus: The Ohio State University Press, 2017.

Mandel, Bernard. *Samuel Gompers: A Biography*. Yellow Springs, OH: Antioch Press, 1963.

Margolies, Daniel S. *Spaces of Law in American Foreign Relations: Extradition and Extraterritoriality in the Borderlands and Beyond, 1877–1898*. Athens: University of Georgia Press, 2011.

McCoy, Alfred W., and Francisco A. Scarano. *Colonial Crucible: Empire in the Making of the Modern American State*. Madison: University of Wisconsin Press, 2009.

McGreevey, Robert C. "Empire and Migration: Coastwise Shipping, National Status, and the Legal Origins of Puerto Rican Migration to the United States." *Journal of the Gilded Age and Progressive Era* 11, no. 4 (October 2012): 553–73.

McKeown, Adam. *Melancholy Order: Asian Migration and the Globalization of Borders*. New York: Columbia University Press, 2008.

Merleaux, April. *Sugar and Civilization: American Empire and the Cultural Politics of Sweetness*. Chapel Hill: University of North Carolina Press, 2015.

Mongia, Radhika Viyas. "Race, Nationality, Mobility: A History of the Passport." In Burton, *After the Imperial Turn*, 196–214.

Montgomery, David. "Workers' Movements in the United States Confront Imperialism: The Progressive Era Experience." *Journal of the Gilded Age and Progressive Era* 7, no. 1 (2008): 7–42.

Morales, Julio. *Puerto Rican Poverty and Migration: We Just Had to Try Elsewhere*. New York: Praeger, 1986.

Natal, Carmelo Rosario. *Éxodo Puertorriqueño: Las emigraciónes al Caribe y Hawaii, 1900–1910*. 4th ed. Río Piedras, PR: Editoria Edil, 2001. First published in 1983.

Negrón-Portillo, Mariano. "Puerto Rico: Surviving Colonialism and Nationalism." In *Puerto Rican Jam: Rethinking Colonialism and Nationalism*, edited by Frances Negrón-Muntaner and Ramon Grosfoguel, 39–56. Minneapolis: University of Minnesota Press, 2008.

——. *Las turbas republicanas, 1900–1904*. Río Piedras, PR: Ediciones Huracán, 1990.

Neuman, Gerald L., and Tomiko Brown-Nagin, eds. *Reconsidering the Insular Cases: The Past and Future of the American Empire*. Cambridge, MA: Harvard University Press, 2015.

Ngai, Mae M. *Impossible Subjects: Illegal Aliens and the Making of Modern America*. Princeton, NJ: Princeton University Press, 2004.

Nobles, Melissa. *Shades of Citizenship: Race and the Census in Modern Politics*. Stanford, CA: Stanford University Press, 2000.

Okihiro, Gary. "Colonial Vision, Racial Visibility: Racializations in Puerto Rico and the Philippines during the Initial Period of U.S. Colonization." In *Racial Transformations: Latinos and Asians Remaking the United States*, edited by Nicholas de Genova, 23–39. Durham, NC: Duke University Press, 2006.

Olmeda, Marta Sánchez. *Los movimientos independistas en puerto rico y su permeabilidad en la clase obrera*. Río Piedras, PR: Editorial Edil. 1991.

Paralitici, Ché. *No quiero mi cuerpo pa' tambor: El servicio militar obligatorio en Puerto Rico*. San Juan, PR: Ediciones Puerto Rico Histórico, 1998.

——. *Sentencia Impuesta: 100 Años de Encarcelamientos por la Independencia de Puerto Rico*. San Juan, PR: Ediciones Puerto Rico Histórico, 2004.

Paton, Diana. *No Bond but the Law: Punishment, Race and Gender in Jamaican State Formation, 1780–1870*. Durham, NC: Duke University Press, 2004.

Peck, Gunther. *Reinventing Free Labor: Padrones and Immigrant Workers in the North American West, 1880–1930*. Cambridge: Cambridge University Press, 2000.

Pérez, Louis A., Jr. *The War of 1898: The United States and Cuba in History and Historiography*. Chapel Hill: University of North Carolina Press, 1998.

Picó, Fernando. *Al filo del poder: Subalternos y dominantes en Puerto Rico, 1739–1910*. Río Piedras, PR: Editorial de la Universidad de Puerto Rico, 1993.

——. *Historia general de Puerto Rico*. 7th ed. Río Piedras, PR: Ediciones Huracán, 2000.

——. *History of Puerto Rico: A Panorama of Its People*. Princeton, NJ: Markus Wiener, 2006.

——. "La revolución puertorriqueña de 1898: La necesidad de un nuevo paradigma para entender el 98 puertorriqueño." *Historia y Sociedad* 10 (1998): 7–22.

Poblete, JoAnna. *Islanders in the Empire: Filipino and Puerto Rican Laborers in Hawai'i*. Urbana: University of Illinois Press, 2014.

Ponsa, Christina Duffy. "The Edges of Empire and the Limits of Sovereignty: American Guano Islands." *American Quarterly* 57, no. 3 (September 2005): 779–803.

——. "Empire and the Transformation of Citizenship." In McCoy and Scarano, *Colonial Crucible*, 332–41.

——. "'They Say I Am Not an American': The Non-Citizen National and the Law of American Empire." *Virginia Journal of International Law* 48, no. 4 (2008): 659–718.

——. "United States: American Expansion and Territorial Deannexation." *University of Chicago Law Review* 72, no. 3 (Summer 2005): 797–879.

——. "When Statehood Was Autonomy." In Neuman and Brown-Nagin, *Reconsidering the Insular Cases*, 1–28.

Ponsa, Christina Duffy, and Adriel I. Cepeda Derieux. "Los casos insulares: Doctrina desanexionista." *Revista Jurídica de la Universidad de Puerto Rico* 78, no. 3 (2009): 661–99.

Ponsa, Christina Duffy, and Burke Marshall. "Between the Foreign and the Domestic: The Doctrine of Territorial Incorporation, Invented and Reinvented." In Burnett and Marshall, *Foreign in a Domestic Sense*, 1–36.

Putnam, Lara. *Radical Moves: Caribbean Migrants and the Politics of Race in the Jazz Age*. Chapel Hill: University of North Carolina Press, 2013.

Quintero Rivera, Ángel G. *Patricios y plebeyos: Burgueses, hacendados, artesanos y obreros: Las relaciones de clase en el Puerto Rico de cambio de siglo*. San Juan, PR: Ediciones Huracán, 1988.

Robertson, Craig. *The Passport in America: The History of a Document*. New York: Oxford University Press, 2010.

Rodríguez, Clara E. *Changing Race: Latinos, the Census, and the History of Ethnicity in the United States*. New York: New York University Press, 2000.

——. *Puerto Ricans: Born in the USA*. Boulder, CO: Westview Press, 1991.

——. "Racial Themes in the Literature." In *Hispanic New York: A Sourcebook*, edited by Claudio Iván Remeseira, 180–200. New York: Columbia University Press, 2010.

Rosario Rivera, Raquel. "Pasaporte a la angustia: Sufrimientos de los emigrados y familiares con destino a Hawaii." *Horizontes: Revista de la Pontificia Universidad Católica de Puerto Rico* 44, no. 87 (October 2002): 211–43.

——. *La llegada del Cíclope: Percepciones de San Ciriaco a cien años de su visita*. San Juan, PR: Fundación Puertorriqueña de las Humanidades, 2000.

Rosenberg, Emily S. *Financial Missionaries to the World: The Politics and Culture of Dollar Diplomacy, 1900–1930*. Cambridge, MA: Harvard University Press, 1999.

——. *Spreading the American Dream: American Economic and Cultural Expansion, 1890–1945*. New York: Hill and Wang, 1982.

Sanabria, Carlos. "The Puerto Rican Organized Workers' Movement and the AFL, 1901–1934." PhD diss., City University of New York, 2000.

Sanchez, George J. *Becoming Mexican American: Ethnicity, Culture, and Identity in Chicano Los Angeles, 1900–1945*. New York: Oxford University Press, 1995.

——. "Race, Nation, and Culture in Recent Immigration Studies." *Journal of American Ethnic History* 18, no. 4 (1999): 66–84.

Sánchez Korrol, Virginia E. *From Colonia to Community: The History of Puerto Ricans in New York City, 1917–1948*. Westport, CT: Greenwood Press, 1983.

Santiago-Valles, Kevin. "American Penal Forms and Colonial Spanish Custodial-Regulatory Practices in Fin de Siècle Puerto Rico." In McCoy and Scarano, *Colonial Crucible*, 87–94.

Saranillio, Dean Itsuji. "Colliding Histories: Hawai'i Statehood at the Intersection of Asians 'Ineligible to Citizenship' and Hawaiians 'Unfit for Self-Government.'" *Journal of Asian American Studies* 13, no. 3 (October 2010): 283–309.

Sassen, Saskia. *Mobility of Labor and Capital*. Cambridge: Cambridge University Press, 1988.

Scarano, Francisco A. "Censuses in the Transition to Modern Colonialism: Spain and the United States in Puerto Rico." In McCoy and Scarano, *Colonial Crucible*, 210–19.

Schmidt-Nowara, Christopher. "'After Spain': A Dialogue with Joseph M. Fradera on Spanish Colonial Historiography." In Burton, *After the Imperial Turn*, 157–69.

——. "From Columbus to Ponce de León: Puerto Rican Commemorations between Empires, 1893–1908." In McCoy and Scarano, *Colonial Crucible*, 230–37.

——. *Interpreting Spanish Colonialism: Empires, Nations, and Legends*. Albuquerque: University of New Mexico Press, 2005.

Schmitt, Robert C. *Demographic Statistics of Hawaii, 1776–1965*. Honolulu: University of Hawai'i Press, 1968.

——. *Historical Statistics of Hawaii*. Honolulu: University of Hawai'i Press, 1977.

Scully, Eileen P. *Bargaining with the State from Afar: American Citizenship in Treaty Port China, 1844–1942*. New York, Columbia University Press, 2001.

Senior, Clarence. *Puerto Rican Emigration*. Río Piedras: University of Puerto Rico, 1947.

——. *Santiago Iglesias: Labor Crusader*. Hato Rey, PR: Inter American University Press, 1972.

Serrano, Susan K. "Dual Consciousness about Law and Justice: Puerto Ricans' Battle for U.S. Citizenship in Hawai'i." *CENTRO: Journal of the Center for Puerto Rican Studies* 29, no. 1 (Spring 2017): 164–201.

Sim, David. *A Union Forever: The Irish Question and U.S. Foreign Relations in the Victorian Age*. Ithaca, NY: Cornell University Press, 2013.

Smith, Rogers M. "The Bitter Roots of Puerto Rican Citizenship." In Burnett and Marshall, *Foreign in a Domestic Sense*, 373–88.

——. "The Insular Cases, Differentiated Citizenship, and Territorial Statuses in the Twenty-First Century." In Neuman and Brown-Nagin, *Reconsidering the Insular Cases*, 103–28.

Sneider, Allison L. *Suffragists in an Imperial Age: U.S. Expansion and the Woman Question, 1870–1929*. New York: Oxford University Press, 2008.

Soltero, Carlos R. *Latinos and American Law: Landmark Supreme Court Cases*. Austin: University of Texas Press, 2006.

Sparrow, Bartholomew H. "The Centennial of *Ocampo v. United States*: Lessons from the Insular Cases." In Neuman and Brown-Nagin, *Reconsidering the Insular Cases*, 39–60.

——. *The Insular Cases and the Emergence of American Empire*. Lawrence: University Press of Kansas, 2006.

Sparrow, Bartholomew H., and Jennifer Lamm. "Puerto Ricans and U.S. Citizenship in 1917: Imperatives of Security." *CENTRO: Journal of Puerto Rican Studies* 29, no. 1 (Spring 2017): 284–315.

St. John, Rachel. *Line in the Sand: A History of the Western U.S.-Mexico Border*. Princeton, NJ: Princeton University Press, 2011.

Stern, Alexandra Minna. "Eugenics and Racial Classification in Modern Mexican America." In *Race and Classification: The Case of Mexican America*, edited by Ilona Katzew and Susan Deans-Smith, 151–73. Stanford, CA: Stanford University Press, 2009.

Tabili, Laura. *"We Ask for British Justice": Workers and Racial Difference in Late Imperial Britain*. Ithaca, NY: Cornell University Press, 1994.

Tansill, Charles Callan. *The Purchase of the Danish West Indies*. Baltimore: Johns Hopkins Press, 1932.

Thomas, Lorrin. *Puerto Rican Citizen: History and Political Identity in Twentieth-Century New York City*. Chicago: University of Chicago Press, 2010.

Thompson, Lanny. *Imperial Archipelago*. Honolulu: University of Hawai'i Press, 2010.

Torruella, Juan R. "The Insular Cases: A Declaration of Their Bankruptcy and My Harvard Pronouncement. In Neuman and Brown-Nagin, *Reconsidering the Insular Cases*, 61–76.

——. "The *Insular Cases*: The Establishment of a Regime of Political Apartheid." *University of Pennsylvania Journal of International Law* 29, no. 2 (Winter 2007): 283–347.

Tuero, Fernando López. *Isla de Puerto-Rico: Estudios de economía rural*. Puerto Rico: Imprenta del Boletin Mercantil, 1893.

Valdés, Dionicio Nodín. *Organized Agriculture and the Labor Movement before the UFW: Puerto Rico, Hawai'i, California*. Austin: University of Texas Press, 2011.

Vargas, Zaragosa. *Proletarians of the North: A History of Mexican Industrial Workers in Detroit and the Midwest, 1917–1933*. Berkeley: University of California Press, 1993.

Vega, Bernardo. *Memoirs of Bernardo Vega: A Contribution to the History of the Puerto Rican Community in New York*. Edited by César Andreu Iglesias. Translated by Juan Flores. New York: Monthly Review Press, 1984.

Venator-Santiago, Charles. "Mapping the Contours of the History of the Extension of U.S. Citizenship to Puerto Rico, 1898–Present." *CENTRO: Journal of the Center for Puerto Rican Studies* XXIX, no. 1 (Spring 2017): 38–55.

Vitalis, Robert. *White World Order, Black Power Politics: The Birth of American International Relations*. Ithaca, NY: Cornell University Press, 2015.

Wagenheim, Kal. *Puerto Rico: A Profile*. New York: Praeger, 1975.

Watkins-Owens, Irma. *Blood Relations: Caribbean Immigrants and the Harlem Community, 1900–1930*. Bloomington: Indiana University Press, 1996.

Welch, Richard E., Jr. *Response to Imperialism: The United States and the Philippine-American War, 1899–1902*. Chapel Hill: University of North Carolina Press, 1979.

Whalen, Carmen Teresa. *From Puerto Rico to Philadelphia: Puerto Rican Workers and Postwar Economies*. Philadelphia: Temple University Press, 2001.

Whalen, Carmen Teresa, and Victor Vázques-Hernández, eds. *Puerto Rican Diaspora: Historical Perspectives*. Philadelphia: Temple University Press, 2005.

Williams, Walter L. "United States Indian Policy and the Debate over Philippine Annexation: Implications for the Origins of American Imperialism." *Journal of American History* 66, no. 4 (March 1980): 810–31.

Willrich, Michael. *Pox: An American History*. New York: Penguin, 2011.

Wright, Micah. "Building an Occupation: Puerto Rican Laborers in the Dominican Republic, 1916–1924." *Labor: Studies in Working-Class History of the Americas* 13, nos. 3–4 (2016): 83–103.

Index

Page numbers in *italics* refer to figures.

Printed in the USA
CPSIA information can be obtained
at www.ICGtesting.com
LVHW050510280124
769982LV00004B/477

9 781501 764608